T0305337

Merger Arbitrage

Merger Arbitrage

A Fundamental Approach to Event-Driven Investing

Lionel Melka
Amit Shabi

A John Wiley & Sons, Ltd., Publication

© 2013 John Wiley & Sons, Ltd

Translated by Andrew Fanko and Frances Thomas from the French edition *Arbitrage sur Fusions et Acquisitions, Le Merger Arbitrage* published in 2012 by Economica

Registered Office
John Wiley & Sons Ltd, The Atrium, Southern Gate, Chichester, West Sussex, PO19 8SQ, United Kingdom

For details of our global editorial offices, for customer services and for information about how to apply for permission to reuse the copyright material in this book please see our website at www.wiley.com.

Wiley publishes in a variety of print and electronic formats and by print-on-demand. Some material included with standard print versions of this book may not be included in e-books or in print-on-demand. If this book refers to media such as a CD or DVD that is not included in the version you purchased, you may download this material at http://booksupport.wiley.com. For more information about Wiley products, visit www.wiley.com.

Designations used by companies to distinguish their products are often claimed as trademarks. All brand names and product names used in this book are trade names, service marks, trademarks or registered trademarks of their respective owners. The publisher is not associated with any product or vendor mentioned in this book.

Limit of Liability/Disclaimer of Warranty: While the publisher and author have used their best efforts in preparing this book, they make no representations or warranties with the respect to the accuracy or completeness of the contents of this book and specifically disclaim any implied warranties of merchantability or fitness for a particular purpose. It is sold on the understanding that the publisher is not engaged in rendering professional services and neither the publisher nor the author shall be liable for damages arising herefrom. If professional advice or other expert assistance is required, the services of a competent professional should be sought.

Library of Congress Cataloging-in-Publication Data

Melka, Lionel.
  Merger arbitrage : a fundamental approach to event-driven investing / Lionel Melka, Amit Shabi.
    p. cm.
  Includes bibliographical references and index.
  ISBN 978-1-118-44001-8 (cloth) – ISBN 978-1-118-44006-3 (ebk.) – ISBN 978-1-118-44007-0 (ebk.) – ISBN 978-1-118-44008-7 (ebk.) 1. Arbitrage. 2. Consolidation and merger of corporations. 3. Stock exchanges and current events. I. Shabi, Amit. II. Title.
  HG4521.M4345 2013
  658.1′62–dc23   2012029646

A catalogue record for this book is available from the British Library.

ISBN 978-1-118-44001-8 (hardback) ISBN 978-1-118-44006-3 (ebk)
ISBN 978-1-118-44007-0 (ebk)   ISBN 978-1-118-44008-7 (ebk)

Cover images: Shutterstock.com

Set in 11/13pt Times by Aptara Inc., New Delhi, India
Printed in Great Britain by TJ International Ltd, Padstow, Cornwall, UK

To our beloved children: Tia, Ilaï, Raphaël and Gabriel

Contents

Foreword

In my professional life I have learned to respect the power and influence of merger arbitrage in the transaction process. Good fortune gave me the opportunity to do so in very different ways: as an investment banker in charge of M&A deals; as an investor in event-driven funds; and most recently as a director of a public company under offer. If you are contemplating being involved in financial markets in any of these capacities, you must read this book.

During my many years at one of the greatest investment banks in history, Morgan Stanley, I had the privilege to execute several of the largest mergers, acquisitions, takeovers, and defenses on both sides of the Atlantic. My career there (from 1986 to 2008) spanned the two decades which saw the greatest M&A bull market in recent history. Activity charts mark the beginning of what became known as "merger mania" towards the end of 1983; one of the deals which started it was Pennzoil's offer to buy 20% of Getty Oil in December of that year. Ultimately all of Getty Oil was acquired by Texaco; the deal was large, complex and contested, a perfect combination for merger arbitrage which provided an early, yet spectacular, opportunity to deploy capital and to take calculated risk. For many of them, playing that situation paid off, and, although it was before my time on Wall Street, I knew it had been a defining moment.

The development of professional merger arbitrage logically accompanied the enormous wave of merger activity which followed, and soon the question "what are the arbitrageurs doing?" became central to understanding and sometimes predicting the outcome of takeovers. To put it simply, merger arbitrageurs analyze transaction risks in public deals and put capital to work, increasingly in scale, by going long or short on financial instruments from different issuers in ways that reflect their risk assessment and ultimate convictions. The combined strength of such convictions and of the capital used to back them might result, for example, in a higher price for the security "in play" – e.g. the stock of a public company under offer. Nowhere would this be more relevant than in contested situations, whether as a result of a hostile bid or competitive offers for a company. To quote a business magazine article from the previous decade, "these are the situations M&A bankers live for". The same could be said of merger arbitrageurs, although more plain-vanilla agreed transactions have long constituted the bulk of the activity for all.

This is clearly a risky business, but so is deal making. As a banker, you know the transactions you've worked on and which never saw the light of day – these are many in number. I always told my colleagues "there will be more reasons for a deal not to happen than for it to happen". A dose of humility is healthy in the banking business, and not just because of the current climate. Investment bankers often felt that the toughest part of the job was to get to the announcement stage; yet this was only the beginning of the story for the market, of which merger arbitrage instantly became a key component. Risk is no longer about pursuing alternative strategies to the deal in question, or testing the CEO's and board's resolve in following it through; attention moves to market reaction, interloper action, regulatory delays, defensive moves, and other execution risks. This is the time for merger arbitrageurs to deploy their skills in assessing these risks, to mitigate them using the range of available securities and derivatives instruments, and to push for their preferred outcome. So for their transactions to be successful, M&A bankers need to know and understand what the merger arbitrageurs are thinking at all times.

The authors of this book have chosen several notable transactions to illustrate these points with competence and clarity. I was involved in the Alcan-Pechiney deal as Alcan's banker, and encourage you to read the case study. It has many of the components of a textbook unsolicited offer: compelling strategic logic, as evidenced by prior discussions between the two companies; vigorous bidding and takeover defense strategies; powerful and positive market reactions for both stocks; and finely conducted negotiations which ultimately resulted in an agreement. I remember the question the board of Alcan asked me the first time I met with them in Montreal: "Can it be done?". The question essentially related to whether it was then possible to acquire a French company via a hostile offer. I replied without hesitation: "Yes it can". Certainly by

2003, European equity markets were driven by institutional shareholders – including merger arbitrageurs – whose objective is to maximize the value of their investment. It was increasingly hard for any target company to successfully reject an opportunity to get a premium without providing shareholders with a better option. Indeed, in my entire career, the "just say no" defense worked only once, in 1999, when Société Générale rebuffed BNP's offer, in an exceedingly complicated situation. Going back to Alcan/Pechiney, it was significant that we received the "Deal of the Year" award in 2003 from the "Club des Trente", an association of major French CFOs, as a mighty French industrial name had fallen to shareholders' power.

Deal stories, and their lessons, could be the subject of another book. But ensuring that you become a successful investment banker is not the only reason you should be familiar with the content of this book. Merger arbitrage provides investors, in the great tradition of other forms of securities arbitrage, with a highly effective way to invest capital. As this book will explain, arbitrage plays a significant role in providing liquidity and ensuring the good functioning of securities markets. Investing in so-called event-driven funds has therefore become a permanent feature of asset management. Many portfolios include allocations to such funds, which are in principle uncorrelated to macroeconomic trends – or indeed the value of securities such as bonds or stocks going up or down. Because the returns produced are based on arbitrage opportunities, such funds provide an attractive diversification from other types of investments. Some of the smartest people I have met on Wall Street run such funds.

Understanding the role of merger arbitrage is also critical for boards. As I write this, GDF-Suez has made an offer for the 30% it does not own in International Power, a company listed on the London Stock Exchange. I am a director of International Power and, for the first time, I was going to live through the deal experience from a board seat: how exciting for someone who has spent most of his life advising boards in such situations! I had not forgotten the grueling rhythm of meetings imposed on the directors of Gucci during the "handbag war" with LVMH (I was Gucci's banker), to the point where we joked "today there is a board meeting, so it must be Sunday". Interestingly, the agreement between GDF-Suez and International Power provided that, for a period of time following the original business combination, all six independent directors must approve any offer for buying out the minorities; here we had the power to just say no. After due consideration, we rejected GDF-Suez' first offer at 390p; our investment banks provided us with relevant analyses and market views to support such a stance, and the stock price actually settled above the offer price. The message from shareholders was clear, yet it must have been challenging for merger arbitrageurs to factor our right to veto into their risk analyses. That additional element of uncertainty must have weighed on many people's decision to intervene: unlike in standard takeovers, the bidder could not bypass the board and take its proposal directly to the shareholders. In the end, we obtained a price of 418p, whereas the market price had stabilized at around 404p (I was involved in the negotiations). By the time you read this, shareholders will have voted on the transaction.

Finally, I would like to say that this excellent book gave me yet another opportunity to learn, this time as a student of merger arbitrage theory. Nowadays, it is impossible to understand how capital markets function without mastering the analyses contained herein. Indeed, you will read how complex such analyses need to be in certain takeover situations – dare I say sometimes in direct proportion to the creativity displayed by those involved? I referred above to the very complicated situation created by BNP's dual offer for Société Générale and Paribas, which had previously agreed to merge, so that all three stocks' movements became interdependent. A five-month rollercoaster was stopped with BNP taking control of Paribas but missing out on Société Générale. Other situations where I led the defense were certainly difficult to analyze at times, such as when Elf, in a bold defense move against Total's hostile offer, launched a counterbid for Total itself. This was an unprecedented defense strategy in 1999, which observers quickly named "Pac-Man" after the popular video game. In this case, which stock do you buy and which one do you short? To end the battle, Total raised its price and Elf agreed to merge. In another famous situation mentioned earlier, what were merger arbitrageurs to do when Gucci issued stock overnight (as could be done then on the Amsterdam exchange), first as part of an employee share ownership plan and then to white squire PPR (at a premium to the market price, of course), to stop competitor LVMH from taking creeping control of its capital? In a second stage which took place in 2004, PPR acquired the rest of Gucci, also at a premium. Merger arbitrageurs must have been surprised again in 2004 when Aventis announced it would issue "Plavix warrants" to holders of its shares should Sanofi (the maker of Plavix) succeed in its takeover plans, undoubtedly creating confusion in the marketplace and prompting a regulatory review of yet another innovative structure. Sanofi increased its offer, and Aventis agreed to merge. In 2006, merger arbitrageurs were taken aback when Arcelor, under a hostile offer from Mittal, agreed to sell a significant non-controlling stake to Severstal in exchange for assets and cash; Mittal had to raise its offer to see off the competition (and I received a bottle of champagne from a happy merger arbitrageur). Ultimately, in all these situations, merger arbitrageurs had to incorporate previously unseen complexities into their analyses; but ultimately, and without exception, these moves resulted in a superior outcome for shareholders, including merger arbitrageurs themselves.

There is a fifth and final reason why you should read this book, even if you do not plan on becoming a better banker, investor, director or scholar of market efficiency theories: it could very well set you on the path to becoming a merger arbitrage professional.

Michael Zaoui

Acknowledgements

We are deeply grateful for the invaluable guidance, ideas, and work from numerous colleagues and friends that have made this book possible.

Throughout the development of this text, many people have provided critical feedback and ideas for improvement. We would like to express our deepest thanks to Coralie Amar, Rachel Chicheportiche, Sébastien Dettmar, Emmanuel Dinh, Romain Geiss, Hako Graf von Finckenstein, Sophie Sassard, and Aurélie Yacoël. We are particularly indebted to them for their insightful suggestions and valuable expertise.

Valuable and constructive observations have also come from Fabrice Anselmi, Séverin Brizay, Thomas Candillier, Christoph Englisch and Donat Vidal-Revel, who have read and reviewed earlier drafts of this text. Without their patience, enthusiasm, and wise comments, this book would not have been the same. The pleasure of discussing these topics with them was worth every moment spent writing this book.

We would like to thank Michel Cicurel, CEO of LCF Rothschild, who wrote the foreword of the French edition, as well as our editors there, Delphine Lautier, Jean Pavlevski and Yves Simon.

Michael Zaoui did us the great honor of contributing to this work by writing its foreword. His experience as Morgan Stanley's Head of Mergers and Acquisitions provided us with invaluable additional expertise and details.

On this same note, we want to thank Serge Benchetrit, Madison Marriage and Matthieu Pigasse for endorsing the book.

We are particularly grateful to Ygal Abergel, David Amar, Dr Teddy Amar, Clarisse Anger, Régis Attuil, Jeremy Benamara, Stéphanie Bianco, Vanessa Bogaardt, Stéphane Bourdon, Antonine Chenevier, Didier Chicheportiche, Nicolas Contis, Itai Dadon, Bertrand Demesse,

Fabien Dersy, Tony Esposito, Grégory Gallais, Ori Gruenpeter, Nicole Guedj, David Haller, Vinh-Thang Hoang, Marc Irisson, Yaël Lebrati-Attuil, Alain Leclair, Mathieu Lemesle, Isabelle Lixi, Sébastien Mathieu, Serge Muller, Roger Nordmann, Dr Marion Nordmann-Amar, Philippe Paquet, Rozenn Peres, Michel Piermay, Bénédicte Provost, Jacques-Henri Rieme, Antoine Rolland, Benjamin Rouach, Yakhara Sembene, Oren Shilony, Edouard Sigwalt, Ludovic Uzan, Serge and Valérie Ventura, Tom Wilner and Marcelle Yacoël for making this possible.

We would also like to thank the editors and staff at John Wiley & Sons – Werner Coetzee, Aimée Dibbens, Bill Falloon, Samantha Hartley, Jennie Kitchin, Lori Laker and Vivienne Wickham – for their constant support as well as their helpful comments and suggestions throughout the realization of this project. The team of editors who worked on this book improved it tremendously.

Special thanks go to Harriet Agnew, Caroline Allen, David Benoit, Deirdre Brennan, Mary Campbell, Marietta Cauchi, Barry Cohen, Nicola Culley, Kris Devasabai, Joy Dunbar, Tony Griffiths, Jessica Hodgson, William Hutchings, Sam Jones, Tara Lachapelle, Margie Lindsay, Bill McIntosh, Mike Prest, Phil Serafino, Mimosa Spencer, Martin Steward, Sten Stovall, Meg Tirrell, Albertina Torsoli and Will Wainewright.

We also want to express immeasurable gratitude to our families and friends for their encouragement and support throughout this project: special thanks to Elad, Hana, Marcelle, Moti and Ofer Shabi, and Marie-Paule, Nicole, Pascal and Raymond Melka.

We would like to thank François Bourriguen for his contributions and the quality of his research. Bright, patient, and creative, he showed great care and dedication in his work – this book could not have been completed without him. All errors are naturally our own.

Finally, we are grateful to our children, Raphaël, Gabriel, Tia and Ilaï, who offered welcome relief from long stretches of writing and rewriting. Although they are only nine, eight, four and one, someday they will grow up and study the principles of finance. We hope this book provides its readers with some of the education and enlightenment that we wish for our own children.

About the Authors

Lionel Melka started his career in 1998 with Lazard Frères, where he undertook numerous M&A advisory engagements for blue-chip clients (LVMH, Saint-Gobain, Casino, France Telecom, Thomson, Air Liquide, Kingfisher) in a large scope of situations: privatizations, friendly and hostile takeover bids, LBOs, asset disposals, and IPOs. He then joined the M&A Department of Calyon, where he worked on various advisory assignments in the TMT-Defense team and LCF Rothschild in 2005, where he led many M&A cross-border assignments in various industry sectors.

Lionel is also a teacher at the University of Paris Dauphine, one of the leading academic institutions in Europe, in the fields of corporate finance, asset allocation, and alternative investments.

Amit Shabi is an ex-commander of an analyst team in a military intelligence unit of the Israel Defense Forces. After completing three years of army service, he moved to Paris to pursue his studies and obtained a Master's degree in Finance from Sorbonne University.

Amit started his career in the asset management department of LCF Rothschild. After this experience in traditional asset management, he worked in the Capital Markets divisions of MAN Group and Cantor Fitzgerald selling sophisticated financial instruments to hedge funds and institutional investors.

In 2006, Lionel and Amit cofounded Bernheim, Dreyfus & Co., a Paris-based asset manager specialized in alternative investments. Since then, they have used a merger arbitrage strategy to manage the Diva Synergy funds.

Introduction

It is Monday morning. Before the markets open, Salinas PLC announces a $50-per-share takeover bid for Migjorn Inc. Shares in the target company closed at $36 in New York on Friday. Trading will begin again at any moment. What price will Migjorn shares open at? Who will buy? Who will sell? Does that really matter in the grand scheme of things? And, perhaps most importantly, is there a way of making money from the situation?

Arbitrageurs spend their working days asking themselves these questions, analyzing operations and taking (or not, as the case may be) positions on the stock market. In friendly operations, they often act in the buyer's favor and facilitate the conclusion of the transaction. In hostile operations, they tend to be more of an arbitrator, in terms of the "fairness" of the final price, by rotating capital as soon as the takeover bid is announced.

Merger arbitrage is one of the event-driven alternative strategies applied by hedge funds, whereby they trade in the stocks of companies that find themselves at a particular stage in their life cycle. This could be a merger, a takeover bid, a restructuring or insolvency proceedings. Merger arbitrage was developed in the 1940s by Gus Levy at investment bank Goldman Sachs and enjoyed its heyday during the fourth big wave of mergers and acquisitions in the 1980s. Let us first give a brief reminder of what a hedge fund is and what merger arbitrage is.

Hedge funds are investment vehicles that aim to deliver absolute returns with no benchmark. They are generally free to invest in any asset class, and insofar as they do not raise money from the public, they are subject to very little regulation, if any. They can use leverage and sell short (something we will come across several times in this book).

Hedge fund managers, who invest significant sums in the funds, are paid according to their performance. They may be vilified by some, but they actually play a positive role by adding liquidity to the markets and helping the prices of the financial assets in which they trade to level off more quickly.

Merger arbitrage aims to make a profit on the difference between the market price of a stock and the price put forward in a takeover bid. The price at which the shares of a target company settle after an operation has been announced is an implicit indicator of whether arbitrageurs feel the transaction will go ahead. Where there is competition (a situation often instigated by the target company's management), the market price is usually higher than the bid price. In general, offer execution risks and uncertainties surrounding the ability of the bidder to complete the transaction are more likely to get an arbitrageur's attention. In these cases, the market price will tend to be less than the bid price, generating a difference known as the spread.

This spread varies depending on how likely the transaction is to fail. There are risks related to:

- the financing of the transaction;
- the intervention of government bodies and other regulatory authorities (such as competition regulators);
- the shareholder vote (or reaching approval thresholds for takeovers);
- the implementation of legal clauses featuring in the merger agreement.

If these conditions precedent are met, the spread will gradually narrow as the transaction completion date approaches.

All these risks can appear after an M&A transaction has been announced, and they must therefore be evaluated by arbitrageurs. In order to capitalize on the control premium usually offered by a buyer, some investors try to buy shares in potential target companies even before a deal is announced. These pre-event strategies are founded on several decisions that relate to risks of varying importance.

The most risky strategy is to take positions on the basis of pure speculation, a practice adopted by Ivan Boesky, who was the inspiration for the Gordon Gekko character in Oliver Stone's film *Wall Street*. At the other end of the scale, there are arbitrageurs who wait until the buyer and the target company have signed a definitive agreement. Others make their move somewhere in the middle: upon the entry of an activist investor, a mere approach, advanced discussions, or a conditional offer. In this book, we will look only at deals that have been formally announced, as these represent the majority of situations targeted by arbitrageurs.

Whatever your opinion of the financial markets (an instrument of economic efficiency and resource allocation, or a sounding box for short-term and copycat behavior), it is these markets that decide the fate of major mergers and acquisitions. This notion of "market" has, however, become increasingly diverse and fragmented. The presence of new types of investor (US/UK mutual funds, arbitrage funds, activist funds, sovereign wealth funds, etc.), each with their own incentives and constraints, makes it increasingly difficult to analyze investment decisions. The M&A market has also undergone major changes: the outbreak of hostile bids; the rise of private-equity firms; the emergence of buyers from emerging nations; and the growing impact of ratings agencies and government bodies (particularly competition authorities). All these mechanisms, changes, and issues are at the heart of this book.

The book is split into three parts. In the first part, we examine the basis of merger arbitrage. Chapter 1 looks at the key role of the market in takeover bids. It also assesses the major changes in the financial markets over recent years and their impact on M&A. Chapter 2 uses recent examples to describe the different types of transaction that provide investment opportunities for arbitrageurs. In Chapter 3, we look at the various M&A risk and return factors, such as the risk of the deal failing, the timetable, and bidding wars. Chapter 4 focuses on the historical profitability of merger arbitrage, the different approaches used by fund managers and the results of academic studies on the subject.

In the second part of the book, we look in more detail at the risks of an M&A transaction failing, which is the key factor in an investment process. Chapter 5 deals with financing risk, Chapter 6 with competition issues, Chapter 7 with the legal aspects of merger agreements and Chapter 8 with other risks, such as administrative and political risks.

The third part of the book examines specificities of M&A transactions. Chapter 9 deals with hostile takeovers and Chapter 10 with leveraged buyouts.

We will examine many recent examples and case studies in order to show how the various theories and notions are put into practice. These include Dow Chemicals' purchase of Rohm & Haas to illustrate financing risk and Oracle's takeover of Sun to demonstrate competition risk. Sanofi's purchase of Genzyme will reveal the dynamics of a hostile takeover, while the takeover of Del Monte Foods by a KKR-led consortium will illustrate the particular characteristics of a leveraged buyout.

Part I
The Arbitrage Process

The first part of this book describes the environment in which arbitrageurs work, as well as the major principles of merger arbitrage. Although they are often analyzed within the context of corporate financing, M&A are essentially tied to the financial markets and to changes therein, as the first chapter will show. In Chapter 2, we will study the financial mechanisms at work in the arbitrage process, as well as their different characteristics depending on the payment method of the transaction. The third chapter looks at the risk and return factors of merger arbitrage. The final chapter in Part I examines the historical performance of merger arbitrage and the different approaches adopted by specialist managers.

1

The Role of the Market in Mergers and Acquisitions

In spite of the many laws governing mergers and acquisitions (M&A), it is always the market that has the final say. Takeover bids may have to comply with various national and international laws, but by accepting or rejecting the terms of these bids the market is the ultimate judge of whether they are successful. Whether they like it or not, the market can sometimes usurp even the decision-making bodies of the target company in this role as the ultimate judge. As you might expect, the market's role of arbitrator is governed strictly by securities regulations, whether during bull periods, such as the beginning of the 1990s, or during more difficult times for financial markets, such as we have seen since 2008.

The concept of "the market" has evolved considerably. It now comprises as many different operators as strategies, and recent changes have served only to make it more fragmented and diverse in terms of the operators it groups together. These market operators include investment funds (arbitrage funds, private-equity funds, etc.), family offices, wealth managers, asset management units of major financial institutions, and individual shareholders. Each operator follows its own investment process in order to achieve its own goals, whether it is managing its own money or someone else's. All this means that the market, now more than ever, is a complex sum of individual interests. The partial or total liquidation of many so-called alternative investment funds, in the wake of early redemption requests from investors following the recent financial crisis, is a prime example. Moreover, the increase in trading volumes on global stock exchanges means a much greater turnover of shareholders in the share capital of companies. Combined with the different behaviors of market operators and the wide range of financial instruments available, this makes takeover bids – and the factors that determine whether they will be successful – more complex.

Such diversity on the financial markets means there can be no broad-brush analysis of takeover bids. As well as the individual characteristics of each operation, the reactions of the many parties involved and their respective dynamics need to be taken into consideration. The success, or otherwise, of takeover bids therefore depends fundamentally on the market. Over the last few decades, the market has undergone many changes that have affected M&A practice.

1.1 STRUCTURAL CHANGES TO THE FINANCIAL MARKETS

Over the last few decades, the global financial markets have experienced several major structural changes as they have risen on the back of the growth and globalization of listed companies. The total stock-market capitalization of all US and international companies listed on the New York Stock Exchange rose from $2,700 billion in 1990 to more than $13,300 billion in 2010. Over the same period, the S&P 500 climbed from 350 points to more than 1,350 – an increase of over 285%.

The first thing to point out is that market liquidity has increased considerably. Average annual trading volumes on the New York Stock Exchange rose from around $1,325 billion in 1990 to more than $11,600 billion in 2010. This significant increase in trading volumes, and therefore market liquidity, enables market operators to position themselves more easily, and above all more quickly, in the share capital of companies. Those wishing to launch a takeover bid can therefore quickly build up significant stakes in the share capital of target companies, whether before or after the bid is actually submitted.

There are many ways of building up blocks of shares, such as purchasing shares on the market, buying blocks of shares off market, and using derivatives. Whatever method is used, it is made easier by a more liquid market. Having said that, all these techniques are subject to strict regulatory control. There are two major determining factors: first, the notion of privileged information held by the potential instigator of the transaction (moreover, different jurisdictions interpret this issue in different ways – does a market operator preparing a takeover bid for a target company have privileged information?); and second, ownership threshold disclosure requirements. These issues are topical and often trigger debate, as shown by the recent creeping takeover of Porsche by its German competitor Volkswagen.

A second significant change to the markets is their integration with international capital flows. Nowadays, foreign capital always represents a large part of the volumes traded on all global financial markets. This change has significant consequences and goes hand in hand with the first change we discussed earlier. It encourages ownership fragmentation and the circulation of capital – both of which are conducive to takeover bids. The greater openness of the markets also means that individual investment choices depend increasingly on economic and financial criteria. In the context of takeover bids, these criteria are particularly crucial in determining whether or not an investor tenders their shares.

There are many reasons for this change. First, EU regulation encourages the free circulation of capital. Second, advances in communication technology have brought about the development of new types of electronic trading platforms, which facilitate market access and allow for faster execution. Lastly, the harmonization of international accounting standards and better access to financial information have also contributed to better global integration of capital markets.

Countries have responded to the opening up of the international capital markets, but it remains to be seen what effect this response will have on M&A. Several countries have created investment structures aimed at protecting "sensitive" assets. There is, of course, nothing new about sovereign wealth funds (SWFs); the first, the Kuwait Investment Board, was set up in 1953. These funds now manage more than $3,000 billion, and their primary aim is to diversify their investments. Until now, they have been most active in taking minority stakes in large US or European groups that have built up a dominant position in their markets. There have been several recent examples of conflict between SWFs and the authorities in the country of the target company, such as the attempted takeover in 2006 of US oil company Unocal by state-controlled Chinese group CNOOC. It remains to be seen what effect will arise from these funds being in the share capital of M&A target companies. As they are largely a recent phenomenon, it will be interesting to see the stance adopted by these funds, especially if their presence in the share capital has come about through a concerted effort with the management team of the target company.

The third major change in the markets is the growing importance of hedge funds. The main aim of these funds is to deliver "absolute" returns, i.e. to generate positive performance whatever the conditions on the financial markets, as opposed to benchmark management where performance is compared to that of a reference index. Other specific characteristics of hedge funds include widespread and sometimes mass usage of leverage, short selling, derivatives, and fee systems that include performance fees. The hedge fund industry currently has $2,000 billion of assets under management, which is fairly small compared with the asset pool of traditional, long-only mutual funds. Redemption requests from investors and many fund liquidations caused hedge fund assets under management to fall sharply during the recent financial crisis. Fundraising has been positive since 2010, however, with investors once again very keen on returns that are uncorrelated to the markets. Furthermore, we need to take into account the leverage used and the actual exposure of hedge funds, which in general is much greater than for other asset management players and therefore increases the amount of assets.

Hedge funds are something of a broad church in that they comprise many different investment strategies, asset classes (equities, bank debt, high-yield bonds, etc.), and financial instruments. And yet the names given to the different styles have become familiar: long/short, event driven, macro, convertible arbitrage, etc. With regard to takeover bids, "activist" funds specialize in acquiring significant stakes with a view to acting as a catalyst, or sometimes with the explicit aim of encouraging a bid, whether under their own steam or on behalf of a third party. The strategies employed by these funds are very similar to the conduct of individual activist investors such as Carl Icahn or T. Boone Pickens. Among other things, Mr Icahn was particularly active in the split of Motorola into Motorola Mobility (housing all the mobile phone activities) and Motorola Solutions (specializing in corporate telecoms services). This separation enabled the acquisition of Motorola Mobility by Google, which was on the lookout for patent buys to help its Android system compete better with Apple's iPhone. A large number of takeover bids are the result of moves by these activist investors or funds.

The final change to the financial markets is that the different markets are becoming increasingly integrated. The connections between the equity and derivative markets and the markets for other products have become much stronger in recent years, partly because hedge funds use all of these financial instruments at the same time.

LVMH's acquisition of a 21.4% stake in Hermès once again provides a good example of how derivative products (in this case, equity swaps) can be used to build blocks of control. It also shows the role that regulation needs to play in market transparency. In most cases, the use of derivatives is not regulated. Since 2009, however, regulation has gradually evolved in its attempts to encourage more transparency by making more information available to market operators, particularly on the existence of such derivative products. Furthermore, intermediaries have developed new ways of financing call and put options. These strategies involve less exposure and greater leverage. Their development has therefore enabled certain highly specialized operators – such as arbitrage, activist, and sovereign funds – to play a greater role in the markets. We can see that all of these financial innovations, brought about by greater market integration, require changes to regulation and have undeniably transformed the markets themselves.

1.2 CHANGES TO M&A PRACTICE

The transformations we have just discussed, which have altered the environment of the financial markets and how they operate, have also affected how takeover bids are conducted. The first thing to note is that the increase in the size of mergers and acquisitions is closely linked to the increase on the financial markets. Since the mid-1990s, M&A volumes have been around 10% of stock-market capitalization on average in a given market. In recent years, as well as the increase in the size of M&A, there have been significant changes to takeover bids and the way they are conducted.

The first change involves the greater role of cash in M&A transactions. Before the dotcom bubble burst in 2000, cash-only deals represented around 35% of all M&A. Since 2005, this figure has climbed steeply to between 60% and 70%. There are several reasons for the rise of cash deals at the expense of all-share and mixed offers:

- Since 2000, large international groups have shaken up their cost structures to generate more cash and therefore improve their liquidity. Since 2005, the trend has been to use this cash, and one of the main uses has been the acquisition of target companies with a view to improving growth prospects.
- The increased role of cash goes hand in hand with fewer share offers, which can be seen as more risky because they depend partly on the share price of the buying company. Some observers believe the number of share transactions has fallen because they are less attractive than all-cash deals to shareholders of the target company. Moreover, all- or part-share offers can create unwanted downward pressure on the buyer's share price as the result of large sell positions being built up.
- The third reason – which we will come back to later – is the emergence and growing importance of private-equity funds in M&A transactions

up to the summer of 2007. Extraordinarily favorable lending conditions saw a sharp rise in the number of leveraged buyouts (LBOs), which involve large amounts of debt. Finally, any credit squeeze would surely see a return to more share offers at the expense of all-cash deals.

A second change has been the increase in hostile transactions. In 2000, this type of operation represented only around 2% of global M&A. Over the last few years, this figure has risen to approximately 15%. Hostile bids are generally a sign that managers of the buying company are confident about the prospects for their business, about macroeconomic stability, and that the transaction is strategically sound. Such bids are less likely to arise in uncertain climates like the present one, which is marred by fears over eurozone debt and global growth. The presence of activist investors, such as the ones we discussed earlier, in the share capital of target companies can encourage a hostile bid, too.

The emergence of LBO funds has also brought about a big change on the financial markets. Starting in 2005, extremely favorable lending conditions and low interest rates encouraged the appearance of these funds and allowed them to play a more important role in the financial markets. They were able to raise considerable sums of money and make full use of debt for most of their transactions. In 2006 and 2007, LBO funds were behind as many as 25% of global M&A. Historically, these funds came about largely for the purposes of financing management buyouts, with a view to maximizing profits and cash flow. They typically have a medium-term investment horizon (three to five years; sometimes more) and target returns that are attractive and partly uncorrelated to the financial markets.

A return to more "normal" credit conditions in recent years, and indeed tougher conditions in the form of the credit crunch, has had a big impact on this kind of transaction and on private equity as a whole. Private equity will remain, however, a key player on the markets and an initiator of takeovers owing in particular to its immense investment power. At the same time, the ways in which these investment funds intervene have changed slightly. These days, some private-equity firms tend to acquire minority stakes and then help managers to take operational decisions (e.g. Blackstone in Leica Camera). Majority transactions now involve lower levels of leverage.

Lastly, M&A are increasingly instigated by groups from emerging nations. Since 2000, the financial markets of emerging nations have changed dramatically. They are playing an increasing role in international transactions, both as a source and a destination of capital. Between 2000 and 2007, stock-market capitalizations in China, India, Russia, and the Middle East increased tenfold to reach around $5,000 billion.

1.3   MARKET EVALUATION OF M&A

Before actually making an offer, the bidder must take into account the often different objectives of the parties involved. The two determining factors are the bid price and how the offer is structured. The price needs to be attractive to shareholders of the target company, and the offer must be structured in such a way that respects the many constraints placed upon the bidder.

1.3.1   The price offered to shareholders of the target company

The bid price is the most important factor:

- it must include a control premium over the various reference share prices (volume-weighted averages taken over different periods; the peak price from the 12 months preceding the offer date is often the best indicator of a company's standalone value);
- it must be greater than the entry price paid by the target company's historic shareholders, hence the need to research as thoroughly as possible the shareholder structure and the entry price paid by the various shareholders;
- it must be analyzed against the price targets set by sell-side analysts and against how much growth potential the board and managers of the target company think the share price has;
- it should be evaluated based on the likelihood and amount of a counteroffer from a rival bidder (and therefore on the synergies attainable by this competitor).

From the buyer's point of view, they need to be able to justify the price by the possible synergies and by the added value that the target company's activities will create for their shareholders.

1.3.2   Structure – the key to evaluating an offer

Offers can be made either in cash or in shares of the buyer, or a mixture of the two.

An all-cash offer is generally considered to be more attractive to shareholders of the target company because they know exactly how much they will be getting. Share offers are unpredictable because the value of the buyer's shares is subject to market fluctuations. Having said that, share offers can be fiscally advantageous because they are generally subject to deferred taxation. Moreover, share offers mean shareholders retain an interest in the performance of the newly merged entity (although there is nothing to stop these shareholders using the money they receive in a cash bid to reinvest in the buyer).

For the bidder, the choice between a cash and a paper offer is determined largely by five factors:

- the cost and availability of financing;
- their financing constraints, debt ratios, and credit rating;
- their share price (issuing shares is often seen as a sign that a company's management team overvalues its shares);
- the accretive/dilutive effect on earnings per share (EPS) (unless the price-to-earnings ratio is very high, cash payment is generally more favorable);
- aspects relating to shareholder structure and dilution of control.

Whether the offer is announced before or during market opening hours, reactions from the different market operators are seen immediately and can be very revealing as to their assessment of the bid.

Attention should be paid to several factors, including the reaction of the share price not only of the target company but also of the bidding company. Indeed, the latter is even more important where the offer is for a similar-sized company or is made entirely or partly in shares. The different reactions provide a first impression of whether or not the market thinks the offer will be successful.

The spread is the gap between the share price of the target company and the value of the offer once the bid has been made public. The size of the spread provides us with an idea of whether the bid is likely to be successful. If the market believes there are likely to be higher counterbids, the share price of the target company will be higher than the offer price, meaning the spread is negative. Conversely, if the market does not expect counterbids and is skeptical about the offer being successful – if there are doubts about financing or regulatory approval, for example – the spread will be very large, with the share price of the target company well below the offer price. If a bid is on track and the transaction is likely to be completed, the spread tends to gradually narrow as the closing date approaches – i.e. the share price of the target company and the offer price converge.

Arbitrage funds make their investments once the bid has been made public, based on their view of the likelihood of success of the bid. We will come back to that later in the book.

In the event of an all- or part-share offer, it is important to keep an eye on how the share price of the bidder reacts to the announcement. After all, the final offer amount depends on the buyer's share price. If the bidder's share price falls, the offer premium is reduced and the bid becomes less attractive to the shareholders of the target company. This can indicate that the market has a lack of faith in the bid and its chances of success. Conversely, a rise in the bidder's share price makes the offer more attractive to the shareholders of the target company. We will take a closer look at this phenomenon in the case study on Alcan's bid for Pechiney, which follows this chapter.

In the event of an all-cash offer, the bidder's share price has no impact on the offer made to the shareholders of the target company, but it does give an indication of how supportive the bidder's shareholders are of the acquisition and should not, therefore, be ignored.

So, we have seen that the markets play an essential role of arbitrator in takeover bids. They judge the quality of the offer made by the bidding company and assess how capable the target company is of resisting this offer.

Having said that, the diversity of the parties involved and their individual objectives and interests make the situation much more complex in reality. The evolving nature of the parties involved, their methods and structures has also brought about changes in M&A practice.

1.4   TYPES OF SYNERGIES AND WAVES OF M&A

1.4.1   Justification for transactions

Buyers commonly justify M&A by claiming that the resulting synergies will create value. These synergies can be grouped together as a series of objectives.

1.4.1.1   Better efficiency

The main aim of any M&A operation is to maximize value for shareholders.

Economies of scale are generally the reason most often given for a business combination. This means a lower average unit cost of production for the quantity of products manufactured. A merger seems to be an effective way of achieving this and spreading fixed costs over a greater number of manufactured units.

The Boston Consulting Group (BCG) determined a few years ago that the unit cost price drops by 20% when cumulative production volumes double. An acquisition is therefore a quick way of enjoying economies of scale, for example in terms of research and development costs (pharmaceuticals) or distribution costs (e.g. Pernod-Ricard's purchase of Allied Domecq in the spirits sector, or the Kraft/Cadbury confectionery deal).

The size of the merged companies also brings improvements in efficiency and gives the buyer the chance to reach the critical mass it needs as part of its development.

Cost synergies can also be brought about through streamlining in the form of sharing nonspecific resources that are present in both companies.

This rationalization, which reduces costs through economies of scope, may involve one or more areas of business. It helps to avoid overlapping and makes the organization more coherent by offering cost-saving opportunities in the form of:

• grouping together sales forces and distribution networks;
• rationalizing certain services or functions;
• optimizing production sites by closing the less profitable ones or allocating resources more effectively;
• centralizing company departments and divisions;
• improving the distribution of human resources and, in some cases, cutting jobs.

1.4.1.2   Obtaining market power

One of the reasons for M&A is the desire to have enough economic power to strengthen the company at the expense of other market operators. This market power can then be used for offensive strategies.

Buyers use M&A to increase their domination or influence over the market, a strategy which is strongly linked to the company's ability to subtly affect the competition by, for example, reducing production volumes in order to increase prices or imposing certain restrictions on its rivals.

The increase in raw-material procurement volumes that arises from the combination gives the new entity an advantage in negotiating contracts with its suppliers (e.g. Carrefour/Promodès). More specifically, it can negotiate lower prices, quicker delivery times, and longer payment terms.

1.4.1.3   Acquiring specific resources

This is important because a company sometimes needs to get hold of new resources, whether these come in the form of expertise or assets, quickly in order to remain competitive.

Such a situation can lead the management of a company to opt for a merger, which is the only choice available if the resources needed are not available on the market.

Buying companies look for resources such as specific expertise (e.g. Google's acquisition of YouTube) and reputable brands (e.g. the purchase of Volvo by Chinese group Geely).

Mergers can be explained by the desire to buy resources that are already available on the market. The transfer of resources from the acquired company to the buyer could involve technology resources or teams with a particular area of expertise.

In such a transaction, the target company is essentially a "resource provider" aiming to add to or improve the capabilities of the buying company.

1.4.1.4   Benefiting from the intellectual property of the target company

Intellectual property can give a company a competitive advantage and is perhaps one of the best reasons for an acquisition. It can include patents, registered trademarks, manufacturing processes, complex databases, and research and development laboratories with a strong track record in product development. Sanofi's acquisition of Genzyme is a perfect example.

1.4.1.5   Hindering the progress of a troublesome competitor

A merger can be an effective way of seeing off the threat of major rivals. It can be a defense mechanism in several situations, with results of varying impact, such as:

- neutralizing a competitor by strengthening market power – this strategy, which has a temporary and direct effect, can be seen in the case of internationalization;

- eliminating a competitor – this strategy, which has a long-term and direct effect, enables the buyer to eliminate a rival that is threatening its market leadership;
- submitting a counterbid – this strategy, which has a long-term and indirect effect, prevents rival firms from merging and enables the company to take control of the target entity of its biggest competitor. The hostile double all-share bid made by BNP in 1999 for Société Générale and Paribas, which were planning to merge, is a good example.

1.4.1.6 Blocking new entrants to a sector

If a company wants to prevent external threats, it can attempt to dissuade potential new entrants to a sector. This kind of threat is even more serious if the costs involved in getting access to the sector are not especially high for potential entrants. A merger can be a vital way of responding to the danger posed by new competitors.

A company can make entry into the sector more difficult by merging with one of its rivals, suppliers, or distributors. This enables it to raise the cost of entry into a sector to such an extent that penetrating the market becomes either too risky or not profitable enough.

By acquiring a potential rival, this kind of merger can also, of course, transform an element of risk into an opportunity for growth. Such a strategy is particularly useful where technology is a strategic resource with clear and sustainable benefits.

1.4.2 Waves of M&A

As shown in Figure 1.1, the M&A market has two main characteristics: an underlying trend of steady growth and a cyclical nature in the form of waves.

Figure 1.1 shows two aspects of the global M&A activity since 1980: the number of transactions and their overall value. The cyclical nature of this activity and the waves of transactions can be clearly observed. In the US, there are generally considered to have been six M&A waves:

- The first dates back to the 20-year period straddling the end of the 19th and the beginning of the 20th centuries, just after the industrial

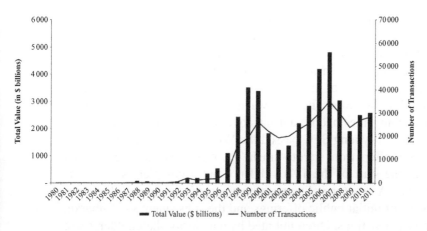

Figure 1.1   Global M&A activity in value and number of transactions since 1980
Source: Bloomberg

revolution in the US. It involved the creation of "majors" through the
horizontal mergers of industry-leading conglomerates. Groups such as
U.S. Steel and Standard Oil were created during this period. Research
shows that the period saw more than 5,000 companies merged into
just 300 conglomerates. The first wave was interrupted by the Panic
of 1907 and prompted many responses from regulators. It was during
this period that the first texts were written regulating the constitution
of conglomerates, and these texts form the basis of the competition
rules still in effect today.

- The second M&A wave was born out of the economic growth that
followed the First World War. Horizontal transactions were less common because new antitrust rules gave government authorities the
power to block anti-competitive deals. The second wave was therefore a large consolidation of existing groups by way of many vertical
M&A. This movement gave rise to oligopolies but did not result in
specific regulation. However, the 1929 Great Depression that brought
an end to the second wave led to the creation of the Securities and
Exchange Commission (SEC) and the adoption of the Exchange and
Securities Acts, with a view to regulating the issue and exchange
of shares.

- The third wave emerged at the start of the 1960s and lasted for a
decade. The trend at the time was for companies to expand and
diversify, with the peak period of 1967–1969 seeing more than 10,000
companies acquired. The stand-out feature of this movement was the

prevalence of hostile takeovers. Previously, offers required the publication of a proxy statement and then the approval both of the target company and of its shareholders. Now, bids took the form of tender offers with payment in cash. This meant the decision was taken directly by the shareholders of the target company, bypassing the opinion of the board of directors. The third wave was a considerable movement because companies had no anti-takeover defense mechanisms at the time. The still-young SEC passed the Williams Act in 1968 to regulate tender offers from start to finish. The recession and stock-market crash at the start of the 1970s did not put a complete stop to the third wave. A new type of transaction emerged, born out of the previous wave of initial public offerings and the subsequent stock-market downturn: delistings. Often initiated by a majority shareholder, these operations were mostly a display of authority. This caused regulators to clampdown on delistings, which saw small investors often rendered powerless and presented with a *fait accompli*. Well after the end of the third wave, the SEC passed a law forcing companies undergoing a delisting to publish their position on the equal treatment of shareholders with no affiliation to the buyer. The aftermath of the stock-market crash at the beginning of the 1970s put a definitive end to the third wave.

- The fourth wave was the wave of corporate raiders. It started at the end of the 1970s and came to a close with the savings and loans and high-yield bond market crisis. The proportion of hostile takeovers rose sharply during this period, mainly in the form of tender offers. An abundance of high-yield credit enabled the financing of large acquisitions by investment banks mandated by investors such as T. Boone Pickens. As a result of the previous M&A wave, companies were now equipped with anti-takeover defense mechanisms, making hostile bids more difficult. But favorable lending conditions meant bidders could offer huge control premiums, making hostile cash offers especially attractive to shareholders of target companies. This wave ended once such credit facilities had disappeared, namely after the 1989 crisis.

- The fifth and penultimate M&A wave came with the arrival of the dotcom bubble and extremely high stock-market levels. The period, which lasted from 1993 to 2000, was also one of "mega deals": six of the 10 largest ever deals took place in the final two years of the period. One of these deals, for example, was the $165 billion merger

of AOL and Time Warner in 2000. The regulatory response came in the wake of the Enron and WorldCom scandals.
* The sixth and final wave was dominated by private-equity funds. It lasted from 2003 until 2008 and will be discussed in more detail in Chapter 10 on LBOs.

There is nothing random about the cyclical nature of M&A; it is the result of interaction between many different economic forces. It can be explained, to varying degrees, by all of the following factors:

* Periods of innovation and technological change – these tend to bring about a wave of mergers between companies. As soon as a new technology appears (e.g. the internet or renewable energies), large numbers of companies are created. Some become market leaders, but others find it tougher, need to finance their development and end up being bought by the success stories. Microsoft's acquisition of Skype in May 2011 is an excellent example.
* Changes in scale or reference markets – companies now operate in a globalized framework that requires major investment and critical mass. The merger between British Airways and Iberia provides a good example of this.
* Changes to the regulatory environment – the majority of western countries have implemented a general regime of deregulation across many sectors (e.g. air travel, telecoms, banking, energy) over the last 20 years. This market liberalization caused a wave of privatizations and then reorganizations of certain sectors (e.g. J.P. Morgan's acquisition of Chase Manhattan in January 2011, and Imperial Tobacco's acquisition of fellow tobacco firm Altadis in 2008).
* A final factor is the structural evolution of the financial markets and the passage from a German model (dominated by bank financing and the weight of major shareholders) to an Anglo-Saxon one, where shareholders apply pressure on managers to improve competitiveness, financial results, and, therefore, the share price. In a context where the outlook for organic growth is fairly bleak (static populations and sluggish economic growth), companies are strongly swayed to sate their craving for growth by means of acquisition.

The phenomenon of waves of M&A has been the subject of extensive academic research, which has generally uncovered two possible explanations on top of the ones we have already seen (which, of course, are not mutually exclusive):

- M&A waves could perhaps be explained by the coexistence of under- and overvalued companies on a market at any given time. In this context, companies which are aware that they are overvalued look to buy undervalued firms in order to improve their value before investors pick up on the situation. It is a way of overvalued companies mitigating against a future sharp fall in value. This approach relies on the different information that different investors get from the market, and the same difference of information can be found between the buyer and the target company. In theory, the target firm, knowing it is undervalued, agrees to be bought in any case because it tends to overestimate potential synergies.
- The other possible reason is the behavioral aspect of finance. Several researchers have found that the psychology of a company's management team plays a crucial role when it comes to M&A, particularly the pride of an executive who buys a rival or another firm and finds himself at the head of an enlarged group. Research also suggests the existence of mass movements at the start of M&A waves, whereby managers are persuaded to embark on an acquisition because they do not want to be seen as the only inactive ones.

The following case study will provide examples of the things we have just discussed. Whether before or after the announcement of the acquisition of French industrial group Pechiney by Canada's Alcan (itself subsequently acquired by Rio Tinto), which began in September 1999, the market and its reactions played a fundamental role in how the operation panned out. We will start to look at M&A arbitrage in its own right in the next chapter.

CASE STUDY: The Alcan/Pechiney Deal

Three-Way Merger Aborted

In September 1999, Canadian aluminum giant Alcan signed a three-way merger agreement with Pechiney and Alusuisse Lonza Group AG (Algroup). The transaction was due to take the form of two independent share-swap offers by Alcan: one for Pechiney and one for Algroup. On November 22, 1999, Alcan shareholders approved the issue of new Alcan shares to be awarded to Pechiney and Algroup shareholders as part of the two offers.

On March 13, 2000, after several months of negotiations with European and US competition authorities, the three companies informed the European Commission that they had withdrawn their notification of the operation concerning Pechiney and abandoned the merger with the French company. The project was abandoned because the European regulator rejected the undertakings proposed by the three companies in response to competition concerns it had identified.

According to the European Commission, the new group would have had dominant positions in certain European markets, notably flat-rolled aluminum products used in the production of beverage and food cans and certain packaging products. The regulator did not consider satisfactory the undertakings proposed by the companies to resolve this issue of a dominant position. The Commission therefore published a press release on March 14, 2000, in which it identified the different problems raised by the proposed merger of the companies and explained its reasons for rejecting the undertakings they proposed.

On the same day, however, the European Commission gave its approval to the share-swap deal between Alcan and Algroup, subject to certain disposals. The combination between the two companies took place on October 17, 2000, with Alcan buying 99% of Algroup's shares. The remaining shares were acquired by Alcan in 2001, prompting the delisting of Algroup from the Swiss stock exchange.

Despite this sequence of events, Alcan had not given up hope of merging with Pechiney.

The First Approach

On October 7, 2002, Travis Engen, the chairman and CEO of Alcan who was still determined to add the French firm to his group despite the setback three years earlier, met in Paris with his counterpart at Pechiney, Jean-Pierre Rodier, for informal talks on whether the two companies might consider another attempt at a combination. The two parties were clearly convinced of the potential of such a deal and decided to continue discussions.

At the end of October, however, Pechiney announced that it had agreed in principle to buy the flat-rolled aluminum products business of Anglo-Dutch group Corus, which represented 14% of its total turnover at the time. This deal was driven by Corus' desire to focus on its core steel business and Pechiney's desire to re-establish itself as the world's third-largest aluminum producer, a position it had lost to Norway's Norsk Hydro. However, Pechiney's acquisition of the Corus business posed a regulatory problem for the potential merger with Alcan – just like in 1999.

Alcan and Pechiney executives held another meeting soon after, where the French firm explained that its priority was to proceed with the Corus acquisition and that, for the moment, it did not want to continue merger talks with the Canadian group. There was, however, another twist in the tale.

On March 11, 2003, Corus announced that the supervisory board of Corus Nederland NV, its aluminum subsidiary, had rejected the proposed sale to Pechiney of its flat-rolled products and shaping activities. On this occasion, Pechiney's expansion plans had been thwarted because the Corus supervisory board was afraid that the deal would have had a negative impact on jobs owing to the considerable losses posted by the aluminum business of the Anglo-Dutch steel group.

Following the abandonment of the Corus acquisition, Mr Engen and Mr Rodier got together again to discuss the possibility of a merger between their respective groups. In the wake of discussions with their respective boards of directors, Pechiney executives informed their Canadian counterparts that the time was not right to discuss such an operation. Alcan and its board of directors continued to look at the possibility of a merger during this time.

On July 3, 2003, Mr Engen's PA organized a telephone conversation with Mr Rodier for the following morning. That same day, Reuters reported rumors of possible takeover bids for Pechiney by both Alcan and Norsk Hydro. Pechiney's share price rose from €32 to €33.70, with trading volumes above average levels.

During his conversation with Mr Rodier the following day, Mr Engen raised the issue of Pechiney's rising share price and assured his French counterpart that Alcan was not involved, either directly or indirectly, in buying Pechiney shares on the market. He asked Mr Rodier to organize a meeting that same day in Paris, and the meeting took place – at Mr Rodier's request – at the offices of Pechiney's lawyers.

During the meeting, Mr Engen presented to Mr Rodier the economic and commercial advantages of a merger between Alcan and Pechiney, the changes that had occurred in both groups and in the aluminum and packaging industry as a whole since the aborted merger in 1999, and Alcan's new approach to the potential competition issues arising from the transaction. Mr Engen said he wanted to establish the headquarters for the combined packaging business in Paris and to examine the economic and commercial reasons for also having the aeronautical and engineered products activities based in the French capital. He also discussed how Alcan would protect Pechiney's French employees, establish its R&D headquarters in France with a view to setting up a center for new reservoir technology, and commit to a meritocratic system for selecting the management team of the new Alcan group. Mr Engen also insisted on reaching an agreement before July 7, 2003 in light of the recent progress of Pechiney's share price, stock-market speculation (this concern related to legal requirements and other market disclosure restraints), and the need for Alcan to protect its own interests.

Mr Rodier said he was not in a position to give a formal response to Mr Engen, but he did raise several difficulties that Pechiney had faced in the wake of the failed operation in 1999.

He indicated to Mr Engen that Pechiney would not respond favorably to any transaction that would be subject to competition regulatory authorizations.

Mr Engen then presented the terms of the initial bid that he envisaged submitting on behalf of Alcan. Mr Rodier said he would have to take into consideration his obligations to his shareholders, employees, and customers in determining whether the offer was the best solution for Pechiney and all its stakeholders. He requested a few weeks to think over the offer. Mr Engen raised the issue of market disclosure constraints and asked if they could continue their conversation the next day. Mr Rodier agreed to meet him on Saturday afternoon.

On July 5, the two protagonists met in the offices of Publicis (Alcan's communications agency) in Paris. Mr Engen explained his understanding of the European Commission's regulatory timetable, of the timetable for takeover bids in France, and of the processes and timeframes available to the management and the board of Pechiney to review the terms of an offer. Mr Engen and Mr Rodier discussed a timetable for a possible bid from Alcan, and the Canadian group's executive again expressed his concerns about the possible need to make public the discussions between the two groups in light of the market speculation. He also stressed the importance of the investigation by the competition authorities getting under way as soon as possible in order to clarify the necessary undertakings and resolve the problems envisaged by Alcan and Pechiney in light of their experiences in 1999. Mr Rodier revealed that he had begun informal talks with the board of directors at Pechiney. He also said that the three key factors in evaluating any offer would be: price; the opinion of senior executives on the bidder; and matters relating to competition law.

Discussions continued, and then Mr Engen informed Mr Rodier that Alcan may issue a press release on the Monday morning (July 7), but he stressed that a final decision had not been taken.

On July 6, during talks with members of Alcan's executive committee, Mr Engen gave his views on the terms and conditions of the initial offer and revealed he had decided to announce and submit the offer the following day.

The Hostile Takeover Bid

On July 7, 2003, Alcan filed its initial offer with the French Financial Markets Council (*Conseil des Marchés Financiers*, CMF), the French Stock Exchange Operations Commission (*Commission des Opérations de Bourse*, COB), and the US Securities and Exchange Commission (SEC).

It was a "mix and match" offer, with a cash element (capped), a paper element (capped), and a mixed element (not capped). This meant shareholders could choose the element they preferred and give Alcan an indication of the final cash/shares mix.

The terms of the offer were as follows:

• The offer values each Pechiney share at €41 (on the basis of the closing price of Alcan's shares as at July 3, 2003 and the US$/€ exchange rate of 1.15).

Table CS1.1 Alcan's offer implied premium

	Pechiney share price** (€)	Implied premium*** (%)
July 2, 2003	32.00	28.1
1-month average*	29.59	38.6
3-month average*	26.78	53.1
12-month average*	30.73	33.4

* Volume-weighted average of closing prices
** Ordinary share
*** On the basis of the closing price of Alcan shares as at July 3, 2003 and the US$/€ exchange rate of 1.15
Source: Analysts' presentation

- Main offer: For every five Pechiney shares €123 in cash plus three Alcan shares (0.6 Alcan shares + €24.6 in cash per Pechiney share).
- Alternative offers:
  - All cash: €41 per Pechiney share
  - All stock: three Alcan shares for two Pechiney shares
  - Total offer mix: 60% cash and 40% in shares.
- Other components
  - For each Pechiney OCEANE: €81.7 in cash
  - For 50 Pechiney Bonus Allocation Rights: €123 in cash and three Alcan shares.

On the day the offer was filed, Alcan's bid included a significant control premium over the Pechiney share price, as shown in Table CS1.1.

The operation would allow Alcan to consolidate its position among the world's leading aluminum and packaging firms and to benefit from economies of scale, increased financial and technology resources, and the greater ability of the new group to reach customers across the globe. The new group would also be better diversified in the low-cost primary aluminum production segment, enabling it to increase profits and manufacture more aluminum products thanks to local sites in many countries across the world, and would enjoy a market-leading position in flexible packaging. The addition of Pechiney would provide the new Alcan group with better R&D capabilities as well as better industrial process and product development capabilities across all business segments. See Figure CS1.1.

Upon the bid announcement, Pechiney's share price was marginally above the offer price and closed at €42 on July 7, 2003. This indicated that arbitrageurs expected an improved offer.

Pechiney's Defense Strategy

On the same day that the offer was submitted, Pechiney issued a press release saying that it had negative implications for the company, its employees and its

Unique Business Opportunity

Greater Range of Strategic Options
and Value Maximizing Opportunities

- Increases presence in core markets

- Broadens technology leadership – core smelting technology

- Benefits customers

- World leader in low-cost primary aluminum

- Enhances aluminum fabrication portfolio – e.g., aerospace

- Creates US$6 billion packaging leader

Figure CS1.1   Alcan's rationale for Pechiney takeover
Source: Analysts' presentation

shareholders, and that Alcan's offer price did not reflect Pechiney's strategic value:

> Pechiney is aware of the unsolicited takeover bid launched by the Alcan group for control of its share capital. There was no consultation between the two groups prior to this decision.
>
> Pechiney is shocked by the hostile nature of the approach.
>
> Pechiney hereby gives notice that the offer is subject to conditions precedent pertaining notably to authorization from the competition authorities. It is therefore very uncertain whether the operation will go ahead, which is damaging for the company, its staff and its shareholders.
>
> Pechiney's leadership in technology and policy of constant growth has consolidated its undisputed market leadership in primary aluminum, enabled it to forge strong positions in the aerospace and automotive industries, and confirmed its market-leader status in packaging. In light of the above, the takeover bid very significantly undervalues the economic and strategic value of the Pechiney Group.
>
> Pechiney's Board of Directors will meet soon to examine the offer in relation to Pechiney's strategic value, from a business perspective and in terms of creating value for its shareholders.

Two days later, Pechiney issued a press release confirming that its board had rejected the initial offer from Alcan during a meeting held the previous day.

Responding to a question from a reporter the same day, Mr Engen said he would seek another meeting with Mr Rodier.

On July 16, the CMF declared Alcan's initial offer to be admissible.

A week later, Pechiney published its provisional results for the second quarter of 2003 and announced it would begin a road show to respond to Alcan's initial offer. Mr Rodier and Pechiney's advisory banks began to hold meetings with investors in Paris, London, New York, and Boston at the end of July.

Pechiney's defense strategy was built around several things:

Standalone strategy

This involved executives meeting with the company's major shareholders and trying to convince them that Alcan's offer price did not reflect the intrinsic value of the company. Pechiney attempted to carry out this strategy, but it had several flaws:

- The French company's management was in no real position to promote a standalone strategy given: (i) the failure of the three-way merger in 1999; (ii) the fiasco of the Corus deal; (iii) a struggling share price; (iv) the company's image as a "fallen angel".
- Pechiney's mooted sale in the summer of its packaging unit, designed to return some cash to shareholders in anticipation of better times ahead, was met with disappointing bids.

The search for a white knight

This involved looking for a third party to come in with a friendly bid at a higher price. With that in mind, Mr Rodier went on the offensive in the press, telling the *Financial Times* that "any offer would be better than Alcan's" and claiming that "several other groups" had already phoned him. The French company's CEO also claimed to have the support of shareholders representing "40% of the share capital," who, he said, "were unanimous in finding the offer [from Alcan] to be ridiculously low."

It appeared, however, that contacts established by Pechiney's advisory banks had not brought about anything concrete. After all, the aluminum sector was already fairly concentrated and there were not many potential buyers around.

Play the jobs card and mobilize employees

This involved mobilizing the trade unions and/or public authorities in order to persuade Alcan to drop its bid. Pechiney's CGT union representatives were the most outspoken against the takeover bid, describing it as part of "the process of concentration of capital that has extended to many industries worldwide and of which we have seen the harmful effects on the day-to-day life of employees and national industries." Alcan had largely defused this threat, however, by making it clear that it did not intend to reduce the number of staff or production sites in France beyond the existing restructuring plans of Pechiney.

Faced with the failure of these various defense strategies, the Pechiney board was rapidly forced to exchange its recommendation for an improved offer price.

Alcan's Attack Strategy and the Issue of Synergies

Since Alcan chose to make a mixed cash and paper offer for Pechiney rather than an all-cash one, it was essential that the Canadian firm's share price did not fall when the bid was announced or in the subsequent days. Such a fall would have devalued the stock offered in exchange and therefore reduced the value of the offer, making it less likely to be accepted by Pechiney shareholders.

Quantifying the synergies that had been announced took on huge importance because it was the assessment of the quality of the business plan and the potential synergies that would determine how the market, and the Alcan shareholders in particular, embraced the deal.

Communication on the synergies had two contradictory objectives:

- announce a large and credible amount of synergies in order to reassure Alcan shareholders that the merger would create value;
- do not announce excessive synergies for fear of letting Pechiney shareholders think that they were entitled to a share of a very large pie and therefore ask for more money.

In the end, Alcan's management team announced annual cost savings of approximately $250 million before tax. By way of comparison, Alcan had achieved annual synergies of around $200 million through the successful integration of Algroup.

The synergies envisaged by Alcan's offer represented around 3.8% of Pechiney's 2002 turnover, excluding revenue from its international commerce business. Again by way of comparison, the synergies achieved through the integration of Algroup represented approximately 3.9% of Algroup's 1998 turnover.

The predicted cost savings were supposed to come from the following areas (see also Figure CS1.2):

- SG&A (31%): lower head-office costs and costs for trading and shared-activity support services.
- Manufacturing (15%): lower production costs from improved production sites and productivity gains.
- Logistics and purchasing (26%): lower raw-material costs, operational costs and financing costs through improved project management, greater purchasing volumes and an extended chain of suppliers.
- Research and development (12%): lower costs through shared research equipment and technical and IT services.
- Corporate (16%): maximizing profits from investments for shareholders by optimizing the investment program for Alcan and Pechiney.

Given that Alcan's share price did not fall when the bid was announced, and that it actually rose during the subsequent weeks owing to the combined effect of rising aluminum prices and good financial results published by the company,

US$250 Million Annual
Pre-Tax Cost Synergies

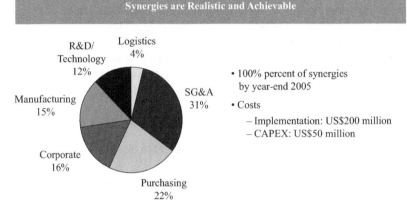

Figure CS1.2 Alcan's estimated cost synergies
Source: Analysts' presentation

the value of the mixed offer kept on increasing, rendering Pechiney's defense increasingly futile. For Alcan, it was simply a case of waiting for Pechiney to back down and collecting its prize. The turnover of capital in favor of arbitrageurs, who by definition favor a "good" offer price, would do the rest.

To give you an idea of the mood at the time, here is an extract from an interview given by Travis Engen on August 20, 2003:

> *Pechiney's share price has risen well above the cash offer of €41 since the Alcan bid was launched. Why do you think that is?*
> It is interesting to note that Pechiney's share price is simply mirroring Alcan's, which has risen sharply since the bid was announced, particularly after we published our second-quarter results. At current share prices, the paper offer (3 Alcan shares for 2 Pechiney shares) is equivalent to €48 per Pechiney share – a price that the Pechiney stock is moving towards. The mixed (paper and cash) offer values Pechiney shares at €44, while the cash offer remains at €41.
>
> *Pechiney said your offer was "manifestly insufficient". Will you be increasing it?*
> Pechiney's share price is low because there is little visibility of the group's prospects. Alcan's shares have also fallen in recent years owing to the difficult climate, but not as sharply as Pechiney's. After the failure of APA [the attempted three-way merger between Alcan, Pechiney and Alusuisse], we have continued to grow, notably through the integration of Algroup, while Pechiney has not managed to capitalize on opportunities for growth. We are now giving Pechiney shareholders the chance to create a major group – something we were unable to do three years ago. If we increased our offer, we would be jeopardizing our future financial room for maneuver. In fact, the acquisition of Pechiney will increase our debt levels and

it will take us one or two years to bring them back down to a normal level. If we increase our offer, we will need more time to recover our financial resources. Pechiney shareholders who want to cash in after the operation will still be able to sell their Alcan shares, which will be listed in Paris.

Negotiations and Announcement of a Non-hostile Operation

In mid-August 2003, Mr Engen phoned Mr Rodier to request a meeting so the two men could discuss their opinions and reach an agreement on the terms of a revised offer that the Pechiney board of directors would be likely to recommend. A meeting was scheduled for the end of the month in Geneva.

In the meantime, Alcan announced that it had formally filed its bid with the European Commission and proposed certain undertakings to resolve some competition issues regarding the European markets for certain flat-rolled products, aluminum aerosol cans, and aluminum cartridges. Following the filing and the proposed undertakings, the European Commission's initial investigation period (commonly known as Phase 1) was completed at the end of September 2003.

At the meeting in Geneva, the management teams of Alcan and Pechiney discussed problems raised in relation to the European competition authorities' approval procedure, and Mr Rodier said the fundamental issue for Pechiney with regard to Alcan's offer was the price. He put forward several arguments for the price being substantially higher, while Mr Engen set out the pertinent factors used to determine the price that Alcan was willing to pay. Mr Engen said that although the support of the Pechiney board could reduce regulatory uncertainty, a price above €50 (i.e. in the range suggested by Mr Rodier) would exceed Alcan's estimation of the fair value of the French company. Mr Rodier suggested that the Canadian group be made aware of certain financial factors that it may want to consider.

Immediately after the Geneva talks, Alcan's advisory banks – Lazard and Morgan Stanley – met in Paris with the advisory banks of Pechiney: BNP Paribas, Goldman Sachs, JPMorgan and Rothschild. Pechiney's banks once again raised arguments relating to the valuation of the French group and how its accounts would be impacted by several recently announced operations. In the days that followed, the two groups' respective banks talked over possible changes that might cause the Pechiney board to recommend the offer. On August 28, 2003, the two sets of bankers met again to provide details on possible changes to the financial terms of the offer. Among these changes was making the bid a simple mixed cash and shares offer, valued at a maximum of €47 per share. Alcan would also have the choice of paying all or some of the paper element in cash. Later that day, the Pechiney banks informed their Alcan counterparts that the French firm considered the offer to be too low.

Negotiations resumed the following day, with Alcan's advisory banks seeking assurances that any revised offer would be considered promptly by the Pechiney board. If this were the case, they explained, it was highly likely that an agreement could be reached over the weekend.

On August 29, 2003, Alcan filed the Hart–Scott–Rodino notification with the US authorities, triggering a 30-day waiting period under US competition laws which would expire on September 29.

Early in the evening on August 30, 2003, Mr Rodier called Mr Engen to inform his Alcan counterpart that he had tried to organize a Pechiney board meeting for Sunday, August 31 with a view to discussing Alcan's bid.

During the subsequent meeting between the parties, a possible increase in the offer price was mooted for the first time, provided that at least 95% of Pechiney shares were tendered into the offer. Still with no assurance as to the response of the Pechiney board, the different parties began to put together their offer for presentation to the French group's board.

After the meeting, Alcan submitted a confidential written offer at the request of Pechiney. The offer was subject to acceptance by the Pechiney board, which was scheduled to meet later that day. The financial terms of the offer were similar to those described above, with an extra euro to be added if 95% of Pechiney shares were tendered into the offer. The offer also raised certain employment issues. A meeting was organized between Mr Engen and some Pechiney directors so the Alcan CEO could present his vision of the business logic behind the operation as well as the reasons for the offer. Later that evening, Pechiney's advisory banks requested a signed copy of the Alcan offer, which had been provided to the Pechiney board before its meeting.

Even later that night, Mr Engen and the Alcan banks were informed that the Pechiney board had rejected Alcan's offer and that the French firm intended to make public the next day both the offer and its decision to reject it.

On September 1, Pechiney issued a press release stating that although Alcan's offer was an improved one, it still fell short of the true strategic value of the company. The press release also specified that the Pechiney board had noted that Alcan's offer remained subject to approval from the European competition authorities under Phase 1. On the same day, Alcan issued its own press release indicating that since its offer had not been accepted by the Pechiney board, this offer was to be considered withdrawn and the talks with Pechiney were over.

However, talks between the two CEOs and the advisory banks resumed in the days that followed.

In addition, on September 5, the French finance minister announced that Alcan had informed him of undertakings it was willing to make should it acquire Pechiney, and that he had given his approval to the transaction. These undertakings concerned defense contracts and their corresponding commitments, the future of Pechiney's existing industrial sites in France, and the location for the headquarters of certain business segments.

On September 8, Pechiney's advisory banks requested another meeting, in which they presented a revised version of the terms of Alcan's offer from

August 31, albeit without indicating a price. On the same day, Pechiney's bankers also indicated that Mr Rodier and another Pechiney director wished to meet with Mr Engen to present a proposition from the French company. Mr Engen accepted the request.

Three days later, Mr Rodier and Onno Ruding, vice-president and director of Citibank and also a director of Pechiney, met with Mr Engen and Alcan's chief legal officer, David McAusland, in Zurich to discuss potential changes to the terms of the Alcan offer that were likely to be proposed to the Pechiney board.

These talks were followed up by meetings in Paris on September 11 and 12 between Alcan's management team and the legal and financial advisory teams of both parties. On September 12, Mr Engen and Mr Rodier exchanged a letter accompanied by terms of the revised offer which had been approved that day by the Pechiney board. The revised terms of the offer were as follows:

- a simple mixed offer – no ancillary cash or paper offers;
  - cash – €24.60 per Pechiney share
  - Alcan shares – €22.90 in Alcan shares per Pechiney share; each Alcan share would be valued at the highest of (x) €27.40 or (y) the volume-weighted average of the Alcan share price on the New York Stock Exchange over 10 trading sessions picked at random from the 30-day trading period ending five trading days before the closing date of the offer.

The Pechiney Board Recommends the New Alcan Offer

The Pechiney Board of Directors met on September 12, 2003 to examine Alcan's new offer regarding its takeover bid for Pechiney.

The new offer is a maximum of €48.50 in cash and shares, comprising €47.50 per share plus an extra euro per share if take-up is at least 95%.

After having studied the terms of the new Alcan offer carefully, and in light of the long-standing business logic of a combination between Pechiney and Alcan and of the various merits of such a combination versus those of a stand-alone growth strategy, which it considers to be a viable option, the Board has concluded that this new offer represents the best available valuation for Pechiney shareholders.

The Board is pleased that the combination will allow Pechiney employees to participate in the creation of a global leader in aluminum and packaging.

The Board has therefore decided to recommend to its shareholders that they accept this new offer, which it considers to be in the best interests of the company's shareholders, employees and customers.

The Board notes that this offer remains subject to prior Phase 1 approval from the European Union and US competition authorities and that Alcan will submit its new offer by Tuesday, September 16, 2003.

On September 15, 2003, Morgan Stanley and Lazard, acting for Alcan, filed the increased mixed offer with the CMF.

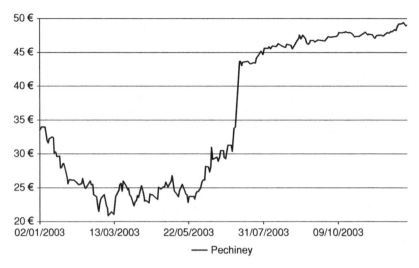

Figure CS1.3   Pechiney stock price evolution
Source: Bloomberg

Alcan's adviser at Morgan Stanley was Michael Zaoui (who wrote this book's foreword). Pechiney's adviser at Goldman Sachs was Yoël Zaoui, Michael's younger brother. Legend has it that the two men started negotiating at a holiday home rented by their respective families and their parents on the island of Ibiza.

Figure CS1.3 shows the Pechiney share price throughout the takeover episode.

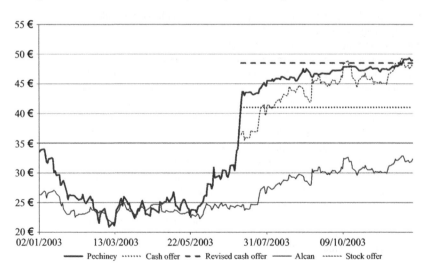

Figure CS1.4   Pechiney/Alcan: changes in stock prices and offer values
Source: Bloomberg

We can clearly see the sharp rise after the various takeover rumors were reported in the press in the days preceding the official offer from Alcan. We can also see that throughout the negotiations which took place after the launch of the initial bid, the share price of the target company went only one way – up. Figure CS1.4 explains this.

We can see that the increase in the Pechiney share price after the launch of the Alcan bid resulted not only from the rise in Alcan's share price given the positive reception to the transaction from the market, which we discussed earlier, but also from the structure of the mixed offer.

Figure CS1.4 also clearly shows the gradual convergence of the Pechiney share price to the Alcan offer price. This is known as the arbitrage spread convergence and it is the subject of the remainder of this book.

2

The Different Types of Transactions

The method of payment used in M&A transactions is one of the most important factors for arbitrageurs. We generally distinguish between three types of transactions: those carried out entirely in cash; those in which remuneration is made entirely in shares; and those that combine payment in cash and in shares. We will also look at a more specific type of share-based transaction: collars.

The reasoning behind the buyer's choice of a certain method and form of payment is all the more important to the arbitrageur because it influences his investment process. The different methods of payment each have specific consequences, which the investor must anticipate and estimate. Whether in terms of financing or of the authorizations required for the transaction to be finalized, which we will discuss later, the different types of transactions pose specific risks to the arbitrage process.

2.1 TYPES OF TRANSACTIONS

2.1.1 Cash transactions

The simplest case is that of a takeover bid with payment in cash. In this type of transaction, the buyer offers to buy the shares held by the target company's shareholders in exchange for a specific cash payment, usually at a higher price than the company's current market share price. Takeover bids can be either friendly or hostile, i.e. accepted by the target company's management board or not, and generally must involve all of the target's shares. We have already seen how important cash settlements have become in recent years.

Example: The Pharmasset/Gilead Deal

On November 21, 2011, US pharmaceutical company Gilead, which specializes in biotechnologies, announced the launch of a takeover bid for Pharmasset. The target is a pharmaceutical firm, still at the clinical-trial stage, which specializes in the treatment of viral infections and, more specifically, of hepatitis C. For Gilead, the objective of the transaction was therefore to acquire Pharmasset's expertise in this field, thereby enabling it to break into rapidly growing markets.

Under the terms of the bid, Gilead offered $137 in cash for each Pharmasset share. The transaction was therefore worth a total of more than $10.3 billion and represented a premium of around 90% over Pharmasset's closing share price prior to the announcement (which was $72.49).

Figure 2.1 shows various factors that are of importance to the arbitrageur:

- the bid price, in this case $137 per share;
- the change in the target company's share price;
- the change in the spread (which we will define later).

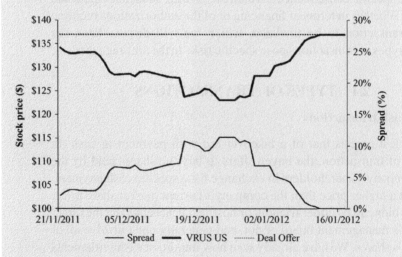

Figure 2.1 Pharmasset: changes in share price and spread
Source: Bloomberg

Figure 2.1 shows an important characteristic of M&A transactions. When the announcement was made, the target company's share price reacted positively, climbing towards the offer price without quite reaching it (in fact, we have seen that, following the announcement, Pharmasset's share price rose by around 90% to reach \$134.14, \$2.86 below Gilead's offer price). This small difference, known as the spread, is the source of arbitrage transactions. In some cases, the spread may also be negative, meaning that, at the time of the announcement, the target's share price is higher than the offer price. In general, this scenario occurs when investors anticipate that other buyers may be able to outbid the bidder to acquire the target.

On the evening of November 21, 2011, the day the announcement was made, Pharmasset's shares closed at \$134.14. Supposing that an arbitrageur bought some of the company's shares at this price, he could expect to make a profit of \$2.86 per share, or 2.13%:

$$Gross\ return = \frac{Offer\ price}{Share\ purchase\ price} - 1 = \frac{137.00}{134.14} - 1$$

$$= 0.02132101$$

We use the term "gross return" because we are not taking into account any taxes that may have to be paid on potential dividends from the target company, or transaction costs or microstructure effects (such as bid–ask spreads).

This return is obtained when the acquisition is finalized. There is a wealth of academic literature (see in particular Hsieh, 2002) on the matter of changes in the shareholder structure of M&A target companies when such transactions are announced. Existing shareholders are often prompted to sell their shares in order to benefit from the rise in the share price caused by the positive response to the announcement. These shareholders are replaced in the shareholder structure by arbitrageurs hoping to benefit from the spread. The entry of arbitrageurs into a company's shareholder structure therefore plays an important role in the success or failure of M&A transactions. We will come back to this point later on.

A second element to take into consideration when calculating the profitability of the transaction is the interval of time between the announcement and the actual closure of the transaction. Generally, when announcements are made, the buyers publish a timetable including an expected closure date. In the case of the Pharmasset buyout, Gilead announced an anticipated closure "during the first quarter of 2012". Consequently, using annualized returns makes it possible to carry out a better comparison between transactions. The interval of time between November 21, 2011, the date of the announcement, and February 15, 2012, the estimated closure date, is 86 days.

There are two formulas for calculating annualized returns: simple interest and compound interest.

Simple interest:

$$R = \left(\frac{Price}{Share\,price} - 1 \right) \times \left(\frac{365}{t} \right)$$

where t is the number of days between the announcement and the closure of the transaction. In our Pharmasset example, we therefore calculate a gross annualized return of:

$$R = \left(\frac{Price}{Share\,price} - 1 \right) \times \left(\frac{365}{t} \right)$$

$$= \left(\frac{137.00}{134.14} - 1 \right) \times \left(\frac{365}{86} \right) = 9.05\%$$

Compound interest:

$$R = \left(\frac{Price}{Share\,price} \right)^{\left(\frac{365}{t} \right)} - 1$$

Using the figures from our example, we calculate a gross annualized return of 9.37%.

The choice between the two formulas depends largely on the objective of the calculation. For comparative purposes, we generally use the simple-interest formula to compare returns that apply to durations of less than a year. Conversely, the compound-interest formula is more appropriate for comparisons involving periods of more than a year.

The choice of February 15 is based on the arbitrageur's estimate of the anticipated finalization date (based on his own analysis, the estimate given by the parties, etc.). Given the information provided by Gilead and Pharmasset, we could just as easily have used more optimistic closure dates, such as January 15, or more pessimistic ones, such as the last day of the quarter, March 31. This choice has a very significant influence on the value of the annualized return, which would be 14.15% in the more optimistic case and 5.94% in the second scenario. We will come back to this aspect in the section on transaction timing.

In this type of transaction, the arbitrageur's position is simple. It consists of buying shares in the target company once the announcement is made and waiting for the transaction to be finalized in order to ensure that he obtains a return equal to the value of the spread. The difficulty lies in assessing the risks that may affect the completion of the transaction.

In this case, Gilead's takeover bid for Pharmasset in theory presented a number of guarantees:

• When the announcement was made, Gilead also stated that it had received bank financing commitments from Bank of America, Merrill Lynch and Barclays Capital, thereby reducing potential uncertainty related to financing.
• It was a friendly takeover bid, meaning that Pharmasset's board of directors and managers accepted the buyout by Gilead and recommended that the French group's shareholders tender their shares into the offer, thereby facilitating the transaction.
• Finally, the control premium offered by Gilead, which was 90%, gave Pharmasset shareholders an additional incentive to tender their shares into the offer.

This lack of uncertainty concerning certain key points of M&A transactions explains the speed with which the share price adjusts towards the offer price and, therefore, the narrowness of the spread.

For the arbitrageur, once the transaction has been announced, four outcomes (two principal outcomes and two subsidiary ones) are possible:

• The two principal outcomes are the closure of the transaction (in which case the profit equal to the value of the spread is known ex ante) or the failure of the offer (in which case the losses are more difficult to predict: at first approximation, we can assume that the share price will return to its prevailing price prior to the offer $+/-$ any changes in the share price of similar companies that have taken place since the announcement). In reality, the impact is generally more pronounced under the combined effect of two factors. The first is technical: the exit of all arbitrageurs, which causes downward pressure on the share price. The other factor is fundamental: the failure of a transaction and the exit of the buyer are sometimes motivated by a MAC clause or the discovery of a problem within the target that is likely to reduce its stand-alone value.

- The two subsidiary outcomes are a counteroffer (every arbitrageur's dream, as in the 3PAR case, which we will discuss in detail later on) and the closure of the transaction by the buyer at a reduced price following a renegotiation of the transaction (which is very rare).

Figure 2.1, depicting the Gilead/Pharmasset case, reveals a major development in the dynamic of the transaction. We can see that, in the days following the announcement of the buyout, the spread began to "open up." In arbitrageur jargon, this means that the target's share price, instead of progressively converging towards the value of the bid, began to fall. Since the amount of the consideration is fixed in cash offers, this means that the gap between the target's share price and the bid price was gradually increasing. We can see, for example, that, just two weeks later, an arbitrageur could acquire Pharmasset shares for $128.44, with an arbitrage spread of 6.66%. The potential gain from arbitrage was therefore bigger. At this stage of the book and of the analysis of examples of arbitrage, we will just say that this opening up of the spread was the result of uncertainties linked to the formulation of the merger agreement between the two parties and therefore linked to an increase, perceived by certain arbitrageurs, of the risk involved in the transaction. The graph shows that this trend continued for some time, with the spread even reaching 11% on December 26, 2011!

However, the transaction was definitively finalized on January 17, 2012. As expected in such a situation, the spread converged towards zero and the arbitrageurs involved in the transaction enjoyed very varied fortunes, depending on their entry and exit levels.

This example perfectly illustrates a fundamental aspect of M&A arbitrage transactions: the spread is not determined once and for all when transactions are announced. It changes according to the dynamic of the transaction, and this enables arbitrageurs to enter into investment opportunities at different times and price levels.

The position of an arbitrageur in a takeover bid, whether friendly or hostile, remains fairly intuitive. The aim is to invest in shares of target companies in transactions that are highly likely to succeed, in order to capture the spread. Therefore, we can see that the difficulty lies in assessing the risks linked to the completion of the transaction. Finally, the distinctive feature of M&A arbitrage transactions is that they present highly asymmetric returns. In the event that the transaction in question succeeds, the arbitrageur's profit is limited to the spread. Conversely, if the transaction fails, the entire premium offered by the buyer is almost always lost. The direct consequence of this, in most cases, is that the target's share price returns to its pre-announcement level, or even falls below it. In addition to the loss linked to the failure of the offer, which is characterized by the loss of the control premium, two elements should be taken into account in the share price reaction: the performance of the market in parallel to the progress of the transaction and the level of interdependence between the movements of the share price and those of the market, characterized by the beta coefficient, as well as the level of liquidity of the shares.

The beta of a stock indicates the degree of correlation between the volatility of a share and that of the market. A share with a beta coefficient of 1 varies in parallel to the market. A share with a beta of less than 1 is less volatile than the market and a share with a beta of more than 1 is more volatile than the market. Therefore, we can see that, if a takeover bid fails, the reaction of the target's share price depends not only on the value of the control premium, but also on the performance of the market since the announcement of the transaction. A stock with a high beta will be much more volatile, and vice versa.

The level of the stock's liquidity also plays an essential role in the share price reaction. In fact, since arbitrageurs' strategies are sometimes similar, they tend to move in the same directions, which is even more obvious in the event of a negative announcement relating to the failure of a transaction. A stock that is not very liquid will therefore tend to fall sharply. This aspect of the potential losses will be dealt with in more detail with the help of examples in Chapter 3.

2.1.2 All-share transactions

From an arbitrageur's point of view, these transactions are a little more complex than transactions that are settled in cash. In all-share transactions, the buyer acquires the target company's shares by paying the shareholders of the latter with its own shares.

We often refer to these transactions as share swap offers. The buyer offers shareholders of the target company a certain quantity of its shares in exchange for their shares in the target. In this case, the arbitrageur's strategy consists of acquiring shares in the target company and simultaneously short selling the buyer's shares, whilst respecting the exchange ratio of the offer. The extremely technical nature of short selling means that access to these transactions is limited to seasoned professionals. Short selling also generates more expenses due to the cost of borrowing the shares from the prime broker. Finally, upon the closure of the transaction, the shares in the target company are exchanged for shares in the buyer, which are then used to repay the shares borrowed for the short selling. In this type of transaction, the reaction of the buyer's share price must be observed very closely. Since these shares serve as a currency for payment, if the buyer's share price falls too sharply on the day of the announcement, the entire transaction could be compromised.

Let's quickly recap what short selling involves. For the investor, this technique consists of borrowing shares from somebody (generally an institutional investor) for a fee and selling them on the market. The investor is responsible for returning them to their owner (and therefore buying them back) at a later date. Short sellers were the first to detect badly run or even fraudulent businesses, such as Enron and Tyco. In such cases, short selling represents a "quest for the truth." Moreover, by favoring arbitrageurs, it acts as a counterweight to the formation of financial bubbles, injects liquidity into the markets, and, consequently, reduces transaction costs and contributes to financial-market efficiency.

In order to properly grasp the subtleties of these transactions, let's use the transaction that took place between Constellation Energy and Exelon as an example.

Example: The Constellation/Exelon Deal

In late April 2011, these two energy operators publicly announced their intention to merge with the aim of creating the biggest integrated energy distribution company in the United States. The new group created as a result of the deal would generate combined turnover of around $33 billion, have total assets of over $70 billion, and carry out a wide range of energy activities in 39 states in the US and Canada. See Figure 2.2.

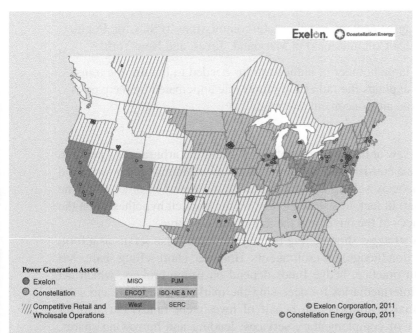

Power Generation Assets

○ Exelon
○ Constellation
//// Competitive Retail and Wholesale Operations

MISO	PJM
ERCOT	ISO-NE & NY
West	SERC

© Exelon Corporation, 2011
© Constellation Energy Group, 2011

Figure 2.2   Complimentary business models and service territories
Source: Available at www.exelonconstellationmerger.com/our-combined-presence

The initial terms of the Exelon bid were as follows:

- at the end of the procedure, 78% of the new company would be held by the buyer's shareholders and 22% by Constellation's shareholders;
- each Constellation share would be exchanged for 0.93 of a share of Exelon;
- the transaction was initially expected to be completed in early 2012.
  In order to be approved, the planned merger needs to obtain a number of authorizations:
- the agreement of the majority of shareholders of Constellation and Exelon;
- the agreement of the US antitrust authorities;
- the agreement of the FERC and the NRC, two US government agencies in charge of regulating the energy industry;

- the agreement of certain state commissions (PSCs, or Public Service Commissions) in Maryland, Texas, and New York.

  The large number of authorizations needed to finalize the transaction explains the rather long timetable anticipated by the parties when the announcement was made.

As we saw at the beginning of this section, the arbitrageur's position in this case consists of acquiring Constellation shares (going long) and simultaneously selling Exelon shares (going short) in order to define the spread. In fact, this strategy rests on the implicit hypothesis that the share prices of the buyer and the target will converge.

In this strategy, short selling the buyer's shares also serves as a form of protection (hedge) for arbitrageurs. However, short selling shares has a cost. In practice, hedge funds depend on prime brokers, which act as their intermediaries for accessing the markets (purchases and sales of financial instruments on behalf of investment funds) but also for a number of complementary services: lending and borrowing shares, financing (for leveraged transactions, among others), etc. Hedge funds can therefore borrow shares of buyers in all-share transactions from prime brokers. They are also sometimes chosen as fund depositories. Moreover, this strategy is not accessible to all merger arbitrage funds. The fund must be able to short sell shares, which not all types of funds are permitted to do. Long-only funds, which are more traditional, therefore cannot become involved in transactions in which at least part of the payment takes place in shares.

The prime-brokerage industry is largely dominated by the biggest international investment banks, such as Bank of America Merrill Lynch, Credit Suisse, Goldman Sachs, Morgan Stanley, and JPMorgan, which share the majority of the market. Using such an institution enables funds to limit counterparty risk, since the prime broker is in effect the counterparty in all their transactions. The prime-brokerage industry has changed considerably since the crisis and is subject to strict supervision from regulators the world over. In fact, a number of observers believe that hedge funds played a role in spreading the financial crisis, but their heterogeneous nature makes them difficult to regulate. It does, however, seem surprising that an industry involving less than 2% of global financial assets could really pose a systemic risk. But that's another debate.

Figure 2.3   Constellation/Exelon share process evolutions
Source: Bloomberg

Figure 2.3 shows the change in the two groups' share prices following the announcement in late April.

It is no real surprise to see that, after the offer was announced, the share prices of the two companies followed a similar trend, since they were linked by the offer involving the two stocks: 1 CEG = 0.93 EXC.

When the announcement was made, Exelon's merger offer represented a premium of around 12.5% over the pre-announcement price of Constellation shares, or a total of around $7.7 billion. When the markets closed on the day of the announcement, Constellation shares were trading at a discount of 8% on the bid offered by Exelon, reflecting to a large extent the anticipation by arbitrageurs of a long process of approval of the transaction by the various government and state commissions.

Figure 2.4 shows the change in the value of the consideration offered by Exelon, as well as the change in the arbitrage spread.

In this type of transaction, the potential gain for arbitrageurs is generated at the moment when they position themselves so as to buy into the share capital of the target company and to sell the buyer's shares. Again, the risk borne by the arbitrageur is that the transaction is not completed and that the spread diverges and changes unfavorably. The risk that competition regulators or the various commissions involved may block the transaction is one example of this, and we will come back to these risks later on in the book.

Finally, the calculation of the return on these transactions is very similar to that used for cash transactions. In addition to the performance

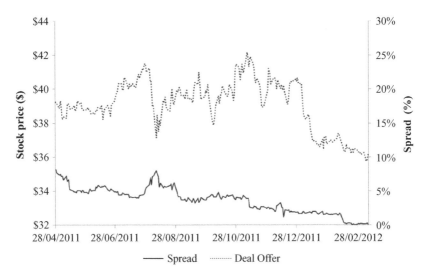

Figure 2.4 Constellation: change in offer value and spread
Source: Bloomberg

of the target company's shares, we must also take into account the performance of the buyer's shares, since they are sold short. We also need to incorporate any dividends paid by the target company and any dividends to be paid in future on the buyer's shares. The cost of borrowing the shares and the remuneration rate of the cash received when the shares are sold short are also factors that influence the final return. A phenomenon that occurs fairly frequently following M&A transactions financed in shares also affects the buyer's share price. Flowback is a downward movement in the buyer's share price and corresponds to the sale of the shares received in exchange for the shares of the target by long-only funds, which are not permitted by law to hold such shares. This situation occurs when the buyer and the target are not listed on stock markets in the same country. By way of example, let's take the case of a buyer listed in the US and a target listed in the UK. UK long-only funds that are shareholders of the target company cannot hold the buyer's dollar-denominated shares and consequently, after the closure of the transaction and the exchange of the target's shares for shares in the buyer, sell the shares in the buyer, causing its share price to fall.

Table 2.1 illustrates this calculation of the return in all-share transactions using the example of the Constellation/Exelon merger.

Table 2.1 Constellation/Exelon: calculation of the return in all-share transactions

Day of the announcement (position entry)	Day of closure (position exit)
Purchase of 1 share of the target: → result: – $36.26 Short sale of 0.93 of a share of the buyer: → net result: + $37.29 (0.93 × 40.10)	Exchange of Constellation shares held for Exelon shares (according to the exchange ratio) Exit from selling position due to repayment of the borrowed shares with the shares received in the exchange
→ net result = + $1.033 per Constellation share bought	→ net result on the day of closure = 0

The following parameters are used:

- Constellation share price when the announcement was made: $36.26.
- Exelon share price when the announcement was made: $40.10.
- Exchange ratio upon closure: 0.93 Exelon shares for each Constellation share.

Table 2.1 demonstrates that, in all-share transactions, the return on the investment is realized when the position is taken, depending on the share price of the entities involved. This is purely theoretical, however, since it omits certain aspects that should be taken into account, such as the cost of borrowing the shares to be sold short and the investment income rate of the cash received from the sale. These two factors also affect the return, as we have previously mentioned.

During the course of the transaction, the arbitrage spread was affected not only by the general decline in the markets in summer 2011 (and a sharper fall for Constellation than for Exelon), but also by the different accounts given by official representatives from Maryland, which questioned how beneficial the merger would be to the state. Constellation is one of the region's principal energy suppliers, and certain regulators feared that its merger with Exelon would damage free competition, which would be unfavorable to consumers. As is often the case with arbitrage transactions on M&A, the spread "opened up" with each announcement that brought the finalization of the transaction into doubt (such as those concerning antitrust issues). However, Constellation and Exelon managed to convince the authorities and obtain all the necessary approvals, and the operation was finalized in March 2012, within a time-frame similar to that anticipated when the announcement was made.

2.1.3 Mixed cash-and-share transactions

The reasons why companies decide to launch mixed buyout offers, with part of the payment in cash and the remainder in shares, can vary greatly. In some cases, a company wishes to compensate for limited access to finance or low cash levels by paying for part of the transaction with its own shares. We can also assume that the advantage of not paying for the entire amount of the transaction in shares is that it enables the company to limit the dilutive effect that would result from a transaction funded entirely in shares. The reasons may vary, but the method is always the same: in addition to a certain amount of cash per share held, the shareholders of the target company are offered a certain number of shares in the buyer.

Consequently, the arbitrage positions involved are essentially similar to those we have seen in the two previous sections, and are close to the arbitrage positions involved in a share-based transaction. The arbitrageur goes long on the target company and short on the buyer, according to the exchange ratio set out in the bid.

Example: The Medco/Express Scripts Deal

The example we will use to illustrate this type of transaction is the buyout of Medco Health Solutions by Express Scripts, which was announced in late July 2011. Medco is a US supplier of health services based in New Jersey, which enables its customers to benefit from more efficient services thanks to its network of pharmacies and the negotiation of wholesale contracts with pharmaceuticals companies and other medical-equipment manufacturers. Express Scripts belongs to the same sector and its biggest clients include the US defense ministry, government agencies, businesses, and trade unions. The anticipated synergies associated with this transaction were valued at around $1 billion upon finalization of the transaction.

The terms of the transaction were as follows: for each share held, the shareholders of Medco would receive $28.8 in cash and 0.81 of a share of Express Scripts. On the day of the announcement, July 21, the bid price was $71.36 per share, a premium of 28% over Medco's share price prior to the announcement, with a total transaction value of around $29 billion. The closure of the transaction was expected to take place in the first half of 2012. Figure 2.5 shows the change in Medco's share price and illustrates the positive reaction on the day the buyout was announced.

Figure 2.5   Medco/Express Scripts: change in share process and offer value
Source: Bloomberg

This transaction took place within a specific context for the health industry in the US because of the future challenges posed by the Obama administration's reforms, forcing operators in the sector to strengthen their positions and diversify their revenue sources.

Moreover, following the vote by the shareholders of the two entities, the transaction would be subject to authorization under the famous HSR antitrust act. In 2006, Express and CVS were in competition in a bidding war concerning the hostile takeover bid launched by Express for Caremark Rx, another health services supplier. After the fight had gone on for more than three months, CVS, which was then the second-biggest pharmacy chain in the US, after Walgreen, finally succeeded in its bid. Despite a final higher offer by Express, Caremark's shareholders chose CVS's offer due to potential antitrust problems. These issues surfaced again in connection with the planned buyout of Medco. The planned merger involved two of the three largest operators in the sector, and these three generated more or less comparable turnover. As always with antitrust regulation, the authorities' objective was to determine whether the planned merger would give the new group resulting from the transaction too much power in the market. More specifically, the regulation authority had to determine whether the competitors of the potential future group would be able to compete with it in calls for tenders involving large clients. As with the Caremark deal, certain groups of industry professionals, such as the National Community Pharmacists Association, attempted to prevent the merger from going ahead.

Figure 2.5, showing the change in Medco's share price, illustrates how difficult it is for arbitrageurs to assess antitrust risk. Once the public announcement is made, the spread narrows almost immediately. However, in the days following the announcement, arbitrageurs can analyze the transaction and the related risks. In this case, the antitrust risk was clearly the obstacle that needed to be overcome to complete the transaction. We can see that, in the month following the announcement, the spread widened considerably, thereby offering other arbitrageurs prepared to assume the antitrust risk the opportunity to take a position if they had not been able to do so sooner. The remuneration for the transaction was therefore adjusted more precisely to the antitrust risk incurred, attracting new arbitrageurs. Figure 2.6 shows the change in the spread in detail:

Figure 2.6   Spread evolution
Source: Bloomberg

We can see that, initially, the transaction spread doubled, reaching 30% on a non-annualized basis. This change reflected arbitrageurs' concerns about the ability of Express Scripts to effectively convince the US competition authorities of the benefits of the merger with Medco.

A number of objections to the transaction were raised by parties ranging from consumer groups to independent pharmacies, arguing that this concentration would result in a significant increase in prices and limited access to a number of generic medicines. The various complaints were directly addressed to the Federal Trade Commission (FTC) and the Department of Justice, the two institutions in charge of antitrust investigations in the US.

However, the progressive narrowing of the spread since October 2011 seemed to indicate that the transaction was on the way to being finalized and that the parties had managed to convince the competition authorities.

The transaction was eventually finalized on March 30, 2012, following approval by the FTC.

Some mixed cash-and-share transactions include clauses enabling any holder of shares in the target company, including arbitrageurs, to choose between different methods of payment when the transaction is finalized. These clauses are used frequently and can have a significant impact on the arbitrage process. As a general rule, these provisions involve:

- an option to receive 100% of the payment in cash;
- an option to receive 100% of the payment in shares;
- a third option involving payment in a combination of cash and shares.

The subtlety of these offers lies in the fact that the maximum amount payable in cash is generally limited. In this type of offer, the details are decisive, and we will illustrate this using the example of the transaction between El Paso (EP) and Kinder Morgan (KMI).

Example: The El Paso/Kinder Morgan Deal

The passage below is an extract from the merger agreement between the two groups, which was published on October 16, 2011:

The merger agreement provides that, at the effective time of the second merger, each share of New El Paso common stock issued and outstanding immediately prior to the effective time of the second merger (excluding (1) shares held by New El Paso in treasury and any shares held by Kinder Morgan, Merger Sub Two or Merger Sub Three, which shall be cancelled and cease to exist for no consideration, (2) any shares held by any other subsidiary of Kinder Morgan or New El Paso, which shall receive the Per Share Stock Election Consideration and (3) dissenting shares in accordance with Delaware law) will be converted into the right to receive, at the election of the holder but subject to proration with respect to the stock and cash portion so that approximately 57% of the aggregate merger consideration (excluding the warrants) is paid in cash and approximately 43% (excluding the warrants) is paid in Kinder Morgan Class P common stock, one of the following:

- 0.9635 of a share of Kinder Morgan Class P common stock (referred to as the "Exchange Ratio") and 0.640 of a warrant (referred to as the "Per Share Warrant Consideration" and with the Exchange Ratio, the "Per Share Stock Election Consideration") to purchase one share of Kinder Morgan Class P common stock (any such election referred to as a "stock election" and such New El Paso shares referred to as the "stock election shares");
- $25.91 in cash without interest (referred to as the "Per Share Cash Election Consideration") and the Per Share Warrant Consideration (any such election referred to as a "cash election" and such New El Paso shares referred to as the "cash election shares"); or
- 0.4187 of a share of Kinder Morgan Class P common stock (referred to as the "Mixed Election Stock Exchange Ratio"), $14.65 in cash without interest (referred to as the "Per Share Cash Amount") and the Per Share Warrant Consideration (collectively, the "Per Share Mixed Election Consideration") (any such election referred to as a "mixed election" and such New El Paso shares referred to as the "mixed consideration election shares").

The agreement makes several provisions. The maximum amount to be paid in cash by El Paso upon finalization of the transaction may not exceed 57% of the total value of the transaction. Consequently, the amount payable in shares must represent at least 43% of the total offer. We can therefore see a first source of potential hazard: since the structure of the offer includes a part that is payable in El Paso shares, El Paso's share price is decisive in calculating the total value of the transaction. This will not be known until the transaction is finalized.

Kinder Morgan shareholders may therefore elect between three options following the finalization of the transaction:

- receive $25.91 per Kinder Morgan share held (100% cash option);
- receive 0.9635 of a share of El Paso per Kinder Morgan share held (100% share option);
- receive 0.4187 of a share of El Paso + $14.65 per Kinder Morgan share held (mixed cash-and-share option).

The investor can therefore choose the option that is most favorable to him at the time of the vote, which will take place before the closure of the transaction.

However – and this is where a second source of risk arises – the maximum amounts payable under the first two options are limited. Consequently, if one of these options is oversubscribed by investors, i.e. chosen by shareholders in an amount exceeding the limits set out in the agreement, then each shareholder will receive a prorated amount, according to the extent of the oversubscription.

The final adjustment will therefore be made according to the levels of subscription to each option. It should obviously be borne in mind that some shareholders will not take part in the vote, either deliberately or unintentionally. These shareholders are systematically classed under the third category, the "mixed" option, which is granted in any event.

At the end of the voting process, the exact amount of the cash consideration and the exchange ratio will be determined. Below are two cases by way of example:

- **First case**: 75% of KMI shareholders choose the cash option 25% the share option, meaning that the cash option is oversubscribed:
  - those who have chosen the cash option will receive a prorated consideration and their allocation will depend on the closing price of El Paso shares and the maximum cash/share proportions of 57%/43%. Based on the closing share price on 31 January 2011, $26.88, the allocation is as follows:

  1. $19.53 in cash per KMI share;
  2. 0.2371 of a share of EP per KMI share;

- those who have chosen the share option will not receive a prorated consideration and will therefore receive 0.9635 of a share of EP per KMI share held.
- **Second case**: 25% of KMI shareholders choose the cash option and 75% the share option. The first option is therefore not oversubscribed:
  - those who have chosen the cash option will therefore not receive a prorated consideration. They will receive $25.91 per KMI share held;
  - those who have chosen the share option will receive a prorated consideration. In order to respect the cash/share proportions of 57%/43%, they will receive $10.90 and 0.5583 of a share of EP per KMI share held (based on the share price of 31 January, for example).

These provisions are therefore crucial to the arbitrageur, since he must go short on the buyer's shares in accordance with the exchange ratio. If the ratio is not predetermined and varies according to the change in the buyer's share price, this introduces an element of optionality into the final price of the transaction. The arbitrageur's reasoning is therefore influenced by the assessment of this factor that cannot be predicted when he implements his strategy.

The example above clearly shows how the exchange ratio can vary between 0 (if the cash option is not oversubscribed and a shareholder has voted for the cash option) and 0.9635 (if the cash option is oversubscribed and a shareholder has selected the all-share option). Similarly, based on these same scenarios, the shareholder may not receive any cash or could receive the maximum amount in cash, $25.91 per share. When the transaction is finalized, the arbitrageur may receive fewer shares in the buyer than he shorted and will therefore have to buy back the remainder of his short position, or, conversely, the arbitrageur may receive more shares in the buyer than he shorted, and will therefore have to sell the remainder of his position.

There is also an element of variability as far as the buyers are concerned, since the final payments depend on the shareholders' elections. Collars were devised to mitigate this aspect.

2.1.4   Collars

One of the most important innovations of recent decades as far as takeover bids are concerned is the advent of collar offers. Collars are not a type of takeover per se, but rather a contractual provision that can be included in a merger agreement.

In a traditional all-share offer, the number of shares of the buyer provided per share of the target company is specified in the proposal. This number is normally called the exchange ratio. With a collar, this ratio can be determined when the bid is announced. We therefore talk about a fixed-exchange rate offer (FX), with the target's shareholders receiving a fixed number of shares of the buyer as long as the buyer's share price remains within specified limits. The ratio may also be calculated during a specified period. In this case we talk about a fixed-value offer (FV), with shareholders of the target company receiving a fixed amount (expressed in cash) per share held. The exchange ratio is therefore flexible as long as it is within specified limits. The generic name "collar offer" is often used to refer to this type of provision, since it is the most frequent.

Numerous academic studies, such as Gaughan in 1999, have demonstrated that, on average, all-share transactions take longer than cash transactions. The shares of the buyer and of the target company may therefore undergo more changes prior to the closure of the transaction. Consequently, a collar provision in the buyout offer makes it possible to take into consideration these possible changes in value during the period specified in the terms of the transaction. In fact, regardless of whether the offer is FV or FX, if the buyer's share price varies too much, the terms of the transaction are adjusted.

In addition to considerations relating to the buyer's share price, collars generally give the target company the possibility to have the transaction annulled if the share price falls below a given threshold. This is known as a walk-away provision. Sometimes, the buyer also obtains this right in the event that the share price of the target company rises too much following the announcement of the buyout. This type of provision is therefore basically similar to traditional options.

Example: The Virgin Mobile USA/Sprint Deal

By way of an example of a fixed-value collar transaction, we will now look at the buyout of Virgin Mobile USA by Sprint in summer 2009, which was announced with the following press release:

OVERLAND PARK, Kan. & WARREN, N.J. – (BUSINESS WIRE) – Jul. 28, 2009 – Sprint Nextel Corporation (NYSE:S) and Virgin Mobile USA, Inc., (NYSE:VM) announced today that their boards of directors have approved a definitive agreement for Sprint to acquire Virgin Mobile USA for a total equity value of approximately $483 million, which includes the value of Sprint's current 13.1% fully diluted ownership interest in Virgin Mobile USA. In addition, at closing Sprint will retire all of Virgin Mobile USA's outstanding debt, which is $248 million net of cash and cash equivalents as of March 31, 2009, but is expected to be no more than $205 million net of cash and cash equivalents on Sept. 30, 2009. This acquisition will strengthen Sprint's position in the growing prepaid segment by bringing together under one umbrella the iconic Virgin Mobile brand with Sprint's successful Boost Mobile business. These complementary prepaid brands, each with a distinctive offer, style and appeal to different customer demographics, will continue to serve existing and prospective customers following the completion of the transaction.

[. . .]

Virgin Mobile USA Public Stockholders:

Each public stockholder, holding in aggregate approximately 39.7 million shares on a fully diluted basis or 43.3% ownership, will receive Sprint shares having a 10-day average closing price equivalent to $5.50 per Virgin Mobile USA share, subject to the collar referenced below.

(i) The exchange ratio for public stockholders will be based on Sprint's 10-day average closing share price ending two trading days prior to closing.
(ii) The exchange ratio will be subject to a collar such that in no event will the exchange ratio be lower than 1.0630 or higher than 1.3668.

The offer of $5.50 per share of Virgin Mobile USA depends on the closing share price of Sprint on the end date of the transaction. The exchange ratios, 1.0630 and 1.3668, enable us to determine the limits within which the offer of $5.50 is situated.

$$\$5.50 \div 1.3668 = \$4.02$$
$$\$5.50 \div 1.0630 = \$5.17$$

If Sprint's share price is between $4.02 and $5.17, then the transaction will take place at a fixed price of $5.50 per Virgin Mobile USA share. However, as soon as the share price moves beyond this range, then the two exchange ratios enable us to determine the final amount of the offer. Figure 2.7 enables a clearer understanding of the terms of realization of the fixed-price offer.

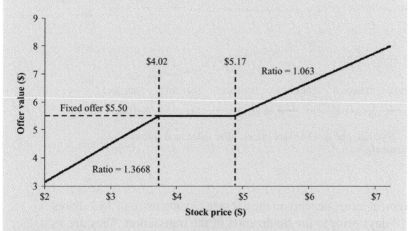

Figure 2.7   Changes in offer value depending on Sprint's stock price
Source: Bloomberg

From the arbitrageur's point of view, transactions involving collars are complex, because the hedging strategy must be planned dynamically. In fact, since the exchange ratio is not constant over time because it depends on the value of the buyer's shares, the number of shares to be sold short varies. In the event of rapid variations in the share price, there are numerous sources of potential losses: the adjustments give rise to considerable transaction costs and the positions may turn out to be losing positions before the arbitrageur has the time to adjust them. It is therefore impossible to have perfect protection.

Figure 2.8 depicts a recent example of a transaction involving a collar. It refers to the buyout of Swiss firm Synthès, which specializes in medical equipment, by US giant Johnson & Johnson (J&J).

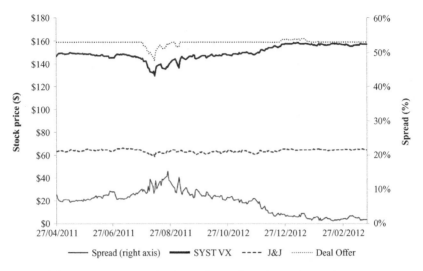

Figure 2.8 Synthès: changes in share prices, offer value, and spread
Source: Bloomberg

The payment terms depend on the average closing price of J&J shares over the 10 days prior to the finalization of the transaction. They are as follows:

- if J&J shares < CHF52.54, then 1 SYST share = 1.9672 J&J shares;
- if J&J shares > CHF60.45, then 1 SYST share = 1.7098 J&J shares;
- otherwise, 1 SYST share = CHF103.35, paid for in J&J shares.

In accordance with the terms of the offer, we can see that when the share price of Johnson & Johnson varies considerably (which is all relative, since J&J shares are among the less volatile stocks on the NYSE) either upwards or downwards, the value of the offer is no longer fixed. We can see two variations in Figure 2.8 (one downwards and one upwards). When J&J's share price returns to within the limits set out in the terms of the agreement, the offer price once again becomes fixed, which is the case throughout most of Figure 2.8. Finally, we can see that, once again, the spread has varied enormously during the course of the transaction (particularly with regard to issues related to competition on the European markets in question), creating numerous entry and exit opportunities for arbitrageurs.

2.2   THE CHOICE OF PAYMENT METHOD

The choice of payment method for the transaction is a crucial decision for the buyer and is the subject of in-depth analyses with the buyer's investment bankers.

Payment in cash involves the following elements for the buyer, as compared with payment in shares:

- It gives the offer credibility due to the psychological effect of payment in cash.
- It increases the buyer's level of debt. It is therefore useful to study in detail the post-transaction level of financial leverage and to consider it in parallel with rating constraints, for example. This also explains why certain transactions (such as major banking mergers and some deals in the pharmaceutical industry), due to their size, can be structured only as share-swap transactions.
- It does not alter its shareholder structure (except in the event of additional refinancing via a capital increase), meaning that the buyer can avoid dealing with the potentially thorny issue of the dilution of the shares held by a reference shareholder.
- It involves taxation of any capital gains made by the shareholders of the target company.
- It does not change the buyer's weight on market indices (because it does not change its market capitalization).
- It involves a defined division of synergies: the shareholders of the target company receive the control premium and the shareholders of the buyer receive all the synergies exceeding this amount.
- It does not involve any post-announcement correlation between the share price of the buyer and that of the target.

Payment in shares presents the following characteristics:

- It enables sellers to benefit from part of the synergies generated by the merger.
- It gives the offer a "friendly" feel, since it involves carrying out a joint "project" together.
- It generally reduces the buyer's financial leverage and increases its weight on the indices.
- The control premium is generally lower than in cash offers, because the creation of value comes after the deal in the form of synergy sharing (and possible re-rating).

- The tax regime is generally favorable, with a suspension of taxation of latent capital gains.
- It usually gives rise to a burst of short selling of the buyer's shares by arbitrageurs, which may be sufficient to artificially cause the share price to fall.
- It involves a mixture of colleges of shareholders of both companies.
- It may send a negative signal about the level of the buyer's share price, since a company normally does not issue any new shares when it considers its stock to be undervalued.

From the arbitrageur's point of view, although an all-share offer has the considerable advantage of generally eliminating financing risk, payment in cash is usually preferred for the following reasons:

- The level of the premium is positively correlated to the success rate (because it boosts the chances of the transaction being accepted by the shareholders of the target company) and is usually higher in cash offers.
- A cash offer generally does not need to be agreed on by the buyer's shareholders, which removes a condition precedent to the deal.
- An all-share offer may be called into question if the buyer's share price falls sharply because the value of the offer may be substantially reduced; this risk does not occur with cash offers.
- Arbitrage on an all-share offer is technically slightly more difficult, because it involves selling the buyer's shares short and therefore incurring the risks related to this short selling: the recall of the shares by the lender (for example, just before the vote by the buyer's shareholders), a change in borrowing costs, or even regulatory risk in the event of a sudden ban on short selling.
- Finally, particularly with an all-share offer, there is the risk that an unsolicited offer may be made on the buyer, which would involve a sharp rise in the buyer's share price, which (as you will have understood) would be catastrophic for an arbitrageur holding a short position on the stock.

3

Risk and Return Factors

Publicly announced M&A transactions can go one of several ways. In this chapter, we will examine the possible scenarios and how they influence the return enjoyed by the arbitrageur. We will then look at issues concerning the timetable and timing of transactions. These also have a big impact on returns from arbitrage.

3.1 THE DIFFERENT OUTCOMES

M&A transactions can have four possible outcomes, and it is down to the investor to predict as soon as the operation is announced which of these outcomes will occur. The first outcome, and the most common, is that the transaction is completed smoothly, on time, and at the initial offer price. The second outcome is the transaction failing altogether. Several events can cause an M&A operation to fail. Arbitrageurs must try and anticipate such events because they are dangerous and usually lead to losses; estimating potential losses therefore becomes a crucial factor. There are two other possible outcomes. Both involve the transaction being completed, but in one scenario the final offer price is lower than the original bid, and in the other the final offer price is higher.

3.1.1 The transaction is completed

3.1.1.1 The probability of success

Analyzing how likely a transaction is to be successful is a delicate process that follows a particular logic. Arbitrageurs look at the different risk factors involved in the transaction and how likely they are to occur. This gives us the following formula:

$$P(\text{Success}) = 1 - P(\text{Failure})$$

Empirical studies (Branch and Yang, 2003; Hoffmeister and Dyl, 1980) have shown that certain factors are particularly important in determining the probability of success of a transaction. The structure of the offer is one of the most important elements. Statistics have shown that, on average, the success rate of hostile bids is unsurprisingly lower than for non-hostile bids, and that mergers are successful more often than takeovers. In theory, a bigger premium also increases the chance of a transaction being successful because it is more likely to be accepted by the shareholders of the target company. Historically, the difference in size between the buyer and the target company is also important. The bigger the buyer is in relation to its target, the more likely the transaction is to succeed. The outcome of operations involving similar-sized companies is less certain.

Although each M&A transaction has its own specific characteristics, some risks are always present and should be taken into account by the arbitrageur as a matter of course. These risks include financing, the votes of the shareholders of the parties involved, and the authorizations required for the operation to go ahead. We will now take a closer look at these factors as they can directly affect how likely a transaction is to succeed.

3.1.1.2 Risks of failure

There are various reasons why a publicly announced M&A transaction might fail, and they can be categorized into two main groups:

- External reasons: the parties still want the tie-up to go ahead, but an external event prevents this, e.g. financing is not available on the completion date or the deal does not receive the clearance it needs from administrative bodies such as competition authorities.
- Internal reasons: one of the parties no longer wants the operation to go ahead. This usually occurs during a financial crisis, with the buyer regretfully wishing to get out of its contractual obligations because the transaction can no longer be justified from an economic perspective.

Some of these reasons, such as financing or competition risk, are mentioned here as crucial factors for risk analysis, but they will be examined more closely in subsequent chapters.

3.1.1.2.1   Financing

The buyer being unable to secure financing for the transaction is one of the biggest risk factors in M&A and is therefore a crucial element for arbitrageurs to take into account. This is especially true for transactions involving a lot of leverage, such as those instigated by private-equity firms. We have dedicated an entire chapter of this book to financing.

There is a fundamental difference between the situation in Europe, where takeovers are governed by regulation that eliminates all or part of financing risk (in France, for example, the irrevocable undertakings made by a bidder are guaranteed by the presenting bank, meaning the financing risk is limited to a default of said bank), and the situation in the US, where the contractual freedom afforded to the parties enables them to insert into the merger agreement (which has been carefully negotiated by experienced lawyers) all kinds of clauses, including ones related to financing.

Chapter 5 will examine more closely the financing risk of an M&A operation, taking into consideration the different structures and regulatory frameworks involved.

3.1.1.2.2 Competition

Competition, or antitrust, law aims to prevent anti-competitive practices. With regard to M&A, it aims to prevent the formation of groups such as cartels or monopolies, which might restrict competition in a sector.

These days, most M&A in all countries require approval from the national competition authorities. Requesting this approval affects the timetable of the operation and also provides an additional risk. If approval is not granted, the buyer may have to adjust its offer. The antitrust authorities can also block the transaction outright.

Competition regulations will be examined in more detail in Chapter 6. We will look at their origin as well as the details of the approval process and the specific risks thereof.

3.1.1.2.3 Shareholder votes

Shareholders of the buyer and of the target company go through different procedures. The former are generally required to vote on the M&A transaction only if the operation requires shares to be issued (more than 20% of share capital in the US).

The latter, on the other hand, are always required to vote on the transaction, whether in the traditional sense or by voting with their feet through choosing, or otherwise, to tender their shares into the offer. Moreover, their vote depends largely on the attitude of the company's board of directors. Shareholders – especially long-only and index funds – tend to follow their board's recommendation.

Approval thresholds at these votes are fixed by the regulations applicable to the company in question. In the event of a takeover bid, the buyer can also fix a minimum threshold. If this figure is not reached, the operation is abandoned.

The attitude of the shareholders of the target company is a crucial factor in determining the success of M&A. The shareholder structure is therefore very important. It is generally harder to seize control of companies whose share capital is held by a majority block or families. Conversely, companies with a fragmented share capital comprising many institutional investors can be easier targets.

3.1.1.2.4   Administrative authorization

The number of administrative authorizations required for an M&A transaction to go ahead depends on the type of transaction, the sector, and the country involved. It goes without saying that a transaction requiring a large number of authorizations is more risky than one requiring fewer authorizations, because its outcome is less certain.

These authorizations fall into several categories. First, there are national authorizations such as:

- the Committee on Foreign Investment in the United States (CFIUS);
- the European Commission;
- Industry Canada.

Some transactions involving "protected" or "sensitive" sectors require additional specific authorization. There are several examples of this in the US:

- telecoms – authorization from the Federal Communications Commission (FCC);
- energy – authorization from the Federal Energy Regulatory Commission (FERC);
- healthcare – authorization from the State Department of Health;
- finance – authorization from the Federal Reserve.

3.1.1.2.5   MAC clauses

The MAC in MAC clauses stands for Material Adverse Change, i.e. any significant change in the target company that alters the economics of the operation and renders it no longer attractive to one or both parties.

MAC clauses are a way for the parties to mitigate risk in the event that a significant unfavorable event occurs between the agreement being signed and the transaction being completed. Depending on their legal formulation and the types of events they take into account, MAC clauses give the parties a certain room for maneuver, to react should such an event take place.

The size of this room for maneuver, arising from the MAC clause inserted into the agreement between the parties, also gives the arbitrageur an idea of how likely it is that the transaction will be successful. These clauses are essential parts of merger agreements, and we will examine them in more detail later in the book.

3.1.1.2.6   Reverse termination fees

A reverse termination fee clause in a merger agreement stipulates the compensation that the buyer must pay to the target company if it decides, for whatever reason, to terminate the transaction. Such clauses first appeared in operations involving private-equity firms. They introduce an element of choice into LBOs because the buyer reserves the right to exit the transaction by paying a penalty, for which the sum is determined upon signature of the merger agreement.

From the arbitrageurs' point of view, their thought process, as for MAC clauses, is that it all depends on the amounts involved. If the penalty is considered dissuasive enough to prevent the buyer from abandoning the transaction, the risk of non-completion owing to second thoughts on the part of the buyer is considerably reduced. On the other hand, if the penalty is low enough to offer the buyer an easy way out, there is a higher risk that the transaction will not be completed.

All these risks can, at one moment or another, affect the chances of a transaction being successful. The arbitrageur must not only identify these risks, but also quantify them and estimate the resulting probability of success of the transaction.

3.1.1.2.7   Opposition from the management of the target company

Hostile bids are so called because the management of the target company has rejected the approach from the bidder. In some cases, bidders pull out because they do not want to get involved in such a situation. Sometimes, though, they decide to try and bypass the opposition from the management of the target company.

At one time, hostile bids came mainly from activist investors with a presence in the share capital of a company. They wanted to make money on an undervalued share price and were convinced that they could run the company better than the management teams already in place. These days, the role of activist investors has changed. Only rarely do they invest directly in companies; more often, they act as catalysts for the arrival of a hostile outside bidder.

We will look more closely at hostile bids and the defense mechanisms of target companies in Chapter 9.

3.1.1.2.8   Fraud and due diligence

Rare though it may be, fraud can of course be a valid reason to cancel an M&A transaction.

The best-known example is that of Dynegy and Enron. In 2001, Enron was debt ridden and its shareholders were low on confidence when its major Texan rival on the energy market, Dynegy, offered to buy the group for $9 billion. Between December 2000 and November 2001, when Dynegy made its offer, Enron's stock-market capitalization had plummeted from its record high of $63 billion.

Just after the Dynegy offer was made public, ratings agency Standard & Poor's downgraded Enron to "junk bond" status, i.e. the level just before default. Enron then revised its financial statements, acknowledging that its profits were lower than originally reported. Dynegy saw this as a material adverse change in the target company and therefore decided to abandon the transaction under the terms of the merger agreement. Enron was soon placed under Chapter 11 bankruptcy protection.

We learned later that the accounting adjustment made by Enron was the final act in a long-running and large-scale camouflage operation that used illegal accounting practices to give the impression that the group was operationally and financially sound. Before signing the merger agreement, Dynegy conducted the usual due diligence on Enron. It was lucky on this occasion that the true situation of the target company was revealed before the transaction was completed.

A more recent example shows that even unfounded allegations of fraud can have a significant impact on M&A and their arbitrage. In October 2011, a Sino-Japanese consortium comprising Winsway Coking Coal and Marubeni announced the takeover of Grande Cache Coal, a Canadian mining group specializing in coke. As shown by Figure 3.1, the transaction was progressing normally until the middle of January

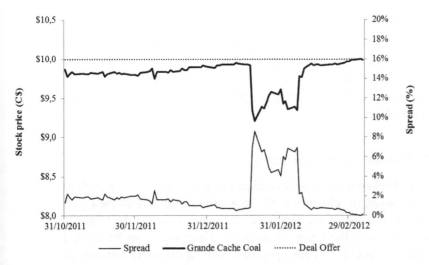

Figure 3.1   Grand Cache Coal: change in share price and spread
Source: Bloomberg

2012, with the share price of the target company converging towards the offer price.

Suddenly, the share price dropped by nearly 10%, causing the spread to widen and bringing about losses for arbitrageurs who had been confident that the transaction would go ahead without any hitches.

The fall came after a short seller published a report accusing Winsway of creative accounting, prompting speculation that the consortium would not be able to complete the acquisition of the Canadian company.

In the week that followed, Winsway went to great lengths to convince the market that its accounts were reliable. During that time, the arbitrage spread remained extremely volatile. As it transpired, the short seller's report was unfounded and the transaction was finalized a few weeks later, with the spread narrowing accordingly.

3.1.2   The transaction fails

It is fairly rare that a publicly announced M&A transaction fails, but it is often disastrous for arbitrageurs when it does. Probability analysis is similar to what we have already seen, but the vital estimation of potential losses is particularly difficult because it involves many factors, some of which are subjective.

3.1.2.1   Estimating failure

The analysis of the failure of a transaction is very similar to credit risk analysis. Evaluating the loss that an event might entail involves two things: the probability that said event is likely to occur (as we have already discussed) and estimating the potential losses if the event does indeed take place.

3.1.2.2   Estimating potential losses

This can be broken down into several cumulative aspects: the premium paid by the buyer, the changes in the shareholder structure of the target company when the deal is announced, the reasons for the deal failing, and the progress of the financial markets. There may also be myriad considerations specific to each operation, but we are interested only in those elements that apply to all transactions.

3.1.2.2.1   Acquisition premium

The acquisition premium reflected in the target company's share price is brought about by the bid and the likelihood that it will be successful. As soon as doubts surface over whether the transaction will go ahead, the share price is likely to fall, meaning the spread gets wider. However, there is no way of quantifying how a share price will respond to the announcement that a transaction has failed. Several parameters need to be taken into account:

- The size of the control premium offered is the most important. Arbitrageurs should be able to estimate potential losses based on the size of this premium. Even if an exact figure is not possible, they can get a rough idea.
- The liquidity of the target company's shares is also very important. This determines how quickly arbitrageurs can reverse their position.
- Other factors should be taken into account. The arbitrageur must consider the behavior of the target company's share price before the deal was made public. If the share price rose sharply even before the first rumors, we can assume that the shares were above their "normal" level and that the loss will be greater in this case.

As we can see, many factors can influence how a target company's share price responds to the failure of a takeover bid. Estimating potential losses is made even harder by the fact that there is no systemic way of conducting the analysis. Another factor to take into account when estimating potential losses is the change in the shareholder structure of the target company.

3.1.2.2.2   Changes to the shareholder structure

After the analysis of returns, one of the most important topics of academic literature on merger arbitrage is changes to the shareholder structure of the target company once a takeover bid has been announced to the market. We will look at how the issue is directly related to liquidity and potential losses.

We have already seen that, as soon as the bid is made public, arbitrageurs enter the fray and buy up shares in the target company. In general, they buy these shares from longstanding shareholders. Arbitrageurs are often described as providers of insurance and liquidity. They allow longstanding shareholders to sell their shares and capitalize on the gains caused by the positive reaction to the M&A announcement. This provides these shareholders with a "certain" profit as they can often benefit from virtually the entire control premium, while the arbitrageurs themselves make their money from the spread (which can be described as a kind of insurance premium or the premium on the sale of a put option).

Hsieh's work (2002) establishes a solid link between the participation of arbitrageurs in M&A transactions, quantified by their positions in the share capital of target companies, and the rate of success of these transactions. He concludes that arbitrageurs facilitate M&A, and his conclusion is consistent with other works that explain how arbitrageurs give up their shares more easily in tender offers in the US. Hsieh even shows how it is in buyers' interests to encourage the entry of arbitrageurs into the share capital of the target company when the bid is made public, in order to improve the chances of the bid being successful. In order to do this, the buyers must therefore propose an attractive control premium.

These changes in the shareholder structure are crucial in explaining potential losses. Upon bad news, whether it is a market movement or a specific event linked to the transaction, the new shareholders – the arbitrageurs – react more quickly than the longstanding shareholders and tend to sell out of their positions almost immediately. This creates a situation where several arbitrageurs want to sell their shares but struggle to find counterparties, which in general take the guise of mutual funds that are investing in a company for its intrinsic qualities rather than whether or not an M&A transaction will go ahead. This is a well-known phenomenon in finance: a liquidity crisis that may cause a share price to fall very sharply.

This aspect of M&A explains why the share price of a target company can fall so sharply when an unfavorable event occurs. It is often said that the skill of an arbitrageur is not in choosing the right deals (90% of bids made public go through to completion) but in avoiding the wrong ones. This explains why a fairly long track record (of at least three, maybe even five, years) is needed to assess the quality of an arbitrageur and distinguish luck from skill. Studying such a track record also proves how an arbitrageur performs in different market conditions.

3.1.2.2.3   Reasons for potential failure

If a transaction is expected to fail, the reasons for this failure must be analyzed carefully because they can affect how the share price of the target company reacts to the bad news.

Most of the time, an operation is abandoned following the occurrence of a significant unfavorable event. These are the same events that feature in the MAC clauses we discussed in 3.1.1.2.5 above.

The main reason for invoking an MAC clause to exit a transaction is a significant change in the underlying business of the target company. This could relate to several things: a natural disaster such as Fukushima; geopolitical events such as war or 9/11; worse-than-expected results; worse-than-expected growth forecasts on the back of regulatory changes, for example; or indeed any event that may have a negative impact on the target company's business or results.

The discovery and subsequent announcement of such an event always impacts on the share price of the target company. Depending on the scale of the damage, the share price will either fall slightly or sharply. In any event, the share price in the wake of the announcement that the M&A transaction has failed should no longer include any premium.

Let us look again at the Pharmasset/Gilead case that we discussed in Chapter 2 when looking at all-cash deals. We saw that Gilead's offer included a premium of nearly 90%, reflecting both the strategic importance of the target company to the buyer and the potential of the hepatitis C treatments it develops. One of the risks associated with this transaction was the potential losses that could have resulted from a premature termination of the deal. If Gilead had invoked an MAC clause to exit the deal, it would have cast doubts over the intrinsic quality of Pharmasset. If the deal had been cancelled, the share price would surely have lost not only the entire acquisition premium but also a significant amount of its pre-merger announcement value, thereby reflecting the new information that had come to light on the true value of Pharmasset's assets. This concern was probably one of the reasons why the arbitrage spread remained wide for a large part of the operation. Thankfully for the arbitrageurs, such a scenario never materialized and the transaction was completed with no hiccups on January 18, 2012. If the deal had collapsed, however, the arbitrageurs would surely have suffered huge losses. It has not been plain sailing since for Gilead. On February 16, the pharmaceutical firm's share price slumped by almost 15% following the publication of disappointing clinical-trial results for a hepatitis C treatment developed by Pharmasset. The fate of both Gilead and Pharmasset would have been quite different had these results been published a month earlier. This is a good example of how the reasons why an M&A transaction may fail are often linked to a significant event relating to the intrinsic quality of the parties involved. Some may even play a decisive role, such as negative clinical-trial results for pharmaceutical companies. It is crucial for arbitrageurs to evaluate these events.

Estimating losses is extremely difficult because it relies on investors' judgment and on how each person evaluates the damage caused by the adverse event. Our look at liquidity and shareholder structure completes this section on the reaction of the target company's share price.

3.1.2.2.4 *Market evolution*

The evolution of the market as a whole can often play second fiddle during M&A. If the transaction proceeds as normal, the target company's share price converges towards the offer price as the completion date approaches.

However, if doubts are cast over the transaction, the progress of the market since the deal was announced, adjusted by the beta value of the target company's share price, becomes a factor to be taken into account.

This means the arbitrageur can try and predict the reaction of the target company's share price based on its beta value. It also explains why when transactions are abandoned in a bear market, the target company's share price sometimes drops by far more than just the acquisition premium.

3.1.3   The transaction is completed at a price lower than the initial offer

The discovery of a material adverse change does not immediately and automatically mean the deal is dead. Sometimes, this kind of unwelcome development can encourage the parties to renegotiate the terms of the offer.

There are two specific dynamics involved in these situations. On the one hand, the buyer does not want to abandon the deal but no longer wants to pay the amount initially offered. On the other, the target company, which has already taken the necessary steps for the transaction to go ahead, still wishes to be bought and cannot afford its share price to fall so sharply. These complementary positions push the parties closer together and force them to revise the offer terms downward.

This type of situation was particularly exploited by private-equity firms during the financial crisis as a way of renegotiating deals that had been struck before the crisis took hold. They often invoked an MAC clause to re-open negotiations. We will take a closer look at these strategies in Chapters 8 and 10 on MAC clauses and private equity. For now, a good example is the takeover of media group Clear Channel by a consortium comprising Bain Capital and Thomas Lee. The original offer price in May 2007 was $39.20 per share ($19.4 billion in total), but the final price when the deal was completed in June 2008 after renegotiation was $36 per share.

3.1.4   Rival bids and bidding wars

Bidding wars between several potential buyers for the same target are an excellent source of revenue for arbitrageurs, but they are difficult to predict and estimate. One recent high-profile example in the US is the battle between Dell and Hewlett-Packard (HP) for Californian data storage firm 3PAR.

On August 16, 2010, Dell announced that it had reached an agreement to buy 3PAR for $18 per share ($1.1 billion in total) with a view to improving its cloud computing offer. Adding the 3PAR business would also enable Dell to cut costs and forge multiple synergies. The offer price included an 80% premium on the most recent share price. 3PAR was financially stable and had an annual turnover of around $200 million.

On August 23, HP wrote to the president and CEO of 3PAR, informing him of its intention to buy his company. HP's offer of $24 per share, valuing 3PAR at $1.6 billion, was 33% higher than Dell's initial offer. With both bidders enjoying considerable cash reserves, financing terms were not an issue.

Just four days later, Dell came back in with a higher offer of $24.30 per 3PAR share. The management of the target company announced that they had accepted this improved offer, just as they had done for the previous counterbid. As it had made the first move, Dell benefited from matching rights, enabling it to bring its offer in line with any rival bid.

The bidding war continued on August 27, with Dell offering $27 per share for the data storage firm and HP responding just 90 minutes later with a bid of $30 per share, valuing 3PAR at nearly $2 billion. At that time, 3PAR's shares were trading at $31, hinting at higher bids to come, which is precisely what happened.

On September 2, Dell again raised its offer to $32 per share but refused to respond further when HP came back shortly afterwards with a bid of $33 per share. HP therefore emerged as the winner of the bidding war and completed its acquisition of 3PAR for $2.4 billion, representing a premium of 83% over Dell's initial offer and 230% over the pre-deal share price. The final purchase price of 12 times revenue left many analysts speechless. Dell received a break-up fee of $72 million under the terms of its initial agreement with 3PAR.

Figure 3.2 shows the 3PAR share price throughout the toing and froing of the bidding war. As we can see, this bidding war provided arbitrageurs who entered the fray upon Dell's initial offer with incredible returns for what started out as a simple arbitrage operation.

The subsequent offers from Dell and HP were pleasant surprises for arbitrageurs who had become involved in the deal when the initial offer was made public. The reaction of the 3PAR share price, which was more often than not above the previous offer, shows that the arbitrageurs had predicted the bidding war fairly well. This kind of transaction always provides the chance for arbitrageurs to make big gains.

Detecting situations that might lead to a bidding war is therefore a key performance quality for an arbitrageur to possess. There is no magic formula, but certain factors are conducive to such a war:

- The relative size of the companies: 3PAR, for example, was a small company (with a stock-market capitalization of $600 million before the deal was announced) up against two corporate giants. No matter how high the purchase price, therefore, it would have little impact on the cash flow or results of the buyer.

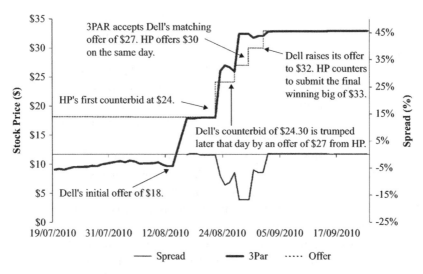

Figure 3.2   3PAR: change in share price, offer value, and spread
Source: Bloomberg

- Strategic interest/rare opportunity: 3PAR, for example, had a knowledge of data-storage technology that was highly coveted by Dell and HP, which wanted to grow in the promising cloud computing sector, and not easy to quickly develop internally.
- Premium or method of payment: when the premium is small, it is obviously easier for a rival bidder to offer a higher price while still creating value for its own shareholders. Similarly, being able to submit an all-cash counterbid to an all- or part-share offer could tip the scales in a company's favor.

Compensation in the form of break-up fees is common when a bidding war decides the fate of an M&A transaction. It allows the unsuccessful bidder to recover some of its investment in the operation. In most cases, the winning bidder ends up paying this break-up fee, even if the initial agreement states that the target company must foot the bill. In the UK, recent changes have led to calls from the Takeover Panel to abolish break-up fees.

These fees have a dual and contradictory effect. They are a deterrent against potential buyers coming in with a counter-bid, but they are also a way of securing a transaction and therefore attracting more potential buyers before the deadline for firm bids. Some research has shown how break-up fees can be beneficial to the sale process. These articles show that the success rate of transactions involving break-up fees is higher than those not containing such a clause. Another study, which examined a broad sample of M&A transactions in the US, shows that the control premium paid to shareholders of the target company is on average 7% higher when the agreement provides for break-up fees.

Some transactions involve "go-shop" periods. This agreement between the potential buyer and the target company provides for a period during which the latter can solicit competing offers. As these periods are concurrent with the normal timetable for the transaction process, they tend not to delay the deal. Arbitrageurs often welcome go-shop periods because they increase the chance of improved counterbids.

These four sections have looked at the different elements that may arise during M&A and their effect on the final price of the transaction. Having looked at price, our focus now moves to the second element in an arbitrageur's return: timing.

3.2   M&A TIMETABLE

After the final deal price, the time that it takes for a publicly announced transaction to complete is the most important factor in calculating a return on the deal. Certain factors that we have already discussed, such as the various shareholder votes and the administrative authorizations, affect the completion date. Other factors, such as the type of operation and the country in which it takes place, also play a part. We will look at all these issues that impact on an M&A timetable.

3.2.1   Timetable considerations according to offer type

Determining the type of offer may be straightforward, but it is particularly important when trying to establish the timeframe for an M&A transaction. Takeovers tend to be over fairly quickly, while mergers generally take longer. We will also look at tender offers.

3.2.1.1   Takeovers

Takeovers are characterized by the speed at which the buyer can take control of the target company. Some deals in the US are completed within a month, but the quickest takeovers in Europe take twice as long. More generally, takeovers take several months – whatever the jurisdiction.

In Europe, timetables vary slightly according to the country in question, but the regulatory provisions are fairly standard. In the UK, a potential buyer has 28 days from the first press releases or speculation to submit a firm bid. Once this bid has been submitted and made public, the target company's board of directors has 14 days to notify the market of its response. All takeover offers must be open for at least 21 days, and the target company has 39 days to publish all the necessary material information. A potential buyer can therefore revise its bid up to 46 days after submitting its initial offer. These last two deadlines can be extended in accordance with City Code rules, with the Takeover Panel responsible for setting new dates. If no deadlines have been extended, the terms of an offer must be accepted within 60 days of the bid submission date. Once an offer has been declared unconditional, it remains open for between 14 and 21 days, meaning the completion date is between 74 and 81 days after the bid was submitted. The last possible settlement date is 14 days after the offer has closed, taking the maximum timeframe to 95 days after the bid was submitted.

In France, once a takeover bid has been filed with the Financial Markets Authority (*Autorité des Marchés Financiers*, AMF), the watchdog has 15 days to give its response. The target company must make the AMF aware of its own response by the same deadline. The bid submission date also triggers the stock-market regulator's investigation period, which may last no longer than 35 trading days. Rival bidders have 32 days from when the initial bid was submitted to file their own counteroffers. The standard procedure generally takes 25 days. After this, the AMF publishes the results of the operation, thereby taking the maximum timeframe to 46 days. If the offer is reopened, there is an extension of 10 working days. The results are then published 75 days after the initial offer was submitted.

In Germany, the potential buyer must submit the offer document to market regulator BaFin (*Bundesanstalt für Finanzdienstleistungsaufsicht*) within four weeks. The watchdog then examines the document and may extend this examination period. Once approval is given, the offer is made public within 10 days. The offer period can last between 4 and 10 weeks, with any modification to the offer terms by the bidder automatically putting things back by two weeks. When the offer period is over, the results are published and the transaction is completed.

The timetables are similar in the US. Antitrust authorization under the HSR Act is automatically required and demands an initial regulatory timeframe of 30 days. However, for cash tender offers (we will study them in the following section), the HSR waiting period is shortened to 15 days. If the authorities quickly determine that the transaction complies with competition rules, approval can be granted before this period ends. With the other formalities concluded in the meantime, transactions are generally completed as soon as there is approval from the antitrust authorities. If the parties are expecting a second request from the competition authorities, the transaction is generally structured as a merger rather than a tender offer.

3.2.1.2   The unique case of tender offers

Tender offers are commonly used unique mechanisms that enable bidders to put their offer direct to the shareholders of the target company. When an offer is announced, the buyer states its price and it is down to the shareholders of the target company to decide whether they accept the terms and wish to tender their shares into the offer. The buyer must also specify the payment form and the offer expiry date.

Most tender offers are friendly operations, i.e. the respective boards of the buyer and the target company have come to a prior agreement on the terms of the offer. However, since tender offers are a way for the buyer to speak directly to the shareholders of the target firm and let them decide the fate of their own company, bypassing the opinion of the board of directors, they are a perfect medium for hostile bids.

The advantage of tender offers is the speed at which transactions can be completed. With no shareholder vote, the timetable is shortened considerably. The shareholders vote with their feet by deciding whether or not to tender their shares into the offer.

As it is practically impossible to acquire all the shares of a company (some shareholders may abstain and others may refuse to tender their shares), a buyer can seize effective control by reaching a pre-arranged threshold in the share capital. When a tender offer is launched, the minimum threshold is determined by applicable regulations, generally at between 85% and 95% (in Delaware, for example, the minimum threshold is 90%) Once the buyer reaches this threshold, it may take control of the remaining shares via a short-form merger.

The 1968 Williams Act in the US states that tender offers shall stay open for at least 20 days. Before then, some raiders used tender offers with very short timeframes to take the target company's shareholders by surprise and almost force them to hurriedly tender their shares. These measures not only prevented the managers of the target companies from putting up effective defense mechanisms but also impeded potential counterbids. Even today, this remains a major disadvantage of tender offers: the speed at which they are concluded gives less time for other possible buyers to emerge.

One of the best examples is the acquisition of Petrohawk Energy, a Texan company specializing in oil and gas exploration and production, by Australian natural resources giant BHP Billiton. The bid announced on July 14, 2011 valued Petrohawk at more than $12 billion, with a premium of nearly 65% over the previous day's closing price, and it was recommended by the Petrohawk board. Comprising mainly institutional investors, the target company's shareholders tendered their shares into the offer immediately – take-up was 97.4% on August 21, the first end date of the tender offer. The various authorizations needed for completion of the transaction were also received in record time. US antitrust approval arrived on July 22, just a week after the bid was announced. As it was a foreign investment in the US, the transaction required authorization from the CFIUS, and this came on August 17. The transaction was completed on August 25, only 42 days after it had been announced to the market.

3.2.1.3 Mergers

Merger timetables are a lot more crowded and involve additional regulatory stages. In general, they take between three and six months to complete from when the agreement is signed.

In the US, the Securities and Exchange Commission (SEC) studies the proxy documents before they are sent out to shareholders. In a takeover situation, however, these checks are carried out simultaneously, which saves some time. The authorities have 30 days to give a merger antitrust approval under the HSR Act, compared with 15 days for takeovers.

In addition, the shareholders of the target company must take a vote on a merger. Eligibility to vote is determined by the holding of shares on a given date between four and eight weeks before the merger was announced. The problem is that, because they want to sell their shares once the deal is announced in order to benefit from the acquisition premium, most shareholders on that given date are no longer present in the share capital of the target company when the vote comes around. They have no motivation to vote for or against the merger because they are no longer shareholders, and their abstention is counted as a vote against. This makes it hard for the buyer to get shareholder approval for a merger. One solution is to stage the vote later so that new shareholders can have their say on the merger project.

Lastly, the conditions precedent of the merger agreement must be met before the transaction can be completed. These clauses will therefore hold up the process even more. There are all kinds of conditional clauses that derive from negotiations between the parties: e.g. getting authorizations, reaching a minimum percentage at a shareholder vote, succeeding with a related offer.

One transaction that perfectly demonstrates timetable issues is the acquisition (announced in June 2007) of US firm Energy East, which specializes in natural gas in the north-east of the country, by Spanish nuclear and water power group Iberdrola.

The usual Energy East shareholder votes and competition and CFIUS approvals were among the requirements for the completion of the transaction. Two further independent administrative authorizations were also needed: one from the Federal Energy Regulatory Commission and another from the Federal Communications Commission. Finally, there were additional conditions that are less common in general but feature heavily in transactions involving firms that provide services to local authorities. These conditions were authorizations from the Public Utility Control commissions in the states where Energy East was active, i.e. Connecticut, Maine, New Hampshire, and New York.

On February 29, 2008, the parties announced that they had received all these authorizations, except from the New York authority. The regulator thought the proposed merger did not contain enough guarantees as to the benefits for consumers in the state. On June 16, a New York administrative judge ruled that the merger should be blocked because it was not in the public interest. If the New York commission were to approve the merger, the judge ruled that there should be some form of compensation for two existing New York gas companies. The New York commission finally approved the merger on September 3, 2008 – more than a year after the deal was announced – and the transaction was completed accordingly. On the day the New York commission initially rejected the merger proposal, Energy East's share price fell by 15%. This is a good example of how M&A timetable issues can have negative consequences for arbitrageurs.

3.2.2   Sector differences

As well as the type of transaction, the sector in which the two parties operate is an important distinction to be made. Using a sample of deals

Table 3.1   Sector differences

Sector	Average duration of transactions (days)
Energy	207
Finance	167
Media and entertainment	160
Telecoms	147
Real estate	138
Basic materials	128
Basic consumer goods	122
Healthcare	115
Retail	114
Industry	106
Discretionary consumer goods	103
Technology	100
Overall average duration	135

Source: Kirchner, 2009: 84. This material is reproduced with permission of John Wiley & Sons, Inc.

conducted in the US, Table 3.1 shows the different timetables involved for different industries:

As we can see, transactions take, on average, between four and five months to complete from when the deal is announced. The longest timetables are in the most regulated sectors, such as energy, finance and telecoms. These are the "protected" sectors that have their own commissions (FERC, FCC, Fed, etc.).

Any risks connected to a possible delay in completing the transaction should be studied very carefully. The regulatory authorization delays are long because administrations want time to make the right decision. If the authorities decide to request additional information from the parties and push back their decision deadline (potentially by several months), it has an immediate and costly effect on the spread.

The overlapping of different timetables and developing a strategy for reusing funds are crucial factors for an arbitrageur building up a diversi-fied portfolio of spreads. When a transaction is completed, arbitrageurs get the rewards for their efforts. They must now reinvest that money in other attractive spreads. As all arbitrageurs are paid at the same time – when big transactions are completed – spreads on the other big deals going on at that time tend to narrow as a result of portfolio turnover. Some fund managers like to play the arbitrageurs at their own game by attempting to profit from these technical aspects.

Dual-Track – When Takeover Meets Merger: Burger King

On September 3, 2010, 3G Capital, the private-equity firm created by Brazilian billionaire Jorge Paulo Lemann (the 48th-richest person in the world, according to *Forbes* magazine), announced the acquisition of fast-food chain Burger King for around $4 billion. The price of $24 per share included a premium of 46% over the pre-speculation share price of $16.45. Before being listed on the stock exchange in 2006, Burger King had been bought four years earlier by private-equity firms TPG, Bain and GSCP, which still held 31% of share capital. The fast-food chain operated 12,150 restaurants across 76 countries, with 90% operated under a franchise.

3G obtained committed financing from JPMorgan and Barclays to buy the shares and restructure the target company's debt. Burger King negotiated a go-shop clause, enabling it to solicit rival offers until October 12.

The merger agreement was innovative in terms of the timetable of the operation. A transaction involving a US-listed company is usually structured either as a tender offer or a merger. In this case, however, the lawyers envisaged a combination of the two in what is known as a dual-track structure. 3G launched a tender offer, while Burger King prepared for and organized a vote on a merger by, for example, filing a proxy statement with the SEC and sending a notice of convocation for a general shareholders' meeting. Whichever process moved fastest would then be implemented.

3G gave no explanation for this unusual structure, but it could have had something to do with the 79.1% threshold for the tender offer compared with the typical 50% plus one vote. If the 79.1% threshold was not reached, 3G could fall back on the merger structure, which requires only a simple majority.

Why the threshold of 79.1%? It can be explained by the top-up clause in the merger agreement. A top-up clause is a mechanism that allows a bidder to take total control of the target company once they have received the shares tendered into the offer. The buyer purchases new shares issued by the target company in order to reach 90% of share capital. It can then organize a short-term merger to squeeze out the remaining shareholders. This short-form merger does not require the approval of the minority shareholders and can be set in motion the day after the securities settlement date. A tender offer can therefore enable a buyer to own 100% of its target company as soon as the 20-day offer period ends.

As the maximum number of shares authorized for issue under the Burger King bylaws did not allow for a top-up clause from 50% to 90%, the threshold was set at 79.1%. With that level established, by issuing the maximum number of shares allowed by its bylaws Burger King could now ensure that the top-up clause took ownership up to 90%.

That explains the dual-track structure. 3G did not want to include a 50% threshold in its tender offer because if the takeup was less than 79.1%, it would be forced to call a shareholders' meeting to squeeze out the remaining minority interests. The vote would have been a formality because 3G itself could have taken part, but it would have set the deal back by two or three months. By instigating the dual-track structure, 3G was ensuring a swift resolution. In the worst-case scenario of failing to reach 79.1%, it could simply fall back on the merger, which had already been prepared. In the end, the threshold for the tender offer was reached comfortably and the transaction was completed on October 15, 2010.

4

The Merger Arbitrage Strategy

As we have already seen, most of the time this investment strategy enables investors to make small profits, represented by the spread, when the transaction is closed (remember that, statistically over the long term, around 90% of deals announced and 95% of friendly deals go to completion). The key to an arbitrageur's profitability is above all to avoid – as much as possible – transactions that fail (in which case the losses may be considerable), whilst also maximizing his participation rate in higher bids. In a way, arbitrageurs act as insurers in M&A transactions, taking clients' premiums but having to provide large amounts of indemnity to the victims in the event of a disaster.

In this chapter, we are going to look at the following:

- the long-term profitability of this strategy;
- the factors that influence the returns generated using this strategy;
- the different approaches to the strategy developed by specialist managers;
- the conclusions of academic studies on the subject.

4.1 THE LONG-TERM PROFITABILITY OF THE STRATEGY

Figure 4.1 compares (for the period from January 1, 1990 to December 31, 2011) the profitability of three indices:

- the S&P 500 (annual return of 8.2% over the period with volatility of 15.2%);
- the Barclays bond index (annual return of 7.0% over the period with volatility of 3.8%);
- the merger arbitrage index (annual return of 8.8% over the period with volatility of 4.1%).

As we can see, over the long term, the strategy can yield an annualized performance similar to that of stocks, with a volatility fairly close to that

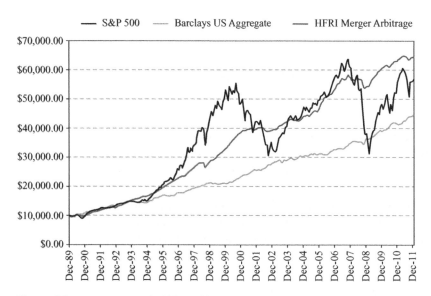

Figure 4.1 Long-term profitability (1990–2011)
Source: Bloomberg

of bonds. The strategy therefore has an excellent Sharpe ratio (a ratio that measures the risk-adjusted return of a strategy).

This suggests that the strategy generates a persistent "excess return," or alpha, over time. We will come back to this point when we review the academic literature on the subject.

On the other hand, M&A arbitrage has proven that it can be resilient in a chaotic financial market like that of 2008 and has delivered positive returns during the last 10 years, with very low volatility, as we can see in Table 4.1.

4.2 THE FACTORS THAT INFLUENCE RETURNS

There is a common saying among arbitrageurs that every deal will have its "judgment day," meaning that at a given moment the transaction will have to either be finalized or fail. The risk involved is therefore an idiosyncratic one that depends on the occurrence of a specific identified event, rather than on an economic or market context.

That being said, since arbitrageurs are essentially insurers of deals for mutual funds, the price of this insurance depends on the prevalent risk aversion at a given time.

Table 4.1 Comparison of hedge fund strategy performances

	2001	2002	2003	2004	2005	2006	2007	2008	2009	2010	2011
Global Hedge Fund	8.67%	4.72%	13.38%	2.69%	2.72%	9.26%	4.23%	−23.25%	13.4%	5.19%	−8.87%
Equity Hedge	8.96%	2.12%	14.46%	2.19%	4.19%	9.23%	3.21%	−25.45%	13.14%	8.92%	−19.08%
Event Driven	5.87%	−1.5%	18.75%	6.93%	2.81%	10.32%	4.88%	−22.11%	16.59%	1.98%	−4.9%
Equity Market Neutral	5.27%	2.83%	−2.37%	0.33%	0.21%	4.76%	3.11%	−1.16%	−5.56%	2.64%	−2.92%
Convertible Arbitrage	13.96%	11.46%	8.86%	−0.14%	−5.69%	9.57%	−0.95%	−58.37%	42.46%	8.76%	−3.07%
Merger Arbitrage	1.47%	0.99%	4.27%	2.8%	3.72%	10.73%	4.89%	3.66%	8.14%	5.69%	−2.09%

Source: Bloomberg

Therefore, when market conditions are difficult, when markets are suffering sharp downward trends and volatility is soaring, we generally see spreads widen and arbitrage funds lose money (at least on paper), because:

- the lowering of valuations and prospects for growth may reduce the likelihood that an offer will be completed (this environment increases the chances that a buyer will invoke a MAC clause, for example);
- in the event that the offer fails, the standalone value of the target company naturally drops when the stock markets are falling;
- in this environment, risk premiums increase (the price of "fear") and – even with the same level of risk – insurance becomes more expensive.

Of course, the most important thing for an arbitrageur is not the mark-to-market of his positions, i.e. their real-time valuation based on their current share price, but knowing whether or not the deals are going to close in the end. While market volatility does not bring the likelihood of the offer's success into question, any widening of the spreads actually provides an opportunity for an arbitrageur to reinforce what he considers to be secure positions.

We can therefore see a fairly good correlation between the merger arbitrage spreads and the VIX volatility index (the volatility index calculated based on the S&P 500). Figure 4.2 illustrates this relationship by showing the change in the spread in the buyout of specialty chemical company Lubrizol by Berkshire Hathaway, Warren Buffett's holding company, and the parallel change in the VIX. Although this transaction was considered particularly secure by the arbitrageur community, during the period of tension and sudden increase in volatility that took place on the markets in August 2011, the spread nevertheless widened considerably, from 0.3% to 1.4%.

The increase in volatility is a sign of anxiety (the market was hesitating; it was no longer able to find the "right" price and reacted violently to any information, in the absence of any fundamental conviction). This conveys a certain risk aversion, which it simultaneously reinforces.

Moreover, the spread systematically incorporates the risk-free rate, because even a certain transaction that must close within six months will not be carried out at the offer price, but at its discounted value. We can therefore see a fairly good correlation between arbitrage spreads and short-term rates, as shown in Figure 4.3 (the gap we can see as of the end of 2008 is due to the crisis: zero-rate policy with a high VIX).

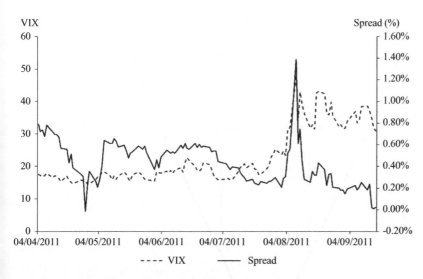

Figure 4.2   VIX and Lubrizol/Berkshire Hathaway spread
Source: Bloomberg

4.3   THE DIFFERENT APPROACHES TO THE STRATEGY DEVELOPED BY SPECIALIST MANAGERS

There are several fundamental differences between the various approaches to this strategy used by specialist managers.

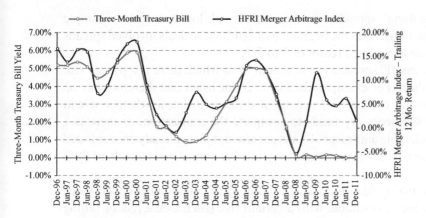

Figure 4.3   Correlation between returns and short-term rates (1997–2011)
Source: Bloomberg

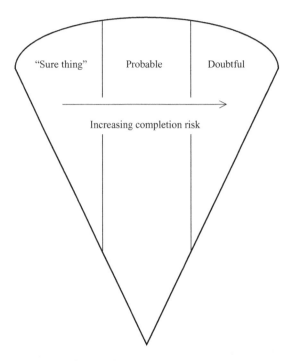

Figure 4.4   M&A transaction breakdown

4.3.1   The deal's risk zone

We normally distinguish between three broad spread zones (Figure 4.4):

- "Sure thing" spreads, i.e. ultra-consensual, low-risk deals on simple transactions. As at the beginning of 2012, these deals involved spreads with an annualized return of 3 to 5%.
- "Distressed" spreads, i.e. transactions in which there is a proven risk of failure. For example, the buyer is not listed and therefore has no disclosure obligations, making it difficult to know whether it will have the necessary funds to complete the transaction, or there is a considerable antitrust risk (merger attempt in an already concentrated market). These transactions may involve annualized spreads of 30% or more.
- High-quality deals that have the arbitrageur community divided, since some are comfortable with a certain risk (such as the risk of falling behind the timetable or of syndication) and others are not. These transactions involve annualized spreads of 8 to 15%.

4.3.2   The use of leverage

The transactions considered by the entire arbitrageur community to be the most secure obviously involve the tightest annualized spreads. Conversely, deals considered more risky yield wide, or even very wide, annualized spreads.

We can distinguish between two main approaches:

- Funds that have a high leverage ratio ($3 \times$, $5 \times$ or even $10 \times$) are generally concentrated in the most-secure-deals segment and "inflate" the returns with leverage. Let's suppose that the average annualized spread of a diversified deal portfolio is 5% and that the fund can borrow from its prime broker at a rate of 2%; the use of a leverage ratio of $3 \times$ (i.e. borrowing 2 from the prime broker) enables the fund to increase its yield to $(3 \times 5\%) - (2 \times 2\%) = 11\%$ gross. The proprietary trading desks of the major investment banks usually use a high level of leverage, which they obtain at a modest price, since they use the bank's balance sheet.
- Funds that do not use leverage may find it difficult to limit their investments to the most-secure-deals segment in order to achieve their return targets and will therefore invest:
  - either in the "distressed"-deals segment;
  - or in the segment of less-consensual deals that yield wider spreads.

Some managers may also arbitrage against transactions (by betting that they will fail), which is known as a Chinese deal in financial jargon.

Finally, when a manager wishes to arbitrage on a transaction in which part of the payment will be made in shares but fears that the buyer itself may be the subject of a takeover bid, he may play a Texan. In a traditional share-based transaction, the arbitrageur goes short on the buyer's shares. He therefore makes a loss if the share price increases. If the buyer is the subject of an offer, the share price will automatically increase and the arbitrageur will be exposed to considerable losses on his original position. A Texan is therefore a way of arbitraging on a transaction involving part of the payment in shares, whilst protecting oneself against an offer on the buyer. It consists of going long on shares in the target company and on shares in the buyer.

4.3.3   The use of options or bonds

Some managers deploy the strategy through shares, which are usually the securities that are the subject of the buyout offer. The profit, if the transaction is completed, is known and is equal to the spread. Other managers also use options (call or put) to arbitrage on certain scenarios. For example:

- the sale of covered calls at the offer price enables the manager to collect a premium, improving the return by abandoning the upside linked to a possible higher bid;
- the purchase of puts enables the manager to cover his losses in the event that the transaction fails (this is a sort of reinsurance against the risks posed by the spread). This purchase of puts may, for example, be financed by the sale of covered calls.

Calls are options that give the investor who holds them the right to buy a certain number of shares of the underlying security at a given price (the strike price) and before a set date (the maturity date of the contract). Conversely, puts give their holder the possibility to sell a certain quantity of underlying shares at a certain price and prior to a fixed expiration date.

The use of options is more common in hostile transactions, in which the uncertainty surrounding the completion of the transaction, the final price, and the timetable creates fertile ground to formulate a better scenario via the option markets. When the announcement was made on September 1 of the (unsolicited) approach of UK confectionery company Cadbury by US agrofood giant Kraft Foods, with an offer of 735 pence per share (in cash and shares), a manager wanting to bet on the final scenario of a friendly offer at 850 pence per share, concluded six months later, could, for example, have bought shares and sold one-month calls with a strike price of 850 pence, rolling his call-selling position forward each month until the transaction closed.

Trading on the option markets requires a certain expertise, since the price of these options depends on a number of variables (particularly the level of volatility) and these instruments are less liquid than shares (due to a fairly wide bid/ask spread).

There are some managers who arbitrage on the spread via the bonds issued by the target company, particularly when these bonds contain early-redemption clauses in the event of a change of control. Arbitrageurs can also bet on the execution of a transaction via the CDS market with the improvement (or deterioration, in the case of an LBO, for example) of the target company's counterparty risk.

4.3.4   Investment portfolio analysis

Managers also differ in terms of their approach to investment portfolios and how they analyze them:

* Some – usually those from investment bank proprietary trading desks – develop deal-scoring tools (using databases containing information on deal success rates and multi-factorial forecasting models) and take a more quantitative approach to analysis. Their task is to carry out, based on a database of thousands of past deals, an analysis that will enable them to identify the main factors influencing the probability that a transaction will be completed. If the model yields a higher probability than that implicitly suggested by the share price, it will be best to take a short position, and vice versa.
* Others – usually those from an M&A consulting background – take a more basic approach and attempt to understand as precisely as possible the individual dynamic of each transaction (considered to be unique), the synergies, and the tactical aspects involved (often by using game theory and scenario analysis).
* Of course, the two approaches can be combined and can complement each other nicely.

The probability-based approach has two structural flaws that should be pointed out:

* The model, which is based on a long history, is slow at detecting changes in M&A market conditions (which can take place quickly), such as changes in access to finance, a stiffening of antitrust authority reviews, or any new elements (e.g. MOFCOM).
* While such models successfully analyze the exogenous risk of non-completion (the risk that an external element will prevent the deal from going ahead), it is much more difficult for them to analyze the endogenous risks, such as the risk that a party no longer wants to proceed with the deal, which depend on the history of the transaction in question.

4.3.5   Portfolio concentration

A specialist manager investing in Europe and North America can choose at any time from between 80 and 150 deals announced (depending on the maturity of the M&A cycle). If we add emerging countries, there are between 150 and 200 "investable" deals.

It is generally considered more prudent to diversify a portfolio in order to reduce idiosyncratic risk on a given transaction. Some managers build a portfolio from 60 lines, while others have just 10 lines. The average is usually around 30 to 40.

4.3.6   The role of trading

Put simply, the strategy consists of taking advantage of the convergence between the share price and the offer price by buying shares in the target company when the announcement is made and tendering these shares into the offer or awaiting payment when the merger is closed. However, this buy-and-hold strategy is rarely used by specialist managers. It is possible for an arbitrageur to improve the transaction's return through trading, by increasing his position when the spread widens and reducing or selling his position when the spread tightens too quickly. Arbitrageurs can "scalp" the spread by calculating its convergence speed, acceleration, etc. Of course, there are certain times at which it is better to take advantage of the spread's volatility, such as the trading sessions prior to an important decision on the deal's fate (typically whether or not the deal has obtained phase II antitrust clearance).

Certain external events can also influence the change in spreads. During the 2008 crisis, the hedge funds whose prime brokers were Lehman Brothers or Bear Stearns were caught up in the difficulties of these two banks and had to considerably reduce their exposure, which is known as deleveraging. Since some of these positions related to M&A transactions under way, arbitrageurs were able to see their spreads widen significantly. This example perfectly illustrates how spread opening can also take place on a purely technical basis.

Figures 4.5 illustrates the different cases using recent transactions. Bearing in mind that each deal has its own unique dynamic, we can observe different convergence profiles that will potentially improve the profitability of each investment.

4.3.7   Classifications

Hedge funds' returns are observed by several databases, which regularly publish classifications of funds by strategy and by performance. Just to give you an idea, Figure 4.6 shows the classification drawn up by data provider BarclayHedge on M&A arbitrage funds over three years.

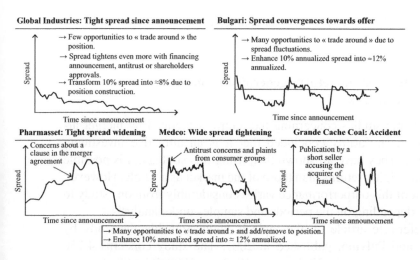

Figure 4.5   Convergence profiles

4.4   THE CONCLUSIONS OF ACADEMIC STUDIES

There is a wealth of academic research on merger arbitrage. It concerns not only merger arbitrage as a portfolio management strategy, i.e. a market and risk management approach, but also its interconnection with the world of business finance and its role in the execution of M&A transactions. We are therefore going to look at the conclusions of academic research into all aspects of merger arbitrage, from the returns

For the period from 4/1/2009 to 3/31/2012. Includes only Hedge Funds managing at least $10 million as of 3/31/2012

	FUND NAME	3-YR COMP. ANNUAL RETURN	SHARPE RATIO	CORR. VS.- S&P 500	STARTING DATE	LAST 12-MO. PERIOD	LARGEST DRAW DOWN	ASSETS UNDER MGMT.($)
1	Diva Synergy Ltd C (USD)	14.43%	1.22	0.54	May-08	1%	12%	64.7M
2	Lion Fund Limited	11.82%	1.98	0.61	Feb-96	5%	1%	268.6M
3	Glazer Offshore Fund Ltd	8.72%	4.51	0.33	Sep-01	5%	0%	168.0M
4	ABCD Opportunities Fund Plc	6.91%	2.24	0.16	Aug-07	13%	1%	45.4M
5	Highland Capital Mgmt LP	6.61%	3.35	0.23	Apr-00	3%	0%	47.2M
6	Hudson Valley Partners LP	6.56%	1.70	0.58	Jun-05	0%	6%	97.2M
7	Diva Synergy Ltd A	6.11%	1.65	0.55	Jan-07	2%	4%	21.5M
8	Gabelli Associates Limited	6.07%	3.49	0.73	Sep-89	4%	1%	116.6M
9	Black Diamond Arbitrage Partners LP	5.74%	1.18	0.00	Feb-98	1%	5%	15.3M
10	Merger Fund Ltd	5.64%	1.67	0.58	Jan-96	0%	6%	97.2M

Figure 4.6   Top 10 – merger arbitrage – 2009–2012
Source: BarclayHedge. Reproduced by permission of BarclayHedge.

generated by the strategy to its other characteristics and its role in M&A transactions.

4.4.1 Studies on the returns generated by merger arbitrage strategies

The academic studies concerning the returns generated by merger arbitrage have uniformly concluded that it is an attractive investment philosophy. They have all shown that, using this strategy, it is possible to generate higher returns than those of the market as a whole. However, the extent of this outperformance varies considerably from one study to the next, depending on the periods and samples under analysis.

The reference article on the topic is unquestionably the study by Mitchell and Pulvino, published in 2001. The study concerns 4,750 M&A transactions in the US between 1963 and 1998. It is an extremely comprehensive account, since the sample covers both cash- and share-based transactions. The authors highlight annualized returns of more than 16% over this period, without taking into account transaction costs. The impact of these costs is significant, since taking them into consideration brings the annualized performance to slightly over 10%. In terms of alpha, the excess return generated is 4% per year.

However, as we have already mentioned, a number of articles have studied the same subject but reached very different conclusions. Jindra and Walking (2004) and Dukes Frohlich, and Ma (1992) exclusively cover offers with payment in cash. The first study is based on 362 transactions between 1981 and 1995, while the second concerns 761 deals between 1971 and 1985. Both studies come to the same conclusion. They show very high annualized returns, of 47% and 117% respectively. The article by Larcker and Lys (1987) covers cash-based, share-based, and mixed transactions but does not include a calculation of the return on short selling the buyer's shares. However, the study still shows a return in excess of 5.3%, or an annualized excess return of 51.9%.

Karolyi and Shannon (1998) focus exclusively on Canadian M&A transactions carried out in 1997. The sample is a small one (37 transactions) representing deals whose targets had a market capitalization of more than $50 million. The authors show that carrying out a merger arbitrage strategy on these operations could generate a performance in excess of the Canadian market index, with a return of 4.78% over 57 days, or an annualized excess return of around 40%.

These results are consistent with other studies, such as the one carried out by Baker and Savasoglu in 2002, which concluded on an alpha of 0.6 to 0.9% per month on a sample of 1,901 US transactions in cash and shares between 1981 and 1996. This corresponds to an annualized excess return of around 12.5%.

Some articles have attempted to explain how arbitrageurs have been able to generate such returns and what factors could influence them. Larcker and Lys (1987) postulate that arbitrageurs are better informed than the market with regard to the likelihood that an M&A transaction will succeed. Consequently, this information asymmetry enables them to generate considerably higher returns than those of the market.

All the articles we have mentioned identify some of the characteristics of M&A transactions that can have an influence on arbitrageurs' returns. We can therefore see that merger arbitrage returns:

- are positively correlated to the control premiums paid by the buyers and to the likelihood of a transaction's success;
- are higher when the target company's management initially opposes the transaction. However, the risk associated with such transactions is greater;
- are positively correlated to the size of the abnormal volumes observed on the target company's shares;
- are lower when the buyer has a large stake in the target company prior to the official announcement of the transaction.

Lastly, some articles contrast with the optimistic conclusions of the aforementioned studies on the size of the excess returns that can be generated through merger arbitrage.

Wei, Ferguson, and Chichernea (2011) show that, after having adjusted the returns for the risks specific to each transaction, for liquidity risk and for volatility, the returns generated by arbitrageurs are in line with those of the market. Therefore, in their opinion, merger arbitrage is not an alpha-generating strategy.

To finish off, let's look at the study by Jetley and Ji (2010) concerning the change in arbitrage spreads. Their sample is broken down into three sub-periods: 1990 to 1995, 1996 to 2001, and 2002 to 2007. The study as a whole covers 2,182 transactions and considers all methods of payment. The authors demonstrate that arbitrage spreads suffered a decline throughout the period. They claim that the spreads for transactions announced since 2002 are 520 basis points (bps) lower than those for deals announced between 1990 and 1995 and 290 bps lower than those for transactions announced between 1996 and 2001. They give three reasons for this decline:

- the decrease in transaction costs;
- the progressive increase in capital allocated to this strategy;
- the reduction in risks linked to the fall in control premiums, which results in lesser losses in the event that the transaction fails.

The authors therefore conclude that many of these changes will probably have a permanent impact on arbitrage spreads and that the profitability of funds that employ merger arbitrage strategies could suffer in future as a result.

4.4.2   The role of arbitrageurs in the execution of M&A transactions

Arbitrageurs play a multifunctional role in the execution of M&A transactions. Their role is often described as that of an insurer for the various market operators. When a transaction is announced and the share price of the target company rises, approaching the offer price, mutual funds usually want to sell their position. Arbitrage funds therefore intervene to provide liquidity (i.e. assurance that the mutual funds can find a counterparty to sell their positions to). This liquidity obviously has a price and depends on the arbitrageur community's absorption capacity (which explains why certain jumbo deals can sometimes involve spreads that are "too" wide, if the arbitrageurs' reserve of capital is insufficient to absorb the mutual funds' paper).

As we have already seen, academic models concerned with merger arbitrage are frequently based on a hypothesis of information asymmetry in the arbitrageurs' favor. In practice, this information bias can be explained by specialist funds' ability to correctly analyze situations, while mutual funds generally do not have this expertise. Mutual funds therefore do not take the risk of quantifying the risk of failure or estimating the potential losses and tend to sell their position so as not to "leave too much money on the table". Even a mutual fund that is capable of assessing the spread will not necessarily want to hold onto the shares for several months, bear the risk of failure, and have its upside limited to the spread (if the markets rise by 30%, the offer price will remain the same, and therefore keeping the shares will automatically reduce the beta of a long-only portfolio and may cause benchmark outperformance problems).

One article, however, has called into question the theory that arbitrageurs possess privileged information. Cornelli and Li (2002) have developed a model in which an arbitrageur acquires privileged information on the transaction only if he decides to participate in it (it therefore arises endogenously). Arbitrageurs do not a priori have better knowledge than other parties regarding the transaction and the likelihood of its being completed. In a way, arbitrageurs are catalysts for M&A transactions, since they largely incline to tender their shares into such an offer. In this sense, they facilitate the completion of these deals. If an arbitrageur decides to participate in a transaction by buying shares of the target company (supposing that the offer will be paid for in cash only), he will have an advantage over other investors with regard to the probability of the deal succeeding, since he already knows that he will tender his shares into the offer. This is how the arbitrageurs' information advantage comes into being in the Cornelli and Li model. Consequently, the authors show that one of the aspects of M&A transactions for arbitrageurs is to attempt to anticipate the conduct of other arbitrageurs.

Another interpretation given in the Larcker and Lys study is that the arbitrageurs who decide to participate in these transactions are more familiar with the workings of such deals than traditional investors, and therefore may refuse to tender their shares into the offer in order to force the buyer to increase its offer. The authors go on to point out that the buyers involved in the transactions in their sample increased their offers by 9% on average.

Lastly, Gomes (2001) studies the behavior of arbitrageurs during tender offers followed by squeeze-outs. He explains that the larger the proportion of arbitrageurs in the target company's shareholder structure, the greater their power to determine the final price paid by the buyer, since it is easier for them to form blocks and refuse to tender their shares into the offer. This conclusion is irrespective of when the arbitrageurs acquired their shares in the target (prior to or during the offer). Moreover, it concurs with the conclusion reached by Kyle and Vila (1991).

Another study, carried out by Hsieh (2002), confirms and complements these results. It confirms that an arbitrageur's position is positively correlated to the probability that a transaction will succeed and to the size of the control premium paid by the buyer. On the other hand, it shows that arbitrageurs reduce their positions when the buyer faces competition from several rival buyers. In fact, although this type of transaction is the most profitable, it is also the most risky, since the investor is exposed to the possibility that the buyers may withdraw from the deal. Finally, the study shows that in transactions involving collars, the likelihood of success and the size of the arbitrageurs' shareholdings are higher than in transactions without these provisions. However, the returns of such transactions are lower.

4.4.3   Other characteristics of merger arbitrage strategies

One of the most striking characteristics of the merger arbitrage strategy is the fact that its returns are not correlated to those of the financial markets. Once again, Mitchell and Pulvino (2001) complement this statement. They show that the returns generated by merger arbitrage are highly asymmetric. On the one hand, their study shows that in most market conditions, these returns are effectively uncorrelated to those of the markets. On the other hand, they show that in environments in which markets are falling, the correlation between the returns generated by merger arbitrage and those of the markets increases considerably. They therefore compare the return profile of this strategy to the sale of naked put options with an underlying market index: in most market situations, a small premium is collected, but a limited number of situations may generate large losses.

Another article (Wang, Wang and Tsai, 2008) deals exclusively with the performance of the merger arbitrage strategy in LBO transactions. The study concerns 299 LBOs between 1991 and 2006, 65 of which ultimately failed. The authors point out the attractive returns generated by merger arbitrage in these transactions, describing an annualized yield of 20%.

Part II
Analyzing the Risk of Failure

The second part of this book looks at the various M&A failure risks that arbitrageurs must consider before deciding whether to invest. This is at the heart of merger arbitrage. Chapters 5 to 8 examine: financing risk; competition risk; legal aspects arising from merger agreements; and other issues, such as administrative and political risks. All these chapters outline the current state of affairs, but they also illustrate each element with the aid of recent examples of M&A transactions.

5

Financing Risk

The assessment of financing risk is one of the key aspects in evaluating the probability of an M&A transaction being completed. Consequently, it is important to understand the different methods of financing a transaction, as well as the level of legal security of such financing.

5.1 THE DIFFERENT FINANCING METHODS

There are two main methods of financing an acquisition: payment in cash and payment in shares. The buyout offer may also be a hybrid offer, involving both cash and shares.

1. *Stock-funded buyout or payment in shares*: In a stock-funded buyout, the buyer pays for the acquisition with its own shares and proposes that the shareholders of the target company receive its shares in exchange for the shares they hold, in accordance with the exchange ratio. A stock-funded buyout does not involve any kind of liquidity and avoids having to exceed certain debt thresholds. On the other hand, it results in a dilution of the voting rights and financial interests of the existing shareholders. It is therefore important to closely follow the result of the vote held by the buyer's shareholders, if it has not yet taken place when the buyout is publicly announced.
2. *Cash buyout*: In a cash buyout, the financing may come from the buyer's existing liquidity, from a capital increase (through a rights issue, for example), or from recourse to debt (through a bank loan, bond issue, etc.).

Since the transaction payment involves a cash component, except where the buyer uses its equity capital, the source and quality of the financing are crucial to the arbitrageur when quantifying risk. Moreover, even in a transaction where the buyer's shares are used as a method of payment, financing can be a problem if the buyer has to refinance the target company's debt.

A deal, whether it is paid for in cash or in shares, and whether it is funded using existing or new resources, can therefore either create or

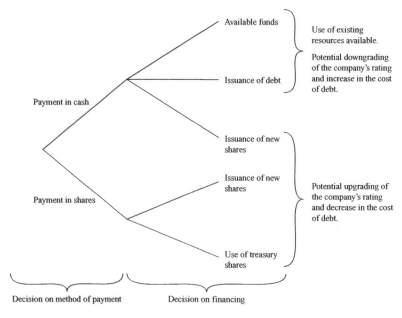

Figure 5.1   Forms of financing and different payment methods

consume cash or available financing capacity. According to the "pecking order" theory of business financing, companies always prefer to use their internal resources, including their treasury shares, first. Once these available internal resources have been used, companies turn to external financing methods. Figure 5.1 groups together the various forms of financing and links them to the different payment methods.

The following extract is taken from the announcement of the acquisition of Anheuser-Busch by InBev in summer 2008. This example will enable us to introduce the different types of bank debt.

Announcement of the Acquisition of Anheuser-Busch by InBev

Press release

Leuven, Belgium – July 14, 2008 and St. Louis, Missouri – July 13, 2008

InBev (Euronext: INB) and Anheuser-Busch (NYSE: BUD) today announced a merger agreement between the two companies to become the world's biggest brewing group. Shareholders of Anheuser-Busch will receive $70 in cash per share, for a total equity value of $52 billion, in a transaction that could transform the sector. The merged entity will be called Anheuser-Busch InBev. The boards of directors of the two companies have unanimously approved the transaction. InBev has received a firm commitment of financing to buy all Anheuser-Busch shares in circulation.

[. . .]

InBev has received a firm commitment of financing with credit facilities signed by a group of major financial institutions, including Banco Santander, Bank of Tokyo-Mitsubishi, Barclays Capital, BNP Paribas, Deutsche Bank, Fortis, ING Bank, JPMorgan, Mizuho Corporate Bank and Royal Bank of Scotland. The transaction will be financed by a $45 billion loan, including a $7 billion bridge loan pending the divestment of some of the two companies' non-strategic assets. InBev has also received commitments for a bridge loan via a share issue of up to $9.8 billion, which will give the company the flexibility to decide on the time and type of the share issue, within a maximum of six months of the finalization of the agreement. The merged company should therefore retain a solid investment grade credit profile, and is expected to reduce its debt levels rapidly thanks to its ability to generate a solid flow of available funds.

The different types of debt are as follows.

5.1.1   Revolving credit

Revolving credit, also known as permanent credit, is a type of senior debt. Senior debt is a debt that is subject to specific guarantees, the repayment of which takes priority over other debts. Revolving credit makes available to the borrower a reserve of money that the latter may use freely and permanently, within the limit of a sum fixed by agreement and for a given period of time. The reserve available decreases as it is used and is replenished following each repayment. In addition to the facility fee, the borrower pays an annual commitment fee on the unused amounts. Revolving credit therefore gives the borrower a great deal of flexibility in terms of its use and is generally used to finance day-to-day needs, such as working-capital requirements. It can also be used for capex, enabling the company to finance certain investments in capital assets and other investments that are necessary for it to operate. Different options can be proposed in a revolving-credit agreement:

- a multi-currency line, which enables the borrower to borrow in several currencies;
- an evergreen clause, which enables the borrower to extend the maturity of the revolving-credit line for an additional year each time;
- a swing line, which is a bridge loan, in conjunction with the revolving-credit line, enabling the borrower to make very short-term (generally overnight) drawdowns in between the repayment of a matured credit line and its renewal;
- a term-out clause, enabling the borrower to convert the revolving credit into a term loan on a given date. This option is generally available only to investment grade borrowers. In many cases, the cost of borrowing increases if the term-out option is exercised.

5.1.2   Bridge loan

If there is a risk that the acquisition of the target company could be closed before bank term loans or a bond issue are put in place, the transaction may be financed in the interim by a bridge loan. A bridge loan is a loan that is put in place in anticipation of future revenues or the arrangement of long-term financing that will be used to pay back the bridge loan, such as a capital increase, a bank term loan, a bond issue, or the disposal of a subsidiary. It is a short-term facility with higher interest charges than conventional financing, and can usually be accessed quickly with relatively little documentation involved. More specifically, it enables a company to reduce information leakage risk in relation to an acquisition in preparation.

5.1.3   Term loan

A term loan or bank term loan corresponds to classic bank lending. In an acquisition financed by debt, it is one of the main sources of financing. It has the following characteristics:

- senior debt with a fixed maturity of 5 to 10 years, but can be repaid in full early at any time, since early-repayment penalties are rare;
- a variable rate with a price based on a spread above Euribor or Libor;
- a loan agreement that generally includes covenants based on the maintaining of certain financial ratios, generally calculated on a quarterly

basis, and restrictions on the operation of the company (such as an investment limitation clause or a no-dividend clause). The breach of a bank covenant may result in early repayment of the loan;
- a structure comprising different tranches, with varying repayment methods and costs.

In LBOs, this debt is usually made up of three tranches:

- tranche A, repayable in installments over six years or fewer;
- tranche B, repayable in a single payment on maturity (bullet repayment) after seven or eight years;
- tranche C, repayable in a bullet payment after nine years. Although tranches B and C are more expensive than tranche A, since they involve greater risk due to the longer maturities and bullet repayment, the proportion represented by tranche A tends to be reduced in favor of tranches B and C in order to reduce the pressure on the company's funds. Tranches B and C are also called institutional term loans, since they became more frequent with the development of a base of institutional investors (insurance companies, mutual funds, structured-finance vehicles, etc.) that buy the loan from the banks. Tranche A, on the other hand, is usually syndicated to other banks. Prior to the 2007–2008 financial crisis, we began to see tranche D in certain transactions, which were repayable with a bullet payment after 10 years, but they have not yet made a comeback (and probably never will).

There are also some other variants of term loans, such as the second-lien and covenant-lite loans.

Second-lien loan

Second-lien loans are slightly more complex than classic term loans. As their name suggests, second-lien lenders are subordinate to senior lenders, which means that second-lien financing cannot be repaid until the senior debt has been repaid, but will be repaid before the company's bonds and mezzanine debt.

Second-lien loans are a classic example of a US import to the European credit market. This asset class first appeared in Europe in 2004, but its usage in the US dates back to the 1990s. It first took off in 2003, when the corporate bankruptcy rate fell. The second-lien loan was used in the US in debt-funded acquisitions to fill certain financing gaps that had arisen due to liquidity problems or maximum senior-debt thresholds. It became very popular from 2005 onwards, and was used to finance a number of acquisitions. When it appeared in Europe, it was seen as an alternative way of financing private-equity transactions and became an essential tranche of LBO financing. Unlike in the US, where second-lien agreements contain less restrictive covenants than those of senior debt (first-lien loans), in Europe, second-lien agreements are subject to the same covenants as first-lien agreements. On the other hand, due to their subordination level, second-lien loans are more expensive than senior debt and prices vary considerably depending on the complexity and the degree of underlying credit risk. Second-lien loans are also more expensive to repay early than senior debt, since early-repayment penalties usually apply in the first two years. They generally mature a year later than tranche C debt.

The second-lien loan seemed to have disappeared from the market following the 2007–2008 crisis, because investors had lost their appetite for this tranche, but it seems to be making a return to the market.

Covenant-lite loan

A covenant-lite loan is a loan that is not subject to traditional protection clauses. As its name suggests, it offers lenders less protection due to the removal of financial covenants, such as the borrower's obligation to maintain a maximum allowable leverage ratio or a minimum interest coverage ratio. Covenant-lite loans disappeared after the credit crunch, but are now making a comeback, since they give borrowers more flexibility.

Example of bank covenants

Extract from a financing document

In relation to the Facilities, the following financial covenants will apply:

(a) Leverage: Leverage in respect of any Relevant Period shall not exceed 2.75:1 (measured quarterly on the basis of Total Net Debt on the measurement date and rolling 12 months Consolidated EBITDA).

(b) Interest Cover: Interest Cover in respect of any Relevant Period shall not be less than 4.00:1 (measured quarterly on a rolling 12 month basis).
(c) Cashflow Cover: Cashflow Cover (i) in respect of the Relevant Period shall not be less than 1.05:1 (in each case measured annually on a rolling 12 month basis).
(d) Capital Expenditure: (i) Subject to paragraphs (ii) to (iv) below, the aggregate Capital Expenditure of the Group in respect of each Financial Year shall not exceed US$2,500,000 on the basis set out below (the "Capital Expenditure Limit").

5.1.4   Syndicated loan

In M&A transactions involving significant amounts of debt, banks syndicate the financing, which means that they redistribute part of the loan to a group of financial entities (other banks and institutional investors) by selling or transferring debt. Syndication enables banks to reduce the risk to which they are exposed to the proportion of the debt that they hold. Almost all types of loans can be syndicated. The syndicated-loan market developed alongside the wave of LBOs in the 1980s. There are three types of syndication: an underwritten deal; a best-efforts syndication; and a club deal.

Underwritten deal

The arrangers (the banks mandated to organize and manage the syndication of the loan) and the lead bank (the principal coordinator) undertake to underwrite the entirety of the loan based on predefined terms. In this case, the financing is guaranteed and the loan can be syndicated to other investors following the closure of the M&A transaction. The banks assume the risk of not being able to redistribute the loan if credit market conditions deteriorate and, consequently, the risk of being forced to hold a larger proportion of the debt than expected on their balance sheets. Alternatively, they can sell the debt at a loss. Thanks to flex-language, an underwritten deal no longer carries the same risk for banks that it once did, since the cost of the debt for the borrower can vary after the closure of the syndication. Flex-language makes it possible to adjust the cost of the debt either upwards or downwards during the syndication, depending on the current liquidity of the market and investors' appetite. It also enables the arrangers to adapt the overall distribution of the debt among the different tranches (A, B, C, etc.) and types of debt (mezzanine, etc.) according to market conditions in order to close the syndication.

Best-efforts syndication

In a best-efforts syndication, the arrangers do not underwrite the entire amount of the loan. The arrangers undertake only to underwrite part of the loan and to place the rest on the syndication market. If the loan is undersubscribed, the credit may not be closed or may need to be radically amended to reflect current market conditions. Best-efforts syndications are generally used for risky borrowers or complex transactions.

Club deal

A club deal is a loan of a relatively small amount that is granted by banks that already have relations with the borrower. Club deals were very common between 2008 and 2009 at the time when the credit crunch had ostracized the majority of institutional investors and affected the large commercial banks' capacity to grant loans.

5.1.5 Mezzanine loans

Mezzanine debt, a hybrid form of financing that combines senior debt and equity capital, is a type of subordinated debt: the principal of a mezzanine loan is repaid only when the senior and junior loans (where present in the financing structure) have been repaid. Mezzanine debt fills a financing gap and enables a company to obtain a more flexible and diversified financing structure. It has the following characteristics:

- A longer maturity than classic credit, at between 7 and 10 years.
- A loan agreement that generally contains the same financial covenants as senior bank loans (although they are sometimes more flexible) and more restrictive clauses on the operation of the company.
- A higher cost than senior debt due to its subordinated position in the company's capital structure, which may involve:
  - cash interest payment: a periodic cash payment based on a percentage of the unpaid balance of the mezzanine financing. The interest rate may be fixed throughout the duration of the loan or may fluctuate with the Libor or Euribor rate or any other base plus a spread;

- PIK (payment-in-kind) interest payment: interest is not paid in cash, but by increasing the amount of the principal by the amount of the interest. For example, a bond worth €100 million with a PIK interest rate of 8% would have a balance of €108 million at the end of the period;
- access to the company's share capital via share subscription warrants that mature at the end of the interest repayment period. These allow lenders to eventually access part of the company's share capital. Mezzanine loans with share subscription warrants are less expensive.

Although historically mezzanine debt has been the financing option of choice for small transactions and the high-yield bond market, over the years this option has become a basic component of LBO financing. Mezzanine debt is attractive to private-equity groups. It enables investors to take advantage of a leverage level that is higher than the bank debt threshold and to put in place a transaction that would have been impossible to carry out using only equity capital and senior debt. It also allows more flexibility in the management of the target company thanks to non-restrictive covenants. The long maturity of mezzanine debt makes it possible to retain the liquidity generated by the company and use it for other purposes. Unlike high-yield bonds, it is a private instrument that is syndicated to a group of lenders ranging from specialist mezzanine funds to hedge funds. Moreover, mezzanine debt agreements often include a one-to-three-year non-call provision and early-repayment penalties in the subsequent years. If the fund decides to sell the company, it will be less expensive to repay a mezzanine debt than to repay high-yield bonds, which generally involve longer non-call periods.

5.1.6 The bond market

The bond market is an alternative to bank financing. Although it is more expensive, a bond issue enables a company to obtain financing with longer maturities and with less restrictive covenants than bank loans.

Bond market glossary

Nominal value – The nominal value of a bond is the amount used to calculate the coupons to be paid by the company to investors.

Coupon (nominal interest rate) – This is the amount paid by the company to investors, calculated by applying the interest rate to the nominal value.

Issue price – In order to attract as many investors as possible, the issue price of the bond is often lower than its nominal value (this difference is known as the original issue discount, or OID). It is also possible for the issue price to be higher than the nominal value, although this is rarer.

Repayment method – There are three ways of repaying the principal: (i) bullet repayment; (ii) in fixed annuities or fixed installments; and (iii) via zero-coupon bonds.

Term – The average term of a bond is between 8 and 10 years for companies, although there are some bonds with a maturity of 15, 20, or 30 years. The longer the term, the greater the risk attached to the bond and, consequently, the cost.

Rating – The credit rating, issued by ratings agencies (S&P, Moody's and Fitch), is a key criterion for investors when estimating the risk involved in an investment.

Credit rating			
Moody's	S&P/ Fitch	Type	Level of risk
Aaa	AAA	Investment grade	Very high quality
Aa	AA	Investment grade	High quality
A	A	Investment grade	Good quality
Baa	BBB	Investment grade	Average quality
Ba, B	BB, B	High yield	Speculative
Caa/Ca/C	CCC/CC/C	High yield	Highly speculative
C	D	High yield	In default

A strategic acquisition or an LBO may also be financed by a bond issue. Transactions in which buyers have raised financing from the bond market include Roche's takeover of Genentech, Pfizer's acquisition of Wyeth, part of which was funded through bonds, and, more recently, Sanofi's acquisition of Genzyme.

Bond issue

Sanofi-Aventis press release: Sanofi-Aventis places bond issue

Paris, France–March 23, 2011

Sanofi-Aventis (EURONEXT: SAN and NYSE: SNY), rated AA–
by Standard and Poor's and A2 by Moody's (with a stable outlook
for both ratings) is pleased to announce that it has successfully
placed a bond issue worth $7 billion in six tranches:

- $1 billion of bonds maturing in 2012, bearing interest at the
  three-month USD Libor rate + 0.05%,
- $1 billion of bonds maturing in 2013, bearing interest at the
  three-month USD Libor rate + 0.20%,
- $750 million of bonds maturing in 2014, bearing interest at the
  three-month USD Libor rate + 0.31%,
- $750 million of bonds maturing in 2014, bearing interest at an
  annual rate of 1.625%,
- $1.5 billion of bonds maturing in 2016, bearing interest at an
  annual rate of 2.625%,
- $2 billion of bonds maturing in 2021, bearing interest at an annual
  rate of 4%.

The issue took place pursuant to a shelf registration statement
filed with the US Securities and Exchange Commission (SEC) on
March 15, 2010. Sanofi-Aventis will allocate the net proceeds of
the bond issue to financing part of its acquisition of Genzyme and
associated expenses. If the share swap offer concerning Genzyme
ordinary shares has not been carried out by the end of September
30, 2011, for whatever reason, Sanofi-Aventis will repay the fixed-
rate bonds and the floating-rate bonds maturing in 2014 at a price
equivalent to 101% of both, plus any interest accrued, by October
31, 2011 at the latest. The rest of the proceeds of the issue of the
floating-rate bonds maturing in 2012 and in 2013 will be allocated
to the company's general needs.

Investment grade issuers, corresponding to borrowers rated between
AAA and BBB – according to the scale used by S&P and Fitch
and rated between Aaa and Baa3 according to the scale used by
Moody's, generally have bond issue programs in place already (such as a

medium-/long-term lending program commonly called an *EMTN* program or a short-term program commonly called a commercial-paper issue program). In order to finance the acquisition of the target company, they can easily launch a bond issue under their EMTN program.

Conversely, high-yield bond issuers often take out a bank loan first (such as a bridge loan or term loan) to finance an acquisition and turn to the bond market later to refinance all or part of their bank loans. A high-yield bond is a subordinated debt which can be repaid only if the senior and junior debts have been repaid. High-yield bonds (those rated between BB + and D according to S&P and Fitch and between Ba1 and C according to Moody's) are issued by companies in administration or with a weak financial base and a high level of debt or to finance a large LBO transaction. In order to offer investors sufficient liquidity, these issues must be worth at least $100 million.

For a long time, high-yield issues were not open to the public, but were made to measure for institutional investors such as insurance companies via a private placement. Junk bonds, the common name used in the US to refer to high-risk bonds, did not appear until the late 1970s.

High-yield bond issues are expensive but enable companies to reduce repayment irregularities by replacing part of their bank debt and extending its maturity. They also offer the advantage of being repayable in bullet form after 8 to 10 years.

5.1.7   Contingent value rights (CVRs)

CVRs are generally used as a sweetener in certain M&A transactions. Sanofi used them in its acquisition of Genzyme. In this case, the buyer undertakes to pay an additional amount to the shareholders of the target company if, for example, expected but uncertain revenues are generated at specified times. CVRs function in the same way as options and, like all options, they can eventually expire without any value. Consequently, for transactions that involve a CVR, an arbitrageur must assess the CVR's value.

Extract from the Sanofi-Aventis press release

Paris, France and Cambridge, Massachusetts – February 16, 2011 – Sanofi-Aventis (EURONEXT: SAN and NYSE: SNY) and Genzyme Corporation (NASDAQ: GENZ) are pleased to announce today that they have signed a definitive agreement pursuant to which Sanofi-Aventis will acquire Genzyme for $74.00 per share in cash, or around $20.1 billion. In addition to the cash payment, each Genzyme shareholder will receive a contingent value right (CVR) for each share held, giving the bearer the right to receive additional cash payments if certain events concerning Lemtrada™ (alemtuzumab for MS) take place over a certain period, as well as certain production levels in 2011 concerning Cerezyme® and Fabrazyme®.

5.2 THE LEGAL SECURITY OF THE FINANCING

The closure of a buyout offer depends largely on the legal security of the financing involved. With regard to this matter, it is important to distinguish between the European legal framework and the US legal framework. In Europe, i.e. if the target company is listed on a stock exchange in one of the member states of the European Union, the financing risk is in actual fact very small, thanks to the "certain funds" provision under UK law. Conversely, for companies listed in the US, it is important to closely examine the documents relating to the transaction's financing to determine how secure it is legally.

5.2.1 The UK legal framework

The reference text on the regulatory framework for takeover bids in the UK is the *City Code on Takeovers and Mergers*, more commonly known as the *City Code*. It contains a list of principles on the forms, structure, and timetable of takeover bids. The Takeover Panel is the body in charge of ensuring that the rules of the *City Code* are correctly applied. The other main regulator of the financial markets is the Financial Services Authority (FSA).

Under UK law, even if the involvement of a financial intermediary authorized by the FSA is mandatory, this intermediary does not guarantee the offer. The obligation of the intermediary is principally a duty of diligence, not of guarantee, as in France. The intermediary must attest that the bidder in a takeover bid is capable of fulfilling its commitments at the close of the offer and has the funds necessary to launch such an offer. The basic principle is that of certain funds and cash confirmation requirements.

Certain funds and cash confirmation requirements

Rule 24.7 of the City Code

When the offer is for cash or includes an element of cash, the offer document must include confirmation by an appropriate third party (eg the offerors bank or financial adviser) that resources are available to the offeror sufficient to satisfy full acceptance of the offer. (The party confirming that resources are available will not be expected to produce the cash itself if, in giving the confirmation, it acted responsibly and took all reasonable steps to assure itself that the cash was available.)

In accordance with rule 24.7 of the City Code, any takeover bid must be accompanied by a certain-funds declaration. Only pre-conditional offers can be announced without a certain-funds declaration. A pre-conditional offer occurs when the buyer announces that an offer will be made if certain conditions precedent are met, such as a major antitrust authorization which is expected to involve a difficult process that will take longer than the timetable implemented pursuant to the City Code.

However, a certain-funds declaration is not an absolute guarantee that the funds are available, but rather an attestation that the buyer's financial adviser is sure that the funds are available. The financial adviser must be careful to ensure the pertinence and irrevocability of the financing sources before the offer is launched, for example by ensuring that the buyer has the liquidity necessary to carry out the offer, frozen in a bank account, or the capacity to access funds pursuant to a loan agreement.

Moreover, the City Code imposes restrictions on financing agreements limiting lenders' capacity to cancel their commitment during a specified period known as the certain-funds period. This is generally a period of 90 to 180 days and should reflect the timetable of the offer, beginning on the day of the announcement and ending upon the closure of the transaction. In general, the only events that give lenders the possibility to cancel the loan agreement during this period are the insolvency of the borrower and the inability to meet the conditions precedent to the offer. Material adverse change (MAC) clauses usually cannot be invoked during this period.

In the UK, financing cannot constitute a condition precedent to the offer and cannot be invoked as a reason why the offer cannot be closed. Consequently, the level of financing risk in the UK is very low.

5.2.2   The US legal framework

In the US, the market authority, the SEC, does not implement any admissibility controls for transactions. There is no legal obligation to present a guarantee that the bidder holds the funds prior to launching a transaction (as in the UK) or an irrevocable guarantee of the offer by a presenting institution (as in France). The transaction may be subject to multiple conditions precedent and subsequent, including financing. Consequently, the crucial question that needs to be asked when reviewing the transaction agreement is this: "who bears the risk? Is it the seller or the buyer? And if it is the buyer, what is the level of commitment of the banks that plan to lend the buyer the funds?" The risk for the arbitrageur may vary in different cases.

***When financing is a condition precedent to the offer
(financing contingencies)***

When financing is a condition precedent to the offer, they buyer may, with or without a penalty, withdraw its offer if it is not able to raise the necessary funds. Traditionally, for all LBO transactions and for certain strategic transactions where the buyer is rated as high yield, financing is usually a condition precedent to the offer. In this case, the target company bears the financing risk.

Traditionally, the acquisition agreement includes the following financing clauses:

- A condition precedent defined as the fact that the buyer must obtain the necessary financing in line with debt commitment letters or under other borrowing terms more favorable to the buyer in order to close the offer.
- A declaration from the buyer attesting that there is no reason to believe that the financing condition will not be met.
- A commitment from the buyer to prove reasonable best efforts to obtain the necessary financing.
- A commitment from the seller to cooperate with the buyer concerning the information necessary to obtain the financing.

In the traditional approach, if the desired financing is not available, despite the buyer's efforts, the buyer is not obligated to close the offer and the seller normally has no recourse against it.

In the years prior to the 2007–2008 crisis, there was an interesting development in merger agreement clauses. Financing contingency clauses were replaced in a number of transactions by reverse termination fee clauses. Under a reverse termination fee clause, if the transaction is not eventually closed because the financing is not available, the buyer agrees to pay reverse termination fees to the seller and/or to guarantee the payment of a capped amount to cover the expenses incurred by the seller as a result of the offer. From 2005 to 2007, the M&A market was extremely dynamic: faced with competition from strategic buyers, for whom financing is rarely a condition precedent, private-equity firms turned to this new approach, enabling them to be on the same level as strategic buyers whilst also limiting their risk. For transactions where financing is not a condition precedent to the offer, the buyer would be in breach of the acquisition agreement, and exposed to damages claims from the seller, if it were unable to close the offer due to a lack of financing. In the case of LBOs, the seller may invoke corporate veil piercing and hold the sponsor liable for damages if the shell company, its counterparty in the offer, is in breach of its obligations but has no assets. Consequently, the reverse termination fee clause in a way makes the transaction optional, enabling private-equity firms not to close the transaction and to cap the amount to be paid to the seller.

There are three main approaches to this type of clause:

- Debt receipt failure fee: this is the most traditional type of clause. The buyer has proven that it has made reasonable best efforts, but has not been able to secure the financing.
- Walk-away fee: in this second variation, the buyer may simply decide not to close the offer, whether the financing is available or not, and subsequently withdraw in exchange for the payment of a predetermined sum. In 2005, the agreement concerning the acquisition of SunGard Data Systems by Silver Lake Partners, Bain Capital, Blackstone, Goldman Sachs, Kohlberg Kravis Roberts, Providence Equity Partners, and Texas Pacific contained this type of clause. The sum to be paid was $300 million, equivalent to around 2.7% of the value of the transaction. This was a first, and the clause was subsequently used in a number of other buyout agreements, particularly those relating to LBOs.

- No fee for termination of the agreement, but reimbursement of the expenses incurred by the seller as a result of the offer, up to a pre-established maximum threshold set out in the agreement.

The basic principle of this clause is that, in exchange for the payment of a pre-determined sum set out in the acquisition agreement, the seller agrees to waive the specific-performance clause and the right to pursue any other recourse against the buyer. During the 2007–2008 crisis, thanks to the precedent set by Cerberus, a number of private-equity firms invoked the walk-away clause in order to be released from their commitments to target companies.

The highly publicized dispute between Cerberus and United Rentals

In November 2007, a shell company controlled by private-equity firm Cerberus invoked the reverse termination provision in the agreement concerning the buyout of United Rentals. In exchange for the payment of $100 million, it would have the option to not close the buyout offer.

United Rentals then decided to bring legal proceedings against Cerberus (before the court of Delaware) based on the specific-performance clause, maintaining that the agreement provided for the specific performance of the financing commitments of the shell company. The legal debate hinged on the ambiguous language used in the two clauses. Cerberus ended up winning the case.

This new approach was also used in certain strategic deals, such as the acquisition of Foundry by Brocade in 2008 and the buyout of Wyeth by Pfizer in 2009.

In July 2008, Brocade Communication Systems announced the acquisition of Foundry Networks for around $3 billion. According to the terms of the agreement, Brocade would be able to terminate the transaction if the financing was not secured, in exchange for a payment of $85 million (or 2.8% of the purchase price). When Brocade's banks raised a question about the interpretation of the clauses relating to the determination of the interest rates to be paid on the $400 million bridge loan, Brocade invoked the financing contingency clause in order to force a renegotiation of the purchase price. The transaction was concluded in December 2008 following a price cut, with the price falling from $18.50 in cash plus 0.0907 of a share of Brocade per share to $16.50 per Foundry share.

Extract from the merger agreement between Foundry and Brocade

Termination Fee: $85m, or 3.03% based on the implied equity value of the deal. The per-share increase required to cover this fee in a superior offer would be $0.58. Under certain circumstances, there would be a reverse termination fee and the parent would owe the company $85m. There would be a reverse termination fee and the parent would owe the company $125m or a reduced termination fee of $85m, if uncured financing failure exists.

Financing Failure: "Financing Failure" shall mean a refusal or other failure, for any reason, on the part of any Person that has executed the Debt Commitment Letter or any definitive financing document relating to the Debt Financing (including the Credit Agreement), or on the part of any other Person obligated or expected at any time to provide or release a portion of the Debt Financing (including the Term Loan and the Applicable Bridge Loan), to provide or release a portion of such Debt Financing; provided, however, that any such refusal or other failure shall not be deemed to be a "Financing Failure" for purposes of the Agreement if such refusal or other failure results directly from a Willful Breach of any of the Parent Financing Covenants.

The Pfizer/Wyeth transaction, however, took a slightly different approach. According to the terms of the agreement, Pfizer was authorized to not close the transaction if the lenders refused to provide the necessary financing, and if this refusal was attributable mainly to Pfizer's failure to maintain its credit rating. Under these circumstances, Pfizer would not be obligated to close the transaction without financing, but would be liable for termination fees in the amount of $4.5 billion (equivalent to 6.6% of the purchase price). Moreover, Wyeth would be able to bring legal proceedings against Pfizer's lenders to force them to comply with the specific-performance clauses contained in the financing document. The financial conditions under which Pfizer would be able to terminate the offer were much more limited than in the Brocade case.

Consequently, in cases in which financing is a condition precedent to the offer, the financing risk may be significant for the target company and therefore for the arbitrageur.

When financing is not a condition precedent to the offer (no financing contingencies)

If financing is not a condition precedent to the offer, the buyer is legally obligated to close the offer, even if the financing is not available upon closure. The lending banks may invoke MAC clauses in order to not grant the loan to the buyer. This disparity between specific-performance clauses, which oblige the buyer to close the acquisition, and the bank's financing terms presents a significant execution risk and, therefore, a risk for the arbitrageur. It is important to closely examine the documents relating to the financing in order to determine how legally secure it is. There are different degrees of financing guarantee that banks may provide in order to support transactions, such as debt commitment letters and comfort letters.

Debt commitment letters or financing commitment letters

A debt commitment letter is a letter of understanding in which a lender sets out the conditions under which it is prepared to lend the money to the borrower. It is usually accompanied by a term sheet, which defines the terms of the loan. The letter is generally delivered to the target company when the acquisition agreement is executed to serve as evidence that the buyer has sufficient funds to complete the acquisition.

Extract from the agreement concerning the acquisition of Blackboard Inc. by Providence Funds

Source: SEC filing

Debt Financing

In connection with the entry into the merger agreement, Acquisition Sub received a debt commitment letter, dated June 30, 2011 (the **"debt commitment letter"**), from Bank of America, N.A., Merrill Lynch, Pierce, Fenner & Smith Incorporated, Deutsche Bank Securities Inc., Deutsche Bank Trust Company Americas and Morgan Stanley Senior Funding, Inc. (collectively, the **"debt commitment**

parties"). The debt commitment letter provides an aggregate of $1,150 million in debt financing to Acquisition Sub, and upon consummation of the merger, the Company, consisting of a $700 million senior secured first lien term loan facility (with the ability to upsize the facility by $80 million if 100% of the outstanding equity interests of a portfolio company of Providence (the "**portfolio company**") are contributed to the Company (the "**additional commitment**")) (the "**first lien term facility**"), a $100 million first lien senior secured revolving credit facility (the "**first lien revolving facility**," and together with the first lien term facility, the "**first lien facilities**") and a $350 million second lien senior secured term loan facility (the "**second lien term facility**," and together with the first lien facilities, the "**credit facilities**"). The first lien term facility will be drawn at closing to finance a portion of the merger, including any refinancing of existing indebtedness of the Company and its subsidiaries and the payment of any fees and expenses incurred in connection with the merger and, (x) to the extent necessary to fund original issue discount or upfront fees in connection with any of the credit facilities and (y) in an aggregate amount not to exceed $10 million, the first lien revolving facility may be utilized at closing, in addition to proceeds from the other credit facilities. In addition, the first lien revolving facility may be utilized to issue or rollover letters of credit at closing. The second lien term facility will be drawn at closing to finance a portion of the merger, including any refinancing of existing indebtedness of the Company and its subsidiaries and the payment of any fees and expenses incurred in connection with the merger.

[. . .]

Conditions

The facilities contemplated by the debt commitment letter are subject to certain closing conditions, including, without limitation (in each case, subject to exceptions):

- the execution and delivery by the borrower and guarantors of definitive documentation, consistent with the debt commitment letter;
- delivery of customary closing documents (including, among other things, a solvency certificate, customary officers' and good standing certificates, legal opinions, resolutions, lien searches requested at least 30 days prior to the closing date, pay-off letters and other

documents as the applicable debt commitment parties shall reasonably request), documentation and other information about the borrower and guarantors required under applicable "know your customer" and anti-money laundering rules and regulations (including the PATRIOT Act), and the taking of certain actions necessary to establish and perfect a security interest in specified items of collateral;

- the accuracy in all material respects of certain representations and warranties in the merger agreement and certain specified representations and warranties in the loan documents;
- the consummation of the equity contribution contemplated by the equity commitment letter;
- the consummation of the merger substantially concurrently with or prior to the initial funding pursuant to the credit facilities substantially pursuant to the terms of the merger agreement, without giving effect to any amendment, consent, waiver or other modification of the merger agreement that is materially adverse to the interests of the lenders or the debt commitment parties that is not approved by the debt commitment parties for the debt financing;
- immediately following the transactions, the Company and its subsidiaries (other than the portfolio company and its subsidiaries, if applicable) having no outstanding preferred equity or indebtedness for borrowed money, in each case held by third parties, other than the indebtedness incurred in connection with the merger, indebtedness permitted to be incurred or outstanding under the merger agreement and certain other indebtedness that the initial lenders have agreed to permit to remain outstanding;
- the absence of a material adverse effect (as defined in the debt commitment letter) since December 31, 2010;
- delivery of certain audited, unaudited and pro forma financial statements of the Company;
- receipt of the required financial information and the expiration of the marketing period of 20 consecutive business days (subject to certain blackout dates) following receipt of the required financial information;
- receipt of applicable borrowing notices;
- payment of all applicable fees and expenses;
- solely with respect to the additional commitment, pro-forma compliance with the financial covenant for the first lien revolving facility;

- solely with respect to the additional commitment, immediately following the transactions, the portfolio company and its subsidiaries having no outstanding preferred equity or indebtedness for borrowed money, in each case held by third parties, other than the indebtedness incurred in connection with the credit facilities, indebtedness permitted to be incurred or outstanding under the merger agreement and certain other indebtedness that the initial lenders have agreed to permit to remain outstanding; and
- solely with respect to the additional commitment, since the date of the last audited financial statements of the portfolio company and its subsidiaries received by the debt commitment parties, there shall not have occurred any change, effect, event, occurrence or state of facts that is, or would reasonably be expected to be, materially adverse to the business, properties, financial condition or results of operations of the portfolio company and its subsidiaries, taken as a whole.

Comfort letter

A comfort letter is a letter provided by a bank or the buyer's financial adviser stating that it is "very confident" in its ability to grant the necessary financing or to help the buyer to raise the necessary financing. However, the level of legal security of this type of letter is very low. A close examination of the letter below, provided by Jefferies to Carl Icahn in relation to his planned acquisition of Clorox, reveals that Jefferies does not ultimately make much of a commitment.

Comfort letter submitted by Carl Icahn for his takeover bid for Clorox

Source: SEC filing

July 14, 2011

Icahn Enterprises L.P.
767 Fifth Avenue, 47th Floor
New York, New York 10153

Attention: Carl Icahn

Ladies and Gentlemen:

We understand that Icahn Enterprises L.P. (the "Sponsor") is contemplating the acquisition (the "Acquisition") of The Clorox Company (the "Company"). It is our understanding that the enterprise value for the acquisition of the Company will be approximately $12.6 billion before fees and expenses. You have further advised us that you plan to raise approximately $7.8 billion of debt financing (the "Debt Financing") in connection with the Acquisition, at a leverage multiple of approximately 7.0x CY 2011 EBITDA. We understand that the balance of the capital will be in the form of equity, from both a rollover of the Sponsor's existing equity ownership position in the Company and approximately $3.8 billion of new equity from the Sponsor.

We are pleased to confirm that Jefferies & Company, Inc. ("Jefferies") is highly confident of its ability to arrange the Debt Financing, subject to: (i) satisfactory market conditions and no material adverse change in the business or prospects of the Company; (ii) receipt of ratings from Moody's and Standard and Poor's and delivery of customary documentation each that are satisfactory to Jefferies and the purchasers and/or lenders in the Debt Financing; (iii) satisfactory completion of our due diligence on the Company; (iv) Jefferies' receipt of an executed engagement agreement with terms, including indemnification, acceptable to Jefferies; and (v) approval from our internal committees.

For the avoidance of doubt, this letter is not a guarantee of the availability of the Debt Financing. Nothing herein shall be deemed to constitute any commitment by Jefferies to purchase or arrange the Debt Financing; such a commitment shall be evidenced only by the execution and delivery of, and shall be subject to the terms and conditions of, the definitive documentation referred to above.

Sincerely,
JEFFERIES & COMPANY, INC.
By: /s/ Jeffrey Whyte
_____

Name: Jeffrey Whyte
Title: General Counsel, Investment
Banking + Public Reporting

5.2.3   The European legal framework in general

The objective of protecting shareholders during a takeover bid is common to a number of countries in the European Union, although their respective legislation varies. The European Union directive on takeover bids, largely based on UK law, is a step towards harmonization.

Directive 2004/25/EC – Article 3.1

An offeror must announce a bid only after ensuring that he can fulfil in full any cash consideration, if such is offered, and after taking all reasonable measures to secure the implementation of any other type of consideration.

In conclusion, it should be noted that, in the European legal framework (meaning in the UK and other European Union member states), the financing risk is small, almost non-existent. In the US legal framework, on the other hand, whether financing is a condition precedent to the offer or not, the transaction may involve a significant level of financing risk. Consequently, it is important for the arbitrageur to examine the merger agreement and the financing documents very closely in order to determine how legally secure the financing is.

CASE STUDY: The Dow Chemical/Rohm & Haas Deal

Deal Presentation

On July 10, 2008, US group Dow Chemical announced the acquisition of Rohm & Haas with a view to creating the world's leading specialty chemical company. The move constituted a transforming deal for Dow Chemical, since it involved overhauling its business profile, which had historically been focused on the petrochemical industry.

The price of the offer was $78 per share ($15 billion in total), representing a premium of 74% over the target company's pre-announcement share price ($45). The financing for the transaction included the subscription of convertible bonds by Berkshire Hathaway (Warren Buffett's investment holding company) and by Kuwait's sovereign wealth fund (the Kuwait Investment Authority) worth $3 billion and $1 billion respectively.

Dow announced that the transaction would have a significant accretive effect on net profits per share as of the second year and calculated the operational synergies resulting from the deal at $800 million. The transaction – approved unanimously by the boards of directors of both companies – would be conditional upon the vote held by shareholders of Rohm & Haas and upon obtainment of the relevant antitrust authorizations.

Financing was not a condition precedent, and Dow declared in the merger agreement that it would have the necessary funds on the closing day:

> SECTION 4.6 Available Funds. [Dow] will have available to it at the Closing all of the funds required to be provided by [Dow] for the consummation of the transactions contemplated hereby and for the satisfaction of all of [Dow's] obligations under this Agreement, including the payment of the Merger Consideration and the Option and Stock-Based Consideration, and the funding of any required financings or repayments of indebtedness (collectively, the "Financing").

The financing was guaranteed by commitment letters from Citigroup, Merrill Lynch, and Morgan Stanley. It consisted of a one-year bridge loan in the amount of $13 billion.

The parties hoped to close the transaction in early 2009.

The share price closed on the day of the announcement at $74.

Early Developments

On September 8, 2008 (several days before the collapse of Lehman Brothers), Dow signed the definitive term loan agreement with the lending banks.

In early December, the share price traded at around $71 when rumors surfaced that the Kuwaitis may have had a change of heart concerning the creation of K-Dow, a joint venture between Dow and the Kuwait Petroleum Corporation (KPC), provided for by a memorandum of understanding signed in December 2007. The transaction, in which Dow would contribute petrochemical assets and KPC cash, would allow Dow to reduce its exposure to these cyclical activities and to raise cash, and would allow KPC to benefit from transfers of technology in a key sector. Shares in Rohm & Haas fell by 10% (from $71 to $64) on the rumors.

On December 29, 2008, Dow was notified that the creation of K-Dow had been formally called into question by the Kuwaiti government. The deal was intended to enable Dow to raise $9 billion in cash from the joint venture, which would, of course, be useful for financing the Rohm & Haas transaction. Shares in Rohm & Haas closed at $53 that day.

During a teleconference on July 10, 2008 to present the transaction, a (visionary?) analyst had mentioned the subject to Andrew Liveris (CEO of Dow) and Geoffrey Merszei:

> [Analyst]: In the same vein, I'm wondering – it looks like that you are very confident now on getting the Kuwait deal done, and it sounds like you are counting on – in fact, counting on that money to do this deal.

ANDREW LIVERIS: Well, I'll get Geoffrey to chime in. But look, no, we are not counting on it. We can do this deal without the Kuwait money, and we will stay at investment grade. . .

GEOFFREY MERSZEI: No, I mean, I would just have to reiterate what Andrew said. I mean, I think it's a very key point here. This deal is certainly not contingent on the closing of our Kuwait joint venture.

On January 8, 2009, the transaction was approved by the European antitrust authorities.

On January 23, 2009, the FTC gave its blessing to the transaction, thereby removing the final condition precedent to the transaction. The transaction should therefore have closed within the next two business days, as provided for by the merger agreement:

SECTION 1.2 Closing. The closing of the Merger (the "Closing") shall take place at the offices of Wachtell, Lipton, Rosen & Katz, 51 West 52nd Street, New York, New York at 10:00 a.m., local time, on a date to be specified by the parties (the "Closing Date") which shall be no later than the second business day after the satisfaction or waiver (to the extent permitted by applicable Law (as defined in Section 3.7(a)) of the conditions set forth in ARTICLE VI (other than those conditions that by their nature are to be satisfied by action at the Closing, but subject to the satisfaction or written waiver of such conditions), or at such other place, date and time as the Company and Parent may agree in writing.

Shares in Rohm & Haas closed at $66 that day.

Dow's Announcement

On January 26, 2009, to the amazement of a number of observers (and arbitrageurs!), Dow published the following press release:

Dow Chemical Confirms Rohm and Haas Acquisition Will Not Close On or Before January 27, 2009

Midland, MI – January 26, 2009

The Dow Chemical Company (NYSE:DOW) confirms it has informed Rohm and Haas that Dow will not close the proposed acquisition on or before January 27, 2009.

Dow has determined that recent material developments have created unacceptable uncertainties on the funding and economics of the combined enterprise. This assessment is based on several macro-economic factors such as the continued crisis in global financial and credit markets combined with the dramatic and stunning failure of Petrochemicals Industries Company of Kuwait (PIC) to fulfill its obligation to complete the formation of the K-Dow joint venture in late December 2008.

"Our long term strategy remains unchanged and the proposed acquisition of Rohm and Haas is consistent with this strategy," said Andrew N. Liveris, Chairman and CEO. Since Dow learned in late December of PIC's failure to close the K-Dow transaction, Dow has been aggressively engaged on multiple paths seeking ways to enable the Rohm and Haas transaction. Dow remains interested in discussions to find a solution to complete the acquisition of Rohm and Haas, but recent events have made closing untenable at this time.

"Dow Chemical has a long history of resiliency in responding to changing market conditions, and that resiliency continues," said Liveris, "but the world has changed significantly and we still do not see the bottom of this unprecedented demand destruction which only accelerated through the fourth quarter and brought December operating rates to historic lows. The Company's commitment to remain financially strong is part of the DNA of this 112-year old company"

Dow previously announced a series of wide-ranging actions to address global economic conditions and is accelerating those actions based on continued deteriorating demand. "We are well-prepared to take the appropriate steps to ensure we retain our options and financial flexibility to see our way through what we anticipate will be an extremely challenging year," said Liveris.

Shares in Rohm & Haas closed at $57 that day.

Rohm & Haas immediately brought legal proceedings against Dow before the court of Delaware (the state in which both companies were registered), demanding the forced execution of the agreement (pursuant to the specific-performance provision) provided for by article 8.5 (a) of the merger agreement.

The parties agree that irreparable damage would occur in the event that any of the provisions of this Agreement were not performed in accordance with their specific terms or were otherwise breached and that the parties would not have any adequate remedy at law. It is accordingly agreed that the parties shall be entitled to an injunction or injunctions to prevent breaches or threatened breaches of this Agreement and to enforce specifically the terms and provisions of this Agreement . . . The foregoing is in addition to any other remedy to which any party is entitled at law, in equity or otherwise.

The argument put forward by Rohm & Haas, set out by lawyer Marc Wolinski of Wachtell Lipton, was as follows:

- Dow is contractually obliged to close the transaction and has not invoked any legal argument (such as a MAC clause) in order to be released from its contractual obligations.
- The transaction is not conditional upon obtaining financing and, in any case, Dow has the funds necessary to pay the price ($13 billion of bank debt and $4 billion in convertible form, i.e. $2 billion more than the $15 billion required).
- The transaction is not conditional upon the joint-venture transaction with the Kuwaitis.

- Dow should therefore be ordered to close the transaction as soon as possible. Dow's reply, dated February 3, was brilliant, since the buyer did not invoke any legal argument to justify its refusal to close the transaction, but stated:

A confluence of dramatic and unforeseeable shocks – to Dow, to the chemical industry as a whole, and to the banks and financial markets – has made it impossible to consummate Dow's planned acquisition of Rohm and Haas at once without jeopardizing the very existence of both companies.

Dow's lawyers asked Judge Chandler not to rule on a legal basis (!) but from a perspective of "fairness," since they believed that the closure of the transaction would endanger the viability of the merged entity and therefore risk the redundancy of tens of thousands of US employees. They therefore asked the judge to simply ignore the specific-performance clause!

The judge replied during a teleconference:

THE COURT: Well, I have several thoughts as I listen to both of you. Obviously, you both make very compelling arguments for your side. One thing that sort of strikes me – not knowing as much about this case as either of you or your colleagues – it strikes me that, A, there is a fundamental business problem here, and it is always my view that business problems are better resolved by business people; and that to the extent that the Court is called upon to resolve a legal issue, the Court will do that, of course, and will do it as promptly as possible. This Court obviously tries to accommodate parties who come and ask for expedited proceedings or accelerated proceedings because of the business necessities that a particular legal question implicates.

A proceeding was scheduled to begin on March 7, 2009.

Legal Negotiations and Conclusion

As is often the case in the US, the lawyers negotiated behind the scenes and, on the eve of the proceeding, an agreement was reached between the parties, the outline of which was as follows:

- Dow agreed to close the transaction at the agreed price ($78 per share).
- The two biggest shareholders of Rohm & Haas (the Haas family and the fund Paulson & Co.) agreed to subscribe $2.5 billion of perpetual bonds convertible into Dow shares.
- The Haas family agreed to subscribe $500 million of Dow shares.
- Dow renegotiated its bridge loan and extended it by 12 months for an amount of $8 billion, as well as implementing a plan to dispose of assets worth $4 billion.

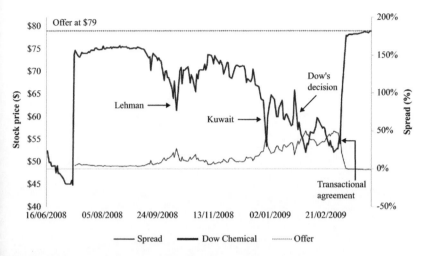

Figure CS5.1   Rohm & Haas: change in stock price and spread
Source: Bloomberg

In summary, Dow probably knew that, legally speaking, its case had no chance of succeeding. However, its press campaign enabled it to restructure its debt and to maintain its investment grade rating. For arbitrageurs, this saga, with its numerous twists and turns and the resulting volatility of Rohm & Haas's share price (Figure CS5.1), presented countless opportunities for profits (or losses).

6

Competition Risk

Competition, or antitrust, risk is one of the most important risks for an arbitrageur and also one of the hardest to evaluate. It is a technical subject – there are numerous regulatory texts and knowledge of previous legal decisions is essential – but also a political one given that the regulatory framework of a period is always dictated by the people in power at the time. Just getting to grips with regulatory texts is never enough. Over the course of time, for example, the US Supreme Court has altered its interpretation of the law on many occasions, meaning the current climate is formed just as much by previous rulings as by the laws themselves.

Whatever the jurisdiction, the goal of competition laws is the same: to limit the market power of companies and regulate competition between operators in a given sector. Antitrust laws aim not to prevent monopolies but to control the way in which groups obtain and maintain their market power. The underlying principle is the search for economic efficiency, which is taken to mean the maximum consumer satisfaction allowed by market conditions.

6.1 ORIGINS AND REGULATORY FRAMEWORK OF COMPETITION LAW

6.1.1 United States

The first competition laws in the US were enacted by the Sherman Act of July 2, 1890. The act was named after Ohio senator John Sherman, who wanted to challenge the power of certain companies, particularly the oil groups exhibiting quasi-monopolist behavior in his state. Before the act, certain practices such as price-fixing agreements had been controlled by jurisprudence, but there had never been a formal written text to bring together and codify these issues. The Sherman Act was adopted at a time of great change in the US economy, with large companies being created by a particularly strong wave of M&A. Lamoreaux studied this wave in 1985 and found that between 1894 and 1904, more than 1,800 companies were combined to form 93 conglomerates, known in those days as trusts. The aim of these trusts, which were formed by grouping together

rivals from the same industry by mergers or informal production agreements, was to achieve price and volume stability. One of the first trusts to
fall foul of the Sherman Act was Standard Oil, which was established in
1870 and run by John D. Rockefeller. When it was created, the group had
10% of the US' total refining capacity. It soon struck an agreement with
the railroad companies, giving it an even greater competitive advantage
and enabling it to impose higher prices. In 1906, the Court found that
Standard Oil: "purchased and obtained interests through stock ownership and otherwise in, and entered into agreement with, various persons,
firms, corporations, and limited partnerships engaged in purchasing,
shipping, refining, and selling petroleum and its products among the
various states, for the purpose of fixing the price of crude and refined oil
and the products thereof, limiting the production thereof, and controlling
the transportation therein, and thereby restraining trade and commerce
among the several states, and monopolizing the said commerce" (Standard Oil Co of New Jersey v. United States, No 398). The following
year, the group represented 87% of the country's refining capacity. In
1911, the Supreme Court ordered the dissolution of Standard Oil.

A second type of competition problem emerged during the 19th century: collusion. The major players in several markets realized that by
acting in concert they could reproduce to some extent the effects of
a monopoly. In theory, a monopoly involves just one company in the
market, charging sky-high prices and maximizing profits. Monopoly
situations tend to be characterized by specific elements such as significant barriers to entering the market and all the information being in
the hands of the manufacturer rather than the consumer. There are two
major problems with monopolies: inefficient allocation of financial and
human resources, and unequal distribution of wealth. Such situations
can arise through technological innovation. That is why Microsoft was
a perfect example of a natural monopoly with Windows, before Apple
came on the scene with its own operating system.

The Sherman Act has two major areas of focus: it prohibits restrictions to trade between states, such as unlawful cartels, and bans market
monopolization, i.e. strategies used to abuse a dominant position. It also
enables public authorities, such as the US Department of Justice (DoJ),
to file criminal lawsuits. Having said that, as with any first attempt at a
legal text, the Sherman Act had its faults. First, it made no mention of
the consolidation of companies. Nor was it effective initially because
the judges decided to enforce it retrospectively. Some groups, however,
were broken up as a result of the act, such as American Tobacco and

Standard Oil in 1911. In order to resolve the aforementioned problems, the Clayton Antitrust Act and the Federal Trade Commission Act (FTC) were adopted in 1914.

The Clayton Act focuses on four practices that were ignored by the Sherman Act: price discrimination, where it lessens competition or creates a monopoly; tying and exclusive dealings, where these lessen competition; mergers or consolidations of companies, where these lessen competition; and the creation of cartels between companies that are normally rivals:

> No person engaged in commerce or in any activity affecting commerce shall acquire, directly or indirectly, . . . where in any line of commerce or in any activity affecting commerce in any section of the country, the effect of such acquisition may be substantially to lessen competition, or to tend to create a monopoly (Clayton Antitrust Act, 1919, Section 7).

The Clayton Act also enables victims of unfair competition to seek punitive damages and injunctions against the companies concerned. The FTC Act complemented the Clayton Act by introducing an institutional support in the form of the Federal Trade Commission, whose job is to enforce competition laws and rule on related disputes.

In 1976, US antitrust regulation was strengthened by the Hart–Scott–Rodino Antitrust Improvements Act (HSR), which added more provisions on M&A and amended some parts of the Clayton Act. Under HSR, each M&A transaction has to receive prior authorization from the FTC and the DoJ. The text therefore brought about a significant improvement in the approval process. Before it was introduced, the government would approve or reject transactions retroactively. This led to newly created groups sometimes being dissolved and endless cases being dragged through the courts. The FTC's position on competition law in M&A is as follows:

> Most mergers actually benefit competition and consumers by allowing firms to operate more efficiently. But some are likely to lessen competition. That, in turn, can lead to higher prices, reduced availability of goods or services, lower quality of products, and less innovation. Indeed, some mergers create a concentrated market, while others enable a single firm to raise prices.
>
> In a concentrated market, there are only a few firms. The danger is that they may find it easier to lessen competition by colluding. For example, they may agree on the prices they will charge consumers. The collusion could be in an explicit agreement, or in a more subtle form – known

as tacit coordination or coordinated interaction. Firms may prefer to co-operate tacitly rather than explicitly because tacit agreements are more difficult to detect, and some explicit agreements may be subject to criminal prosecution.

When a merger enables a single firm to increase prices without coordinating with its competitors, it has created a unilateral effect. A firm might be able to increase prices unilaterally if it has a large enough share of the market, if the merger removes its closest competitor, and if the other firms in the market can't provide substantial competition.

Generally, at least two conditions are necessary for a merger to have a likely anticompetitive effect: The market must be substantially concentrated after the merger; and it must be difficult for new firms to enter the market in the near term and provide effective competition. The reason for the second condition is that firms are less likely to raise prices to anticompetitive levels if it is fairly easy for new competitors to enter the market and drive prices down.

Document published by the Federal Trade Commission, September 2002, available at www.ftc.gov.

A transaction needs to be examined under HSR provisions only if certain thresholds are reached:

- The size of the transaction: this is measured according to the value of the assets or voting rights that the buyer will hold after the transaction. The threshold is deemed to be reached if this value is at least $68.2 million.
- The size of the parties: this threshold is deemed to be reached if one of the parties has annual sales or total assets of at least $136.4 million and the other party has annual sales or total assets of at least $13.6 million.

Once it has been established that a transaction requires approval under HSR, the FTC and the DoJ decide which of them will preside over the ruling.

6.1.2 Europe

The origins of European competition law can be traced back to the Treaty of Rome in 1957, which created the European Economic Community. Free competition was one of the founding principles of the common market. Article 3 of the Treaty of Rome states: "the activities of the Community shall include [. . .] the institution of a system ensuring that competition in the common market is not distorted". Despite this, the original treaty contained no provision regulating M&A transactions. This situation was rectified in 1990, when the Merger Regulation was adopted in the wake of the Continental Can and Philip Morris cases.

European competition laws comprise four areas: the regulation of cartels, including collusion and anti-competitive practice; the regulation of monopolies (preventing abuse of a dominant market position); the control of M&A; and the control of direct and indirect state aid to companies. Some of the original articles were amended following the new codification arising from the 2007 Treaty of Lisbon (TFEU).

There are many similarities with US antitrust regulations, especially the Clayton Act. The M&A test set out in the TFEU aims to establish whether the proposed combination would damage free competition within the Community. The treaty states that, under certain conditions, the parties must seek prior approval from the EU authorities. These authorities become competent if the combined global annual turnover of the companies involved is at least €5 billion or if at least two of the companies involved have an individual turnover of at least €250 million, unless all the companies involved generate more than two-thirds of their revenue in a single member state, in which case national competency remains.

6.2 COMPETENT AUTHORITIES AND APPROVAL PROCESS

6.2.1 United States

In the US, the FTC and DoJ are the two bodies responsible for enforcing antitrust laws. If the DoJ is handling the case, it is judged by a federal tribunal. The FTC is responsible for the civil aspects of implementing competition policy. As an independent administrative authority, the FTC's creation ended the state's monopoly (in the form of the DoJ's Antitrust Division) on antitrust implementation. It complements the competitive and criminal sanctions administered by the DoJ with civil actions brought on behalf of those who feel they have been damaged by anti-competitive behavior. Under the Antitrust Improvement Act of 1976, prior notification of proposed business combinations must be given to both bodies. The FTC Bureau of Competition assesses the overall impact of the proposed deal on competition. In order to do this, it uses the expertise of the Bureau of Economics.

The second special characteristic of the US institutional system is the strict separation between the investigative and decision-making bodies – something that is not the case in Europe. The US agencies prepare the cases and then take on the role of prosecutors before a court.

Merger control is based on a substantial lessening of competition (SLC) test. Combinations that are likely to reduce competition by way of higher prices or lower volumes must be blocked. A comparison is made between the pre- and post-merger competitive balance. This involves examining the unilateral effects of the deal, e.g. rival companies may also increase their prices after the merger.

Since the Hart–Scott–Rodino Act of 1976, US antitrust policy has been based largely on economics, which has taken over from formal legal considerations and the exclusive consideration of scope.

Analysis focuses on defining the market in question, measuring the effects on concentration and competition, and taking into account entry barriers and efficiency gains (more streamlined production, lower fixed costs, better R&D, etc.).

The DoJ's Antitrust Division plays a crucial role in introducing economic criteria to US competition policies. One example is the hypothetical monopolist test introduced along with merger control guidelines in 1982. By defining the market in question, this test gives an idea of how likely it is that, after the deal, the combined entity will impose a small but significant and non-transitory increase in price (SSNIP), of 5% for example, without suffering a big drop in demand.

To that purpose, the competition authorities evaluate market power through cross-price elasticities of demand. These elasticities quantify changes in demand, expressed as a percentage, for product A in response to a change in the price of product B. If the elasticity is zero, there is no economic link between the two products. The closer the elasticity gets to one, the more demand is sensitive to price variations. The Supreme Court has explained the use of the notion of elasticity as follows:

> The outer boundaries of a product market are determined by the reasonable interchangeability of use or the cross elasticity of demand between the product itself and substitutes for it (see *Brown Shoes Co. v. United States*, 370 US 294 (1962), p. 325).

When the US antitrust authorities study an M&A transaction, they consider a group of criteria which, rather than being examined successively and individually, are grouped together to form an integral analysis of the competition risk posed by the transaction. Market structure and concentration indicators are just some of the many criteria involved. In fact, market shares and concentration indicators can be poor indicators of antitrust decisions, unless they are extremely high. Structure indicators are mainly used only as thresholds for triggering more detailed investigations.

Investigations into the consequences of a business combination are based on the successive analysis of unilateral and coordinated effects.

The unilateral effects of a merger are analyzed using econometric models. Where the products are similar, the analysis focuses on the incentives that the parties involved in the concentration may have, once the deal is completed, to reduce production or increase prices without expecting a conciliatory response from their rivals. In such a case, the analysis of two substitute products involves estimating the percentage of demand for the second product following a change in price of the first product. Although US guidelines state that a merger is likely to have significant unilateral effects if the cumulative market share of the two companies involved is greater than 35%, the FTC is far more reluctant than the DoJ's Antitrust Division to take its decisions on the basis of such quantitative criteria.

The notion of coordinated effects involves the incentives (and capabilities) of the parties involved in the merger to compete with other market operators once the deal has been completed. It therefore means the likelihood of collusion resulting from a merger that strengthens the oligopolistic nature of the market.

The authorities are interested in efficiency gains and how these are passed on to consumers. In other words, a merger that simply boosts the profits of the two companies by lowering their costs, without price transmission mechanisms coming into play, is likely to be frowned upon by the competition authorities. The criterion used is consumer surplus.

The first economic analysis of the consequences of horizontal mergers dates back to the end of the 1960s and Williamson's "naive" model, which clearly presents the cost/benefit trade-off during the monopolization of an industry in a context of perfect information. The subsequent development of economic tools has allowed us to refine this model to take into account the strategic behavior of rivals in different market structures. Modern analysis of horizontal mergers produces relatively simple definitive results concerning merger profitability and the effect on retail prices. It reveals that retail prices will come down after a merger only if there are sufficient cost synergies, learning effects, or economies of scale.

The European Commission initially focused its analysis on market structures, but now it makes the same distinction between unilateral and coordinated effects. The Commission may block or modify any merger project that is liable to significantly lessen competition, especially by creating or consolidating a dominant position. In other words, it is about ensuring that market structures are not too far removed from the ideal situation in terms of competition.

Unlike the situations we have seen so far, non-horizontal M&A transactions occur at both ends of the value chain (and not between rivals in the same sector). These operations also concern conglomerate deals where a company buys a firm in a sector different from its own. With its finance, aircraft engine, electrical appliance and TV broadcasting divisions, among others, General Electric is the prime example of a modern conglomerate. Government antitrust authorities usually look at two theories when dealing with non-horizontal transactions:

- Potential competition: non-horizontal transactions do not affect competition in a market. They can, however, have a negative impact on potential competition by indirectly dissuading companies from entering the market. If one company joins forces with another that may have targeted the same market, the competition in that market is reduced. Antitrust authorities may challenge a deal on the basis of the threat to potential competition.
- The creation of entry barriers resulting from vertical M&A: these transactions can reduce competition by creating significant entry barriers that dissuade companies from entering a market. If a company combines with another operating in a similar market, a potential new entrant would have to compete with the new entity on the two different markets at the same time – something that would demand a huge, and possibly dissuasive, initial investment.

The antitrust regulatory investigation timetable is established clearly in legislation. The FTC or the DoJ have 15 days to respond in the case of an all-cash offer. This deadline is extended to 30 days for share offers. The transaction cannot be completed during this period. If the competent authority finds no violation of antitrust rules, it can either bring early termination to the investigation period or let it run its course. Data published by the FTC show the number of HSR approval requests and how these figures have changed over time (Figure 6.1). Although

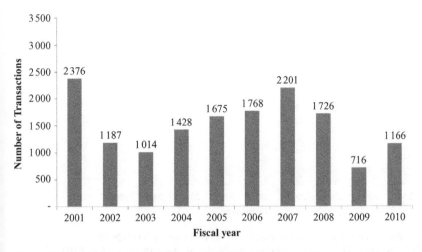

Figure 6.1 HSR merger transactions reported 2001–2010
Source: FTC & DoJ, HSR annual report. Available at www.ftc.gov/os/2011/02/1101hsrreport.pdf.

the figures seem to be rising again from the very lowest levels seen during the financial crisis, they remain well below pre-crisis levels.

If approval is not granted during the first investigation period, the transaction enters a second, more detailed investigative phase known as second requests. The authority asks the parties to voluntarily submit more documentation before conducting its own investigation into the possible consequences of the transaction. This second-request waiting period lasts 57 days. If approval is still to be granted at the end of this period, the authority imposes on the parties compulsory submission of what it deems to be the necessary documentation. Second requests are usually bad news for arbitrageurs because they bring negative headlines and cause the spread to widen. Companies sometimes avoid this situation by withdrawing their approval request and then re-submitting it with the appropriate documentation. The process then starts again from scratch. Data on second requests show that they have become more common over the last few years (see Figure 6.2), meaning that transactions are becoming subject to more scrutiny.

6.2.2 Europe

The competent authority in Europe is the Merger Task Force at the European Commission's Directorate General for Competition. It takes

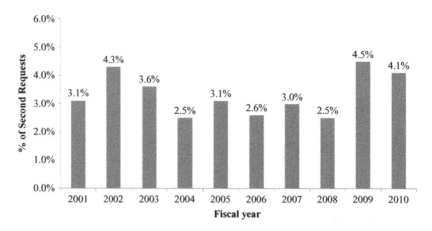

Figure 6.2 Percentage of transactions resulting in second request 2001–2010
Source: FTC & DoJ, HSR annual report. Available at www.ftc.gov/os/2011/02/
1101hsrreport.pdf.

a decision on a transaction, and this decision can then be appealed at the European Court of First Instance and the European Court of Justice. The courts are not shy of annulling a decision if they feel it lacked sufficient reasoning. Under the provisions of the Merger Regulation, the Commission has one month to conduct its first investigative phase. This first period ends with a decision from the Commission taken within 25–35 days of notification. The Commission may: (i) decide that the operation should not be ruled on at EU level; (ii) approve the transaction (possibly subject to certain conditions); or (iii) trigger a more detailed investigation (Phase II) if there are serious concerns over the effects that the deal might have on competition. In this latter scenario, the Commission may request up to four months for Phase II if the transaction is deemed to be incompatible with the principles of the common market.

By focusing on market shares and concentration indicators, such as the Herfindahl–Hirschman Index (HHI), European guidelines pay more attention to market structures than their US equivalents. If the market share of the merged entity is below 25%, the Commission rules that the deal will not have a negative impact on competition. Conversely, if one of the parties has a share of more than 50% of the relevant market, the Commission begins a more detailed examination. The HHI does not define approval thresholds, but it does provide an indication of the level of investigation required. Further investigation by the Commission is required if the post-merger index is above 1,000 points. The index is the sum of the squares of the market share of each player in a sector:

$$HHI = \sum_{i=1}^{N} s_i^2$$

where N is the total number of companies active in the market and s_i is the market share of company i. A more detailed investigation is launched where the HHI is between 1,000 and 2,000 points and the merger brings about a 250-point change in the index. If the HHI is above 2,000 points, any merger that brings about a 150-point change is subject to a more detailed investigation. The market is not deemed to be concentrated if the HHI is below 1,000 points.

However, the Commission considers certain factors as likely counterweights to these market structure measures. These include buyers' market power, market fluidity (the possibility of new entrants in the medium term), and efficiency gains likely to result from the M&A transaction. The Commission can also show great tolerance if one of the M&A parties is in significant financial difficulty.

The economic effectiveness of merger control therefore depends on the quality of cost/benefit analysis of the transaction. This case-by-case analysis is a difficult and expensive process. The new balance of power in an industry will depend not only on the production choices and costs of the merged entity but also on the response of its rivals. Moreover, the parties involved in the transaction are better informed than the competition authorities, particularly on their cost structure, which is crucial in evaluating gains.

Data published by the European Commission show that, in terms of M&A, 2011 was just as busy for Europe as for the US (see Figure 6.3). Just like the situation across the Atlantic, competition approval requests are higher than in the previous two years but remain lower than pre-crisis levels.

Similarly, the proportion of transactions requiring Phase II investigation is up sharply on the previous two years (see Figure 6.4). These figures indicate that the Commission is now adopting a more rigorous approach to requests, although this does not necessarily mean that more deals are being blocked.

Figure 6.5 provides a summary of the review process of the European Commission's Merger Task Force, as well as the timeframes of the different investigative stages (Phase I and Phase II).

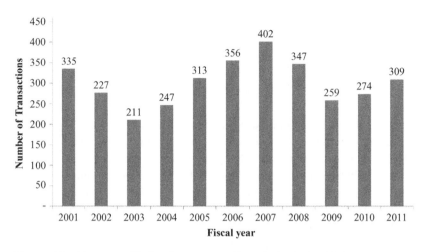

Figure 6.3   Mergers notified to the European Commission 2001–2011
Source: European Commission Statistics. Available at http://ec.europa.eu/competition/
mergers/statistics.pdf.

6.2.3   China

The birth and implementation of competition regulation is much newer
to China, and it has borrowed from both the US and European systems.
The body that regulates competition in China is the country's Ministry
of Commerce (MOFCOM).

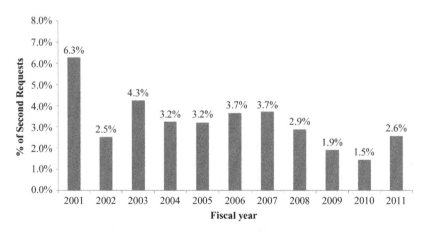

Figure 6.4   Percentage of transactions resulting in a Phase II investigation 2001–2011
Source: European Commission Statistics. Available at http://ec.europa.eu/competition/
mergers/statistics.pdf.

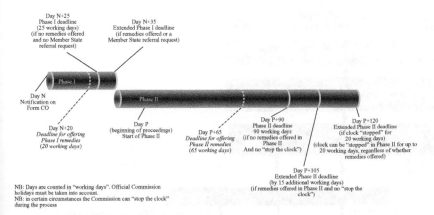

Figure 6.5   Summary of the review process of the European Commission's Merger
Task Force
Source: European Commission

MOFCOM investigates an M&A transaction in any of the following
situations:

- the target company generates a certain part of its turnover in China;
- the buyer has a "decisive influence" over the target company in the
  wake of the transaction, even if it has acquired only a minority interest;
- it is an "asset and share" deal;
- it is a 50–50 joint venture.

As in Europe and the US, China has certain thresholds relating to
turnover. An investigation is compulsory if the total combined annual
revenue of the two parties involved exceeds CNY10 billion (around
$1.5 billion) or if the following two conditions are met: the total com-
bined annual revenue of the two parties exceeds CNY2 billion (just over
$300 million) and the revenue generated in China by each party exceeds
CNY400 million (approximately $60 million). The revenue calculation
method depends on the nature of the transaction, e.g. whether it is a
takeover or a merger.

Once it has been established that the deal requires the approval of the
Chinese authorities before it can be completed, the buyer must take the
necessary steps with the Anti-Monopoly Bureau at MOFCOM. The process that follows is very similar to the ones we have seen in Europe and
the US. The only differences are that the Chinese authorities are less experienced than their western counterparts and the approval process is not
as transparent. Figure 6.6 shows the different stages of the investigation.

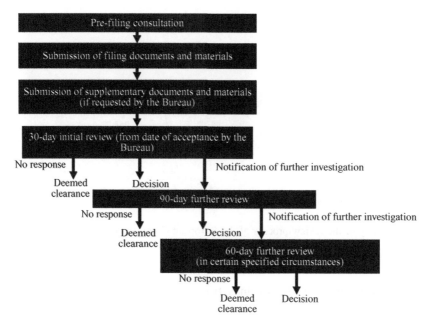

Figure 6.6 Stages of an investigation by the Anti-Monopoly Bureau at MOFCOM
Source: MOFCOM

As a general rule, the process cannot officially begin until the two parties have signed a binding agreement. The pre-filing period usually lasts two weeks.

The role of MOFCOM has taken on greater significance in recent years in the eyes of deal-makers and arbitrageurs, and there are several reasons for this. First, and not at all surprisingly, deals involving Chinese companies are increasingly common, whether they are targets for big groups from developed countries looking for growth and keen to establish themselves in the world's fastest-growing economy, or whether they are buyers looking to establish a presence outside China. In addition, MOFCOM has played a crucial role in some major recent transactions – a sign that it is keen to get more involved in the years to come.

On November 15, 2010, Caterpillar, the giant US manufacturer of construction, mining and forestry equipment, announced the acquisition of rival mining equipment specialist Bucyrus. At close to $9 billion, the deal was the biggest in Caterpillar's history and enabled it to consolidate its market-leading position. However, as the two groups were present on the same market in practically all the natural-resource countries in the world, approval was required from the competition authorities in these different countries before the deal could be completed. These authorities included the European Commission, the US Department of Justice, and China's MOFCOM.

Approval from the US and European authorities arrived simultaneously in May 2011 following a second request by the DoJ in January, but there was a delay in the approval from MOFCOM which had a big impact on the arbitrage spread. Caterpillar finally got the green light from the Chinese authorities in July, some 143 days after notifying them of the deal.

The Caterpillar–Bucyrus case also highlights another aspect of competition risk. While the US and European authorities tend to work together on deals that require their respective approval, this is not yet the case with MOFCOM. Another, more recent, example paints the same picture. Google's acquisition of Motorola Mobility, which was valued at nearly $12.5 billion, also needed authorization from Europe, China and the US. The deal was announced in August 2011, and the US and European approvals arrived on the same day in February 2012 – again underlining the cooperation between the two sets of regulators. The Chinese approval was received eight months after the transaction announcement, or three months after the European and American agencies. On May 19, 2012, MOFCOM conditionally approved the deal and Google announced that it would close the transaction in the following two business days.

6.3   COMPETITION REMEDIES

The principles of free competition are threatened by some, though not most, M&A transactions. The objective of competition law is to prevent these transactions, and the role of government agencies is to identify and prevent such situations. These agencies carry out an additional role: examining solutions (known as remedies) put forward by buyers to resolve competition problems created by the proposed transaction.

In the US, remedies are proposed only where the transaction is not endorsed by the FTC or DoJ for competition reasons. The parties propose remedies with a view to resolving the antitrust issue arising from the structure of the transaction and to avoiding a drawn-out dispute. These solutions must allow for competition to be maintained in the relevant market. Whether this means blocking the transaction or approving it if the proposals are acceptable, it is the only effective remedy.

The competent agencies must preserve free competition without favoring a particular market participant. Before accepting a remedy as a viable solution, these bodies must ensure that the buyer's revised measures satisfy all the questions raised when the initial project was rejected. The investigation must focus both on the consequences or possible consequences of antitrust violation on competition in a sector and on the responses put forward in the proposal.

The different types of M&A generally require different remedies. There are horizontal transactions, vertical transactions, and transactions that are a mix of the two. Horizontal transactions involve rival firms or firms that are potential rivals. They can result in a greater market power for the post-merger entity owing to the reduction in market participants or increased risk of coordination between the different operators. Competition is lessened by the combination of similar assets that would have been in competition had the deal not taken place. Vertical transactions involve firms operating in different markets and whose combination would not result in overlapping assets. In theory, a pure vertical transaction has no impact on the number of companies producing particular goods or providing particular services. It can, however, increase a company's ability to change the competition process. Transactions combining elements from horizontal and vertical operations pose very specific challenges.

Each type of transaction requires a particular brand of remedy for the competition problem in question. There is therefore a whole range of solutions that can be split into structural and behavioral remedies. If none of the remedies is acceptable, the competent authority's only option is to block the transaction. For vertical transactions, structural remedies are the most effective. They aim to preserve competition by forcing the buyer to withdraw from a particular market by selling fixed assets (property, plant, etc.) or intangible assets (patents, trademarks, etc.). In order to examine this type of remedy, the assets in question must be clearly identified and must enable their buyer to become a competitor in the relevant market in its own right within a reasonable timeframe. The disposal of entire divisions is generally more effective than the sale of individual assets. It comprises not only the production assets but also things such as personnel, customers, and IT systems. This is the solution often preferred by government agencies. The sale of individual assets can be accepted, however, if the market in question is already deemed to be competitive. The disposal of intangible assets can take place either through out-and-out sales or through licenses. This can cause problems for the potential buyer because it will have to share the technology concerned and will find it harder to make its products stand out. Behavioral remedies can be effective for horizontal and vertical transactions. They look at the way in which the buyer goes about its business, making recommendations or imposing restrictions where necessary. As with structural remedies, the first step is to identify the antitrust violation and the ways in which it can be rectified. The fundamental principle of these behavioral remedies lies in their implementation. Some of the most common behavioral remedies include: firewall measures, which regulate the dissemination of certain information within a company; anti-discriminatory measures, which are based on the principles of equal access, effort, and terms; or sometimes transparency, non-retaliation, or banning measures relating to specific contractual practices. There are also all sorts of hybrid solutions that mix elements from structural and behavioral remedies.

The timetable for implementing these much-needed remedies is an important part of the approval process. Some companies adopt a "fix-it-first" approach, whereby they aim to resolve the competition problem before the government agencies have to deal with it. Such an approach removes the questions surrounding free competition and absolves the parties from having to submit remedies. Other approaches include agreeing to sell certain assets to a given buyer upon signature of the merger contract or setting in motion a plan for the sale of said assets.

All these steps are taken with a view to avoiding situations like the one endured by Procter & Gamble (P&G) and Clorox Chemical in 1969. It may be a long time ago now, but it remains hugely significant. Having bought the liquid-bleach manufacturer 11 years earlier, P&G, which did not make liquid bleach at the time, was forced by the Supreme Court to split from Clorox because it was already a major player in the household-goods sector and therefore a potential entrant to the bleach market.

6.4 COUNTRY DIFFERENCES IN EVALUATION

A transaction can have both a European and a US element. In such a case, both sets of regulators need to give their approval.

A merger that gets the green light in Europe because it would not create a dominant position could be blocked in the US because it would lessen competition to too great an extent. Conversely, a merger that gets blocked in Europe because it creates or consolidates a dominant position could be waved through in the US because the potential efficiency gains are sufficient to offset the threat to competition.

The Airtours/First Choice case is a perfect example. The post-merger situation on the tour operator market would have seen the emergence of three big players and the squeezing of all other competition. The three big hitters would have had respective market shares of between 20% and 35%, meaning none would have had a dominant position. However, the merger would have reduced the number of major players on the market from four to three.

The European Commission feared that this would be detrimental to competition in the marketplace but it did not have the means to block the deal, so it tried to establish the presence of a collective dominant position, i.e. the possibility that, after the merger, the companies might be able to indulge in tacit collusion given their reduced number. Although the Commission had a perfectly legitimate and economically sound fear that the market would become much more collusive, the Court of First Instance in Luxembourg ruled that its case was not strong enough and that, with the burden of proof on its shoulders, the Commission needed to have better arguments.

Perhaps the best example of the differences between Europe and the US is the aborted General Electric/Honeywell deal, which was a hugely painful experience for all arbitrageurs.

The European Commission had already shown in 1997 that it could be very obstructive in the aerospace industry by imposing several conditions on the Boeing/McDonnell Douglas merger. Four years later, after a string of blocked mergers involving European companies, the GE/Honeywell case – involving two US groups – brought things to a head. The Commission refused to authorize the merger on grounds that were almost diametrically opposed to those on which the US authorities were inclined to accept the deal.

The Commission argued that the two companies would use their strong respective positions to launch bundled offers with which none of their rivals could compete. The deal was approved in the US in July 2001 but was then blocked by the European Commission. The argument sidestepped the dominant-position test and focused instead on the "portfolio effects" that the Commission argued were at work in the various markets affected by the deal. The proposed merger was particularly difficult to analyze because it involved both horizontal (GE and Honeywell were both manufacturers of engines for large regional planes) and vertical (partly because GE made engine control systems used by Honeywell, but also because GE subsidiary GECAS bought planes made by Honeywell) aspects, as well as "conglomerate" aspects. This third category identifies the effects of both parties being active in different markets but being able to propose bundled offers. The potentially anti-competitive effects of the merger arise from one of the companies, having a dominant position in one market, being able to tie its product sales to forge a dominant position in another market. Proving these effects first requires the dominant position of one of the two companies in one of the markets to be established (in this case, the dominant position of GE in the market for large-aircraft engines). The Commission believed that this domination was reinforced by maintenance services. It felt that all present and future revenue flows should be considered when estimating sales. The Commission feared that the merged entity would tie its engine sales to sales of avionics and non-avionics equipment (i.e. various onboard equipment) – a market where Honeywell, but not GE, was present. This tying would have involved offering buyers packages including a range of products offered by the merged entity. Owing to the existence of demand for these packages and of the dominant position of one of the parties involved in the merger on one of the markets, the EU argued, this would have been harmful to competition. The Commission's report reads as follows:

> The proposed merger would have led to the creation/strengthening of dominant positions on several markets as a result of horizontal overlaps between some of the parties' products and the combination of Honeywell's leading market positions with GE's financial strength and vertical integration in aircraft purchasing, financing, leasing and aftermarket services. The merged firm's incentive and ability to foreclose competition through, inter alia, bundling/tying and other anti-competitive means would have also contributed to the creation/strengthening of dominant positions on several of the relevant markets (De Luyck et al., 2001).

This transatlantic dispute stirred up a debate on the respective merits of the two systems and their differences. The US system appeared to focus on protecting the consumer, while the European system seemed designed to protect rival companies. The episode confirmed the view that the EU's control procedures were more strict but less rigorous than those in the US. Following the decision by the European Commission, the US DoJ published its opinion on the process and on the differences with its European counterpart:

The theories of competitive harm relied heavily on the claim that GE was already dominant in the market for larger aircraft engines. We found little support for that argument. Under US law, a firm must have "the power to control prices or exclude competition" in order to be found to have market power or to be "dominant". While GE currently enjoys a large market share (due largely to its position through its CFMI joint venture with SNECMA as the exclusive supplier of engines for the Boeing 737), we concluded that the market for large aircraft engines is a big market with three strong competitors – GE, Rolls-Royce and Pratt & Whitney. In such a market, historic market shares are only weakly indicative of future success, as illustrated by the fact that recent contract awards have been quite evenly divided among the three firms, with GE winning 42%, PW 32% and Rolls-Royce 27% (even including CFMI engines in GE's share). We could see no basis, therefore, for finding that GE would be able to impose restrictions on its engines customers (for example, by tying Honeywell avionics to its engine sales) without disadvantaging itself in its battle against Pratt & Whitney and Rolls-Royce to have its engines selected on future platforms. And, in the case of CFMI engines, GE's ability to impose such restrictions would be further constrained by its joint venture partner, SNECMA, who would gain nothing from such restrictions.

We were also unpersuaded that GE would be able to leverage its strong position in engines to gain a decisive competitive advantage in the markets for avionics and non-avionics systems through either mixed bundling or technological tying . . . The empirical evidence we examined convinced us that mixed bundling, to the extent it may be practiced in aerospace markets, is unlikely to convey a decisive competitive advantage. We found little, if any, evidence that aerospace suppliers have been able to gain significant market share through bundling tactics in the past. With respect to technological tying, we could likewise see no way to determine, ex ante, whether physically integrating engines and avionics/non-avionics systems together would have any foreclosure effect, much less whether any potential foreclosure effect would outweigh the efficiencies that might be produced by such integration. Even assuming arguendo that bundling conferred a competitive advantage, we were unable to find any evidence suggesting that other firms would be unable to match the merged firm's offerings through teaming arrangements of the type that are common in this industry . . . We also could not believe that large, sophisticated buyers, like Boeing and Airbus, would permit GE/Honeywell to monopolize the market for such important aircraft components as engines and avionics. We also examined the claim that GE uses its aircraft-leasing arm, GE Capital Aviation Services ("GECAS"), to gain an advantage in engine competitions and would be likely, post-merger, to use GECAS similarly to expand Honeywell's market share for avionics and non-avionics systems. This was characterized as vertical foreclosure . . . We concluded that GECAS's share of aircraft purchases – less than 10% of all planes worldwide – was too small to give rise to a significant foreclosure effect. This being the case, to the extent GECAS is shifting share towards GE by offering more attractive financing, and it is unclear why GE's competitors should not be able to match these discounts.

All of the theories of consumer injury from the GE/Honeywell merger were dependent on the argument that the merger ultimately would drive competitors from the market or would decrease their share to a point where they could no longer effectively constrain GE's competitive behavior. This argument was critical to consumer injury because prices could rise only after GE's competitors were either forced to exit or could no longer compete effectively.

We found no evidence supporting the notion that competitors would not be able to keep up or would be forced to exit as a result of the merger. GE's and Honeywell's rivals are mostly large, financially healthy companies with large shares in many of the relevant markets and ready access to capital. Since the engines and avionics and non-avionics systems have already been selected for all existing airframe platforms, and since very little or no new platform competition is expected in the near term, these competitors have an assured revenue stream for many years and any exit scenario seemed wholly implausible. We found no historical evidence of aerospace firms exiting or withdrawing from the market because they could offer only a narrow range of products, other than through mergers which kept their productive assets in the market.

In summary, we found no factual support for any of the key elements of the range effects theories of competitive harm with respect to the GE/Honeywell merger. To the contrary, we concluded that to the extent those theories were based on the argument that the merged firm would have the ability and incentive to offer customers lower prices and better products, that meant the merger should benefit customers both directly – through the lower prices and better products offered by the merged firm – and indirectly – by inducing rivals to respond with their own lower prices and product improvements. That, in our view, was a reason to welcome the merger, not to condemn it.

'Range Effects: the United States Perspective', Department of Justice Antitrust Division Submission for OECD Roundtable on Portfolio Effects in Conglomerate Mergers, October 12, 2001. Available at www.usdoj.gov.

The second major difference in interpretation between the European and US authorities is the taking into consideration of economic efficiencies. The US authorities apply the "efficiency defense" principle by trying to determine whether the negative impact that an M&A transaction has on competition can be offset by the economic benefits for consumers, such as lower prices. The European Commission's approach is much less direct. It has never clearly acknowledged that a concentration can be offset by economic benefits. The Commission's guiding principle is one of "efficiency offence," whereby cost synergies bring about increased market power and a dominant position. However, article 2(1b) of Europe's Merger Regulation states that efficiency gains from M&A transactions should be taken into account. As a result, the Commission is expected to review its stance on the matter in due course.

We should also mention several arguments commonly put forward by critics of competition law:

- The way in which regulations are applied is motivated broadly by the political leanings of the authorities. This means there are significant differences depending on context and country, whether in Europe, the US, or China.
- Thresholds and other accepted practices are entirely arbitrary. Whether we talk about thresholds for the HHI or other concentration indicators, the critical value is an arbitrary, and often debatable to say the least, choice by the regulator.
- Large groups do not necessarily have an advantage. If the trend for a time was for the expansion of groups and the creation of conglomerates, this no longer appears to be the case. There are many examples of companies disposing of assets through sales, IPOs, or other methods. Introducing competition law was therefore absolutely appropriate and necessary at one time, but there is plenty to suggest the context is now totally different.
- The competition investigation process is often affected by rival firms. As the process is led by committees at government agencies, most requests for more detailed investigations come from companies in competition with the M&A candidates. William F. Schugart (1998) said: "Antitrust has a dark side. Opposition to mergers, though in theory based on worries that competition may be impaired, often in practice comes not from consumers whose interests antitrust is supposed to defend, but from competitors faced with the prospect of a larger, more aggressive rival. Because they respond to the demands

of competitors, labor unions and other well-organized groups having a stake in stopping mergers that promise to increase economic efficiency, the antitrust authorities all too often succeed, not in keeping prices from rising, but in keeping them from falling.

- Antitrust regulation is founded on the belief that concentrations bring about price rises. Certain leading competition experts such as US judge Richard Posner, however, have suggested that the relationship between price and concentration is a long way from being officially proven by academic research. All competition regulation is therefore based on shaky foundations.
- Lastly, oligopolies are being subjected to many internal and external pressures, making them vulnerable and threatening their very existence. The internal pressures involve the tendency of members of the oligopoly to break away from the common purpose and cheat at the expense of their partners. The external pressures involve macro-economic changes such as deregulation, technological innovation, and liberalization which will eventually destabilize the existing structures.

6.5   THE ALLOCATION OF COMPETITION RISK BETWEEN THE PARTIES

As with all other risks, competition risk is allocated between the parties in the merger agreement. The clear aim is to establish upon the signature of said agreement which of the two parties shall bear the risk of having the competition approval request rejected and seeing the transaction blocked at any stage. The agreement therefore stipulates which of the parties is responsible for implementing remedies if required.

The buyer generally seeks to minimize its contractual obligations relating to the possible sale of assets or other post-deal behavioral restrictions. The seller, on the other hand, generally hopes to force the buyer to accept all concessions in the shortest time possible in order to get approval from the regulatory authorities. The remedies proposed by the buyer do not really matter to the target company, whose aim is to secure (as much as it can) completion of the transaction.

There is a wide range of ways in which competition risk can be allocated between the parties. The most restrictive is the "hell or high water" clause. These clauses involve the parties, and the buyer in particular, undertaking to implement all possible measures to ensure that the conditions imposed by the regulators are met and the transaction does not violate competition law. The different remedies are a way of allocating competition risk, and they can be supplemented. A remedy providing for the disposal of certain assets may include certain clauses limiting its scope of application, such as a material adverse effect (MAE) clause or even a cash amount. The provisions in the agreement depend on several factors, including the balance of power between the parties, the extent to which the transaction may raise competition issues, and the type of remedy likely to be requested by the regulator. The final type of clause is a disclaimer inserted by the buyer saying that it will not engage in any action ex ante. "Best-efforts" clauses are not in any way a guarantee; they are simply a promise to implement appropriate measures.

The different approaches adopted by US and European regulators ensure that there are different types of allocation clause. In Europe, the merger candidates are subjected to both EU and national member state regulations. Their motivations may be similar, but the most frequently used clause is the disclaimer. The other clauses are beginning to feature more heavily but remain less common.

One example of the allocation (or non-allocation) of competition risk comes from the Medco/Express Scripts deal, which we discussed earlier in the book. The $29-billion transaction, which was announced on July 21, 2011, involved the merger of two of the three biggest pharmacy distribution companies in the US. The following is an extract from the merger agreement:

(c) In furtherance and not in limitation of the foregoing, (i) each party hereto agrees to make an appropriate filing of a Notification and Report Form pursuant to the HSR Act with respect to the Transactions as promptly as practicable and in any event within ten (10) Business Days of the date hereof, unless otherwise agreed to by the parties, and to supply as promptly as practicable any additional information and documentary material that may be requested pursuant to the HSR Act and use its reasonable best efforts to take, or cause to be taken, all other actions consistent with this Section 5.8 necessary to cause the expiration or termination of the applicable waiting periods under the HSR Act as soon as practicable and (ii) each of Plato and Aristotle (merging entities) shall use its reasonable best efforts to (x) take all action reasonably necessary to ensure that no state takeover statute or similar Law is or becomes applicable to any of the Transactions and (y) if any state takeover statute or similar Law becomes applicable to any of the Transactions, take all action reasonable to enable the Transactions to be consummated as promptly as practicable on the terms contemplated by this Agreement and otherwise minimize the effect of such Law on the Transactions.

In the event of the competition authorities refusing to approve the transaction, the two parties agreed to terminate the deal. The contract goes on to stipulate that, in such a scenario, neither party would be liable to pay damages to the other. This type of clause is just one of many possible responses we have seen to the issue of allocating competition risk between parties.

CASE STUDY: The Oracle/Sun Deal

Background

On April 20, 2009, US software developer Oracle took many observers by surprise by announcing the planned acquisition of IT group Sun Microsystems for $9.50 per share ($7.1 billion in total). Sun had just rejected a bid from IBM of $9.40 per share. Oracle president Safra Catz claimed the deal would add at least $0.15 per share to earnings in the first full year after completion.

The two companies had worked together for more than 20 years. The Fusion Middleware range of software, the Oracle product that had seen the most growth, was based on Sun's Java technology. Sun's Solaris operating system was also the major platform for Oracle's database software.

The Sun group had grown sharply in the 1990s, but it had never fully recovered from when the dotcom bubble burst at the beginning of the new millennium, causing a collapse in demand for its servers. It had apparently been on the lookout for a buyer for several months.

Under the terms of the agreement, the merger would be put before Sun shareholders, and the outcome was not really in doubt given the premium offered and the tough situation in which the loss-making target company found itself. Financing was not a condition of the transaction and was not really a risk given that Oracle had enough cash on its balance sheet to meet the acquisition price.

The transaction was, however, subject to competition approval in the US and Europe.

Oracle said the deal would be completed at the end of August.

How the Transaction Panned Out

Sun shareholders voted in favor of the deal in July and Oracle received approval from the US antitrust authorities in August. The only remaining condition precedent was approval from the European Commission, whose Phase I investigation period ended on September 3.

On the eve of the decision, Sun's shares were trading at $9.32 – a spread of 1.9% from the offer price.

To most people's surprise, the Commission decided to launch a more in-depth Phase II investigation:

European Commission Press Release:

Mergers: Commission opens in-depth investigation into proposed takeover of Sun Microsystems by Oracle

The European Commission has opened an in-depth investigation under the EU Merger Regulation into the planned acquisition of US hardware and software vendor Sun Microsystems by Oracle Corporation, a US database and application software company. The Commission's initial market investigation indicated that the proposed acquisition would raise serious doubts as to its compatibility with the Single Market because of competition concerns on the market for databases. The decision to open an in-depth inquiry does not prejudge the final result of the investigation. The Commission now has 90 working days, until 19 January 2010, to take a final decision on whether the concentration would significantly impede effective competition within the European Economic Area (EEA) or a substantial part of it.

Competition Commissioner Neelie Kroes said: "The Commission has to examine very carefully the effects on competition in Europe when the world's leading proprietary database company proposes to take over the world's leading open source database company. In particular, the Commission has an obligation to ensure that customers would not face reduced choice or higher prices as a result of this takeover. Databases are a key element of company IT systems. In the current economic context, all companies are looking for cost-effective IT solutions, and systems based on open-source software are increasingly emerging as viable alternatives to proprietary solutions. The Commission has to ensure that such alternatives would continue to be available".

Oracle is active in the development, manufacture and distribution of company software, including middleware (i.e. software that connects software components applications), database software and business application software and related services.

Sun offers computing infrastructure, including server and storage solutions and middleware and database software.

The proposed transaction would bring together two major competitors in the market for databases. The database market is highly concentrated with the three main competitors of proprietary databases – Oracle, IBM and Microsoft – controlling approximately 85% of the market in terms of revenue. Oracle is the market leader in proprietary databases, while Sun's MySQL database product is the leading open source database.

The Commission's preliminary market investigation has shown that the Oracle databases and Sun's MySQL compete directly in many sectors of the database market and that MySQL is widely expected to represent a greater competitive constraint as it becomes increasingly functional. The Commission's investigation has also shown that the open source nature of Sun's MySQL might not eliminate fully the potential for anti-competitive effects. In its in-depth investigation, the Commission will therefore address a number of issues, including Oracle's incentive to further develop MySQL as an open source database.

The European Commission was clearly concerned that Oracle would deny companies access to MySQL so it could promote its own products, thereby limiting choice and artificially inflating prices on the database market.

On November 9, the Commission sent a statement of objections to Oracle, in which it outlined its reasons for opposing the deal. Although not putting a definitive stop to the merger between the two companies, this statement was nevertheless the first step towards blocking the transaction.

The Commission's focus was exclusively on the acquisition by Oracle of MySQL, the world leader in open-source databases and still owned by Sun. Larry Ellison's Oracle, on the other hand, was the world's leading proprietary database firm, ahead of IBM and Microsoft.

The tension was mounting every day between Oracle and the European Commission:

- Jonathan Todd, a spokesman for Neelie Kroes, issued a strong statement to say that the Competition Commissioner "expressed her disappointment that Oracle failed to produce, despite repeated requests, either hard evidence that there were no competition problems or a proposal for a remedy to the competition concerns identified by the Commission".
- Sun announced plans to cut 3,000 jobs and put the blame on the European Commission, saying the redundancies had been decided "in light of the delay in the closing of the acquisition of the company".
- A group of 59 US senators wrote to Neelie Kroes to ask her to speed up the process to avoid several thousand US jobs being threatened.

It should be remembered that Ms Kroes is a member of the liberal Dutch People's Party for Freedom and Democracy. She was responsible for privatizing the Dutch post office.

During this episode, Sun's share price fell to $8.20, some 13.7% below the offer price of $9.50.

What Did the Merger Agreement Say?

On the subject of competition risk, the merger agreement said as follows:

1. Oracle was not obliged to complete the transaction if it did not secure approval from the European competition authorities:

   (c) the applicable waiting period . . . applicable to the Merger under . . . any Foreign Competition Law set forth in Section 7.01(c) of the Company Disclosure Schedule shall have expired or been terminated; any affirmative approval of a Governmental Authority required under any Foreign Competition Law set forth in Section 7.01(c) of the Company Disclosure Schedule shall have been obtained.

2. Oracle was under no obligation to accept remedies to obtain approval from the authorities:

> In connection with the receipt of any necessary governmental approvals or clearances (including under any Antitrust Law), neither [Oracle] nor [Sun] shall be required to sell, hold separate or otherwise dispose of or conduct their business in a specified manner, or permit the sale, holding separate or other disposition of, any assets or business of [Oracle] or [Sun]. . .

Unlike other merger agreements, this one did not mention a materiality threshold concerning disposals that may be demanded by the authorities, nor did it contain an even more beneficial clause (hell or high water) for the target company obliging Oracle to make even bigger disposals.

3. Oracle had to make its "best efforts" to obtain approval from the competition authorities:

> The parties hereto shall (i) provide or cause to be provided as promptly as practicable to Governmental Authorities with regulatory jurisdiction over enforcement of any Antitrust Laws . . . including . . . filings under any Antitrust Laws as promptly as practicable following the date of this Agreement (but in no event more than fifteen (15) Business Days from the date hereof except by mutual consent confirmed in writing) and thereafter to respond as promptly as practicable to any request for additional information or documentary material that may be made under the HSR Act and any additional consents and filings under any Antitrust Laws . . .

Oracle therefore had to be prompt in its exchanges with the authorities and respond to any questions "as promptly as practicable" – something which is clearly subjective.

4. Oracle was not obliged to appeal against a negative decision from the European Commission:

> iii) use their reasonable best efforts to contest on the merits, through litigation in United States District Court and through administrative procedures in relation to other Government Authorities, any objections or opposition raised by any Governmental Authority; provided, however, that nothing in this Section 6.10 shall require [Oracle] to appeal any Order from a Governmental Authority.

Oracle could therefore abandon the deal upon refusal from the competition authorities. As we can see, the competition risk was borne almost exclusively by Sun and its shareholders:

- Sun and its lawyers perhaps thought that the competition risk was very small and were therefore willing to take it on.
- Oracle perhaps knew that the competition investigation might throw up a few surprises and wanted to ensure it had an escape route.

SUN CUSTOMERS

Oracle Plans To:

1. Spend more money developing SPARC than Sun does now;

2. Spend more money developing Solaris than Sun does now;

3. Spend more money developing MySQL than Sun does now;

4. Dramatically improve Sun's system performance by tightly integrating Oracle software with Sun hardware;

5. Have more than twice as many hardware specialists selling and servicing SPARC/Solaris systems than Sun does now.

"We're in it to win it. IBM, we're looking forward to competing with you in the hardware business."
– Larry Ellison

Sun.
microsystems

ORACLE

Figure CS6.1   Oracle's plans

It was therefore crucial for the arbitrageurs to evaluate the true strategic motivation for Oracle to complete the transaction because the buyer could now use the refusal of the European competition authorities to withdraw from the deal unharmed.

A communication issued by Oracle in October 2009 provides some clues as to the firm's motivation (see Figure CS6.1).

Outcome

Oracle eventually decided to sit down at the negotiating table and proposed certain remedies to respond to the concerns raised in the statement of objections, particularly in relation to the acquisition of MySQL.

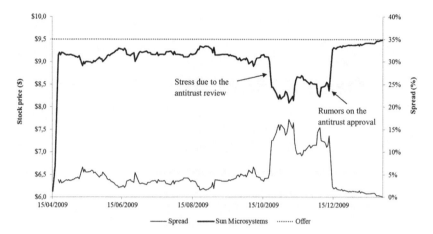

Figure CS6.2   Sun Microsystems: change in stock price and spread
Source: Bloomberg

Oracle undertook to: maintain the availability of application programming interfaces for a storage engine in MySQL; extend OEM licenses until December 2014; continue the development of MySQL; and publish the different versions under a GPL license.

The European Commission eventually decided there was enough competition in the database market to ensure that users were protected. Moreover, companies wanting an open-source solution had alternatives to MySQL, such as PostgreSQL.

"I am now satisfied that competition and innovation will be preserved on all the markets concerned," said Neelie Kroes in December.

The transaction was completed (at $9.50 per share) on January 26, 2010. Figure CS6.2 presents the evolution of the spread since the announcement of the Transaction. It clearly shows the spread widening due to the uncertainty relative to the antitrust review. It subsequently tightened following rumors relative to the antitrust approval.

7

Legal Aspects of Merger Agreements

The merger agreement is the reference document in M&A transactions. It forms the legal basis for the transaction, and will be referred to in any disputes that may arise as the transaction progresses. However, there are also other documents that can provide additional information in such situations, whether it concerns legal clarifications, the context of the transaction, contact between the parties, or any other matters. This chapter will firstly study the different documents and the information they each provide, before looking at the legal aspects of these documents.

7.1 THE DIFFERENT DOCUMENTS

As an M&A transaction progresses, different documents are published by the parties. The nature of the documents depends on the type of transaction, and the timetable according to which they are published may vary. All these documents provide (sometimes fundamental) clarifications about the transaction:

- The merger agreement: this is a firm commitment between the parties concerned, and is usually known as the DMA (definitive merger agreement). It is generally published shortly after the official announcement of the transaction and contains the essential information about the deal. It follows a standard structure, which is described in the next section.

    The proxy statement: when a merger takes place between several parties, the target company is invariably required to submit the transaction for the approval of its shareholders via a vote at the shareholders' meeting. The proxy statement is the document used to convoke the meeting, and it explains what the vote is for, the context of the transaction, and the contact between the parties. The proxy statement also provides details of the terms of the offer and its conditions, as well as the financial reasons for the fairness opinions issued by the advisory banks. The statement is filed with the SEC in two forms: a preliminary form and, subsequently, a definitive form. It contains a section (*Background of the transaction*) describing the main stages that led to the transaction, which is extremely useful in helping to understand the origin of the deal.

When an M&A transaction includes a component involving the buyer's shares in the final payment, if the quantity of shares to be issued exceeds 20% of the shares issued prior to the operation, then the transaction is also subject to the approval of the buyer's shareholders. The buyer must therefore also call its shareholders to a shareholders' meeting, and a proxy statement is published in order to do so.

- In tender offers, it is not a merger agreement that is published, but a tender document called Schedule TO/Schedule 14D-9. Since the offer is directly addressed to the target company's shareholders, the tender document is sent to them. Schedule 14D-9 is the document issued by the target company *in response to the bidder*'s offer, and is generally published within 10 days of the announcement. In its response, the board of directors of the target company must clearly state its recommendation concerning the buyer's offer and how shareholders should respond (whether they should tender their shares into the offer or not). The target company's response usually includes a fairness opinion from its advisory banks. The information contained in a tender document is similar to that contained in a merger agreement in every detail. Finally, in friendly tender offers, the boards of directors of the buyer and of the target company work closely together and the target company's document responding to the buyer's tender offer is published very soon after the announcement.
- During a transaction, if the buyer needs to issue shares or debt securities to finance the deal, certain documents, the S-4 and the 424B respectively, must be published and filed with the SEC. These documents contain useful information concerning the issue in question (shares or debt), the terms of the transaction, and the financial statements of the parties.
- Finally, a Schedule 13E-3 must be published in the event of a transaction in which a listed company delists. For example, in an LBO in which an "affiliate," i.e. a member of the company's management or one of its significant shareholders, participates, a Schedule 13E-3 is required to publish certain financial and other information.

There are other documents published by the parties during an M&A transaction, such as the 8-K form, which is used to notify investors of any material event that may occur. We have covered the most important documents, which usually provide all essential information relating to the transaction. It is then up to the various parties involved to locate and analyze the information they need.

7.2 STRUCTURE OF A MERGER AGREEMENT

As we have already mentioned, the DMA is the reference document for all parties involved in an M&A transaction. It sets out the rules and distributes the different risks among the parties between the announcement and the finalization of the transaction. It is usually filed with the SEC within three days of the announcement of the transaction.

Although we will discuss the main clauses of merger agreements in the next section, we will start by studying the structure of this type of agreement. It consists of several clearly identified sections.

The first section describes the terms of the offer and the timing of its finalization. This section is particularly important in share-based transactions, and explains aspects such as the different final-price determination, proration, and collar mechanisms. With regard to the timing, this section sets out an indicative timetable for finalization once all the conditions have been met. This part is particularly important in private-equity transactions, which are usually subject to a marketing period for syndicated loans to finance them. Such potential delays should be taken into account by arbitrageurs, since they can affect the profitability of a transaction.

The second part concerns the conditions precedent and is essential, since the agreement cannot be executed until these conditions have been met, giving one of the parties the possibility to withdraw from the transaction. It is usually divided into four sub-sections:

- Representations & warranties: these clauses address the problem of differences in information between the buyer and the target company with regard to the target company's situation. The target company provides a description of its situation in this section, guaranteeing the truthfulness of the information provided at the time of signing and of closing.
- MAC or MAE clauses: MAC clauses are determining clauses and are covered exclusively in the next section. To give a brief overview, MAC clauses enable a buyer to withdraw from a transaction should a significant material event occur, thereby bringing the economics of the agreement into doubt.

- Covenants: covenants are provisions that govern the functioning of the target company. The most common covenants forbid dividend payments, asset disposals, and any other action that may have a significant impact on the value or the operations of the target company. In the event of a breach of covenant, the buyer may be authorized to terminate the transaction and demand damages from the target company.
- Exogenous conditions: these usually relate to the financing of the transaction or to the regulatory approvals required to finalize it. The details of the financing already obtained at the time of signing are usually set out in this section.

Lastly, merger agreements contain other important information, such as the cut-off date, or outside date. This can be extended, however, using a number of mechanisms that the parties set out in the agreement. Another determining aspect of the agreement is the indication of the applicable law. In the US, company law varies from one state to another, and these differences may be significant in terms of the protection given to the target company's shareholders, for example. The next two sections will explore in more detail certain clauses that are frequently found in merger agreements, the most important of which are probably MAC clauses.

7.3   MAC CLAUSES

In a merger agreement, so-called MAC clauses are often among the most bitterly negotiated between the lawyers of the two parties.

The MAC clause aims to protect the buyer against the occurrence of a material adverse change between the signing of the agreement and the closing of the transaction.

While it is in the buyer's interest that the notion of material adverse change be defined in the broadest sense possible, the seller will usually attempt to restrict the scope of the term by identifying various exceptions.

The MAC clause therefore serves to contractually distribute the risk of adverse events that may arise in between the signing date and the closing of the transaction between the two parties. As a general rule, the buyer will be liable for all the market risks that may call the subject of the agreement into question. More specific risks that may materially affect the target company are incurred by the target, however.

The example MAC clause below is taken from the merger agreement published on August 31, 2009 in relation to the buyout of Marvel Entertainment by Disney for around $4 billion.

For Disney, the world's leading entertainment group, the acquisition of Marvel enabled it not only to obtain the rights to all the target company's characters, including Iron Man, Spider-Man and X-Men, to name just a few, but also to take advantage of the latest technological innovations developed by Marvel.

MAC clause from the agreement between Disney Company and Marvel Entertainment

"Company Material Adverse Effect" means any event, occurrence, fact, condition, change, development or effect that is materially adverse to the business, assets, properties, liabilities, results of operations or condition (financial or otherwise) of the Company and its Subsidiaries, taken as a whole, except to the extent that such event, occurrence, fact, condition, change, development or effect results from (a) general economic or political conditions or changes therein, (b) financial or security market fluctuations or conditions, (c) changes in, or events affecting, the industries in which the Company and its Subsidiaries operate, (d) any effect arising out of a change in GAAP or applicable Law, (e) actions taken pursuant to this Agreement or at the request of Parent, (f) any changes in the price or trading volume of the Company's stock, in and of itself, (g) any failure by the Company to meet published or unpublished revenue or earning projections, in and of itself or (h) any legal claims or other proceedings made by any of the Company Stockholders (on their own behalf as Company Stockholders or on behalf of the Company) arising out of or relating to this Agreement, in and of itself; provided, that (i) in the cases of clauses (a) through (c), any such event, occurrence, fact, condition, change, development or effect which disproportionately affects the Company and its Subsidiaries relative to other participants in the industries in which the Company or its Subsidiaries operate and (ii) in the case of clauses (f) through (h), the underlying cause of any such change or event, in each case of clauses (i) and (ii), shall not be excluded from the determination of whether there has been a Company Material Adverse Effect.

7.3.1 A negative definition of the MAC clause

The defining characteristics of a MAC clause lie in the content of its text. While the above provision of the agreement between the two parties starts by defining what constitutes a material change ("any event, occurrence, fact, condition, change, development or effect that is materially adverse to the business, assets, properties, liabilities, results of operations or condition (financial or otherwise) of the Company and its Subsidiaries, taken as a whole"), it then sets out a number of exceptions, which may vary depending on the individual transaction, that are the focus of attention. In actual fact, therefore, MAC clauses are defined in a negative way, by exclusion, thanks to the various restrictions set out, rather than in a positive way.

A MAC clause therefore makes it possible to determine, at the time of signing, the situations that the buyer may not invoke in order to be released from its contractual obligations and walk away from the transaction. Depending on the scope of the exclusions set out in the agreement, the clause may be considered more favorable to the target company (if the definition of "material event" is narrow and consequently there is a high number of restrictions), since the buyer's room for maneuver will be considerably restricted in that the number of situations in which it can invoke the MAC clause to terminate the transaction is limited, or, on the contrary, more favorable to the buyer. The content of the clause therefore makes it possible to get an idea of the balance of power between the two parties at the time of signing the deal.

The exclusions most frequently inserted into agreements by sellers include a change in interest rates, a change in markets, a legislative change, and a change in general economic conditions. MAC clauses also often state a number of exogenous events as exclusions, such as those related to climate conditions, terrorism, or war.

Certain more precise restrictions can also be found frequently in merger agreements, such as a change in the projections for the sector, in prices or volumes on the market, in exchange rates (which may be important in cross-border transactions), or in financing, which we will discuss later on. However, when it comes to the clauses in an agreement, the diversity of MAC clauses is limited only by the imagination of the parties' legal advisers and the negotiations that take place.

All these restrictions are illustrated in the Disney/Marvel example. This is a classic MAC clause, demonstrating both the trust and motivation of both parties and the good conditions under which the transaction was concluded. The MAC clause enables us to judge very accurately the parties' intentions and motivations at the time of concluding the agreement by looking at the number and scope of the restrictions.

Another main characteristic of MAC clauses is that they are never written in quantitative terms. They almost never state that the loss resulting from a particular event must be x euro or that the drop in the target company's growth forecasts must exceed y%, etc. This aspect of MAC clauses is a determining one. It partly explains the small number of court decisions relating to MAC clauses and, more specifically, gives the impression that the objective of these clauses is actually something other than merely the retraction of the buyout offer.

7.3.2   MAC clauses and court decisions

On the whole, US case law does not look favorably on the invocation of MAC clauses by industrial investors. The courts tend to see the use of such a clause as an expression of regret on the buyer's part after having made a commitment.

The IBP vs Tyson Foods case laid the foundations of this case law. On January 1, 2001, following a bidding war with Smithfield Food Co., Tyson Foods, a poultry company, announced the acquisition of IBP, the US's leading producer of meat (particularly pork), for around $4.7 billion. However, shortly afterwards, IBP published its first-quarter results and announced figures well below analysts' forecasts. Following the announcement, Tyson Foods declared its intention not to finalize the transaction, invoking the fact that these negative results constituted a material adverse event for IBP. The target company decided to bring legal proceedings against Tyson Foods before the Delaware Court of Chancery, which ruled on the matter in accordance with the law of the state of New York, which was the law elected by the parties in the agreement. The Court of Chancery refused to give validity to the MAC clause on the grounds that it had been written up in such broad terms that it was impossible to determine whether a material adverse change had taken place, and particularly because, as a professional in the sector, the buyer had sufficient knowledge to foresee the changes that occurred. The ruling also stressed that the effect on the buyer, as a professional in the sector, could be measured only in the long term, thereby removing much of the need for the MAC clause's force. It concluded that, though significant, the impact on Tyson would be corrected after several years and that IBP's announcement concerning the temporary drop in revenues therefore did not constitute a material change.

Similarly, in the Frontier Oil vs Holly case in 2005, the same Delaware court transposed the rule pronounced in the IBP vs Tyson Foods case into state law and applied it to refuse Holly, the seller in this case, the right to invoke a MAC clause on the grounds that the target company had not provided evidence of the long-term negative impact of the event in question.

These decisions made by the Delaware Court of Chancery still form the foundations of case law on MAC clauses. They are particularly important because a great many US businesses are registered in this state, but also because the law of Delaware is the basis for that of a number of other US states. These two decisions set out two fundamental principles: in order to prove the existence of a MAC clause, a buyer must prove, simultaneously, (i) that a significant material adverse event has occurred, and (ii) that said event will have a long-term impact on the target company.

These two principles were confirmed in two other cases. The first is the Genesco/Finish Line case, which was ruled on by a Tennessee court. Finish Line's initial strategy was based not on the invocation of a MAC clause, but on the fact that the agreement with Genesco obliged the latter to provide the buyer with additional information. The court acknowledged that Finish Line's claim was well founded and ordered Genesco to provide the information. Following this episode, Finish Line invoked the MAC clause with a view to not closing the deal. According to the court, the drop in Genesco's quarterly revenues was not disproportionate to market conditions and was directly attributable to these conditions. After consulting an expert, the court concluded that this change, resulting from a change in global economic conditions, fell under one of the exclusions provided for in the agreement: "except . . . any event resulting from . . . general economic or political conditions". Finish Line did manage to terminate the transaction, however, through amicable negotiations with Genesco.

The second case to reaffirm these principles is the dispute dating back to September 2008 between chemical company Huntsman and Hexion Specialty Chemicals, a company owned by private-equity group Apollo. Hexion was supposed to acquire Huntsman for $28 per share, but decided not to close the transaction by invoking a MAC clause on the grounds that the merged entity would be insolvent. The judge sided with the arguments put forward by Huntsman, stating that an event classifiable as a MAC would have to have a persistent impact on the target company, which was not the case in this instance. Hexion's defense, based on the interpretation of the exclusions, was not even considered, since the judge stated that the MAC event would have to be proven true before the language used in the exclusions could be analyzed.

7.3.3   MAC clauses and private-equity transactions

The use of the MAC clause by financial investors has had a more welcome reception. This can be explained by the nature of this type of acquisition, which rests on a meticulously planned financial structure, the balance of which can be affected by a simple deterioration in the company's activity.

In practice, most acquisition cases damaged by the financial crisis have been resolved using out-of-court solutions. This can be explained by the fact that the seller runs the risk that a court may set the bar lower than for a strategic/industrial investor, meaning that the investor may terminate the sale without suffering a penalty. The buyer, on the other hand, runs the risk of having to withdraw from the case or pay a break-up fee. Since the financial stakes are extremely high for both parties, these cases are frequently resolved amicably.

In most private-equity transactions, the merger agreement provides for the payment of a reverse termination fee, which is a sum paid by the buyer to the target company that enables it to terminate the agreement (i.e. not close the deal) without having to justify this decision. This amount is predetermined at the time of signing and typically corresponds to around 3 to 5% of the value of the transaction. When they were first introduced into private-equity transactions, reverse termination fees served to compensate the target company in the event that the transaction did not go ahead, and to discourage the buyer from walking away from the transaction. When an agreement contains a MAC clause, the presence of a reverse termination fee provision at least provides the buyer with an extra advantage.

The cases of the buyouts of Harman and Acxiom by private-equity firms (KKR and Goldman Sachs in the first case and ValueAct and Silver Lake in the second) illustrate this aspect. In both situations, the buyers invoked MAC clauses on the grounds of a change in economic conditions in order to be released from their obligations. If the presence of a material event had been proven, the private-equity firms would have been able to walk away from the deals without even having to compensate the target company, as provided for in the MAC clauses. If it had not been proven that a material event had occurred, the total amount of the penalties applicable would be limited to the value of the reverse termination fee.

7.3.4   Why these clauses?

MAC clauses and the invocation of them are a means of negotiation between the parties. That explains why they are never written in quantitative terms. If that were the case, all situations would be directly resolved and the parties would not have any room for maneuver. In the case of qualitative clauses, the parties are placed face to face and forced to negotiate. The small number of court decisions concerning MAC clauses shows how much pressure there is on parties to negotiate out of court. Moreover, buyers have no illusions as to their chances of succeeding in proceedings based on MAC clauses. The objective is therefore actually to renegotiate the terms of the transaction.

The most important case involving a dispute hinging on a MAC clause perfectly illustrates this willingness to renegotiate on the part of the parties that invoke these clauses. Moreover, this case was resolved without the court even having to rule on the existence of such a clause. The case involved the buyout in October 2007 of Sallie Mae (SLM), the entity that manages student loans in the US, by a group of buyers comprising J.C. Flowers (a private-equity firm specializing in financial institutions) and banks JPMorgan and Bank of America, for more than \$25 billion. The buyers' argument was based on the forthcoming adoption of new, more restrictive, legislation (the College Cost Reduction and Access Act) that would have a negative impact on SLM's results and therefore objectively constituted a material event. If the court ruled in favor of the target company, the buyers would have to spend \$900 million in reverse termination fees to put an end to the transaction. The MAC clause contained in the agreement excluded:

> ... changes in Applicable Law provided that, for purposes of this definition, "changes in Applicable Law" shall not include any changes in Applicable Law relating specifically to the education finance industry that are in the aggregate more adverse to (SLM) than the legislative and budget proposals described under the heading "Recent Developments" in the Company 10-K ...

This double negative excluded legislative changes from the MAC clause, and therefore visibly excluded the act in question. However, the clause then goes on to include texts that would have a more adverse effect than those set out in SLM's 10-K form. The views of the two parties therefore diverged on this point: Sallie Mae believed that the difference in impact would be significant, while J.C. Flowers argued that even a difference equivalent to $1 could suffice. The MAC clause, because of its formulation, favored the buyers. They therefore proposed a new offer, reduced by about 17%, which Sallie Mae declined, since its chairman and CEO refused to sell at a lower price than the initial offer. In the end, the two parties agreed to terminate the transaction by mutual agreement after Sallie Mae managed to secure the refinancing of $30 billion of debt with the banks from the group of buyers.

The second-most well-known case in which the invocation of a MAC clause led to the renegotiation of the transaction and, ultimately, to a lower acquisition price than the initial offer is the buyout of Accredited Home Lenders (AHL), a US mortgage lender, by private-equity firm Lone Star. Despite being very strong prior to 2007, AHL suffered the full effects of the subprime crisis that began in the summer of that year. The situation was such that AHL announced that it needed a capital increase or it would have to declare itself bankrupt. Its banker at the time, the now-defunct investment bank Bear Stearns, organized an auction sale of the company. After several rounds of bidding, Lone Star, a private-equity firm that specializes in restructurings, won the auction, with an offer of $15.10 per share, or around $400 million in total. One of the conditions precedent to the closure of the transaction was the obtainment of the approval of the authorities in 95% of the states in which AHL was present, which resulted in a considerable delay before the buyout was able to be finalized. This condition precedent was finally lifted on August 10, 2007.

However, during this delay, the financial crisis worsened, and Lone Star found itself in a position in which it legitimately believed that it had overpaid for AHL. Lone Star therefore informed AHL that it believed that another condition precedent to the completion of the transaction had not been lifted. The private-equity firm did not, however, state the nature of this condition, which presumably was the absence of any events constituting a MAC. On August 11, AHL began legal proceedings before the Delaware Court of Chancery against Lone Star for breach of its obligation to close the transaction. Lone Star filed a countersuit 10 days later, claiming that AHL had in fact undergone a material adverse event, citing the unfavorable report by AHL's auditors and the downward revision of forecast revenues for the company by its managers following the deterioration in market conditions.

The MAC clause in the agreement between AHL and Lone Star contained a large number of exclusions and, as a result of an auction process with multiple candidates, AHL had been able to impose its conditions and negotiate a clause that was largely favorable to it, at least at first sight. The clause contained no fewer than 13 restrictions and, in order to invoke it, Lone Star, like any buyer in this situation, had to prove that the target company had undergone a material adverse event, that the event was unexpected, and that it affected AHL disproportionately compared with other operators in the sector. However, given the economic context in September 2007, one could be forgiven for wondering whether even bankruptcy could constitute a disproportionate event.

The role of the MAC clause in this case is obvious: Lone Star no longer wanted to pay the price initially negotiated following the deterioration of economic conditions, but nevertheless still wanted to buy AHL. A withdrawal from the transaction would have involved the payment of considerable damages to AHL. However, the formulation of the MAC clause was particularly unfavorable to Lone Star. At the same time, in light of the situation, AHL had no other choice but to be sold, and could not afford for its shareholders to lose the acquisition premium in the event of the failure of the transaction. These forces no doubt urged both parties to renegotiate. Finally, on October 12, the two parties announced the conclusion of a buyout agreement at a price of $11.75 per share, which was significantly lower than the initial offer.

A MAC clause can therefore enable the buyer to pursue an objective other than the one that was initially provided for with these clauses (the termination of the transaction). The buyer may attempt to take advantage of a change in market conditions or the occurrence of an adverse event to justify renegotiating the purchase price. In this sense, the qualitative definition of the MAC clause is essential in that it adds a certain degree of judicial flexibility, which is conducive to negotiations. Similarly, this formulation is also preferable for the target company, which may take advantage of ambiguous wording to argue the opposite point.

Therein lies the glorious paradox of the MAC clause, which is often meticulously drawn up and usually bitterly negotiated, but only exceptionally exercised.

7.4   OTHER LEGAL CLAUSES

7.4.1   Go-shop clause

A go-shop clause enables a target company to solicit other competing offers during a period of x days. This type of clause is rarely used when the target company has been the subject of a serious bidding process, because all potential buyers have, in principle, been able to participate and submit an offer. On the contrary, in the event that an unsolicited offer is received and accepted by the target company, the duty of the board of directors to seek the best offer possible requires it to at least carry out a market check (in which the advisory bank calls the other most natural candidates to ensure that none of them is prepared to submit a substantially higher offer) and, ideally, involves the negotiation of a go-shop clause in the acquisition agreement. This clause is most commonly used in the US, since the free play of higher bids makes the clause useless in Europe: a clause forbidding a target company from entering into discussions with companies that may submit a counteroffer would simply be illegal.

In the example of the KKR/Del Monte transaction described in Chapter 10, which deals with LBO transactions, the agreement provided for a 45-day go-shop period following the signing of the transaction. The clause is formulated as follows.

> **Go-Shop Period**. Notwithstanding anything to the contrary contained in this Agreement, during the period beginning on the date of this Agreement and continuing until 11:59 p.m. (Eastern time) on the 45th calendar day after the date of this Agreement (the "Go-Shop Period"), the Company and its subsidiaries and their respective directors, officers, employees, investment bankers, attorneys, accountants and other advisors or representatives (collectively, "Representatives") shall have the right to: (i) initiate, solicit and encourage any inquiry or the making of any proposals or offers that could constitute Acquisition Proposals, including by way of providing access to non-public information to any person pursuant to (but only pursuant to) a confidentiality agreement on customary terms not materially more favorable to such person than those contained in the KKR/Centerview Confidentiality Agreement (it being understood that such confidentiality agreements need not prohibit the making or

amendment of an Acquisition Proposal) (an "Acceptable Confidentiality Agreement"); provided that the Company shall promptly make available to Parent and Merger Sub any material non-public information concerning the Company or its subsidiaries that the Company provides to any person given such access that was not previously made available to Parent or Merger Sub, and (ii) engage or enter into, continue or otherwise participate in any discussions or negotiations with any persons or groups of persons with respect to any Acquisition Proposals or otherwise cooperate with or assist or participate in, or facilitate any such inquiries, proposals, discussions or negotiations or any effort or attempt to make any Acquisition Proposals, including through the waiver or release by the Company, at its sole discretion, of any preexisting standstill or similar agreements with any persons solely to the extent necessary to permit such person to make or amend an Acquisition Proposal or otherwise engage with the Company in discussions regarding an Acquisition Proposal or a proposal that could reasonably be expected to lead to an Acquisition Proposal.

Ultimately, at the end of this period, no competing offer had been submitted, and the transaction progressed in the usual way.

Go-shop clauses generally serve another objective for the board of directors of a company that is the target of a takeover bid. The board has a duty to maximize the amount of the consideration received, while the buyer, on the other hand, is looking to complete the transaction as quickly as possible. The inclusion of a go-shop clause makes it possible to simultaneously initiate the buyout process and give the target company's directors time to fulfill their fiduciary duties.

The proxy statement published after an M&A transaction is announced is generally a wealth of detailed information. More specifically, the *Background of the merger* section describes the context in which the negotiations between the parties are held and, where appropriate, reveals the existence of other bidders. In any case, this section enables the reader to discover the background to the transaction and the details of the process. The short example below describes the successive meetings between the managers of National Semiconductor and Texas Instruments in connection with the buyout of the former by the latter, which was announced in April 2011.

In early December 2010, Mr Richard Templeton, the Chairman, Chief Executive Officer and President of Texas Instruments, made an unsolicited call to Mr Donald Macleod, our Chairman and Chief Executive Officer, to inquire whether National would be interested in meeting with Texas Instruments to discuss potential strategic opportunities between the two companies. Mr Macleod stated that National was not for sale but that he would be willing to meet with Mr Templeton. On December 13, 2010, in order to maintain the confidentiality of discussions between Texas Instruments and National, Mr Templeton and Mr Macleod met at the San Jose Airport. At that meeting, Mr Templeton told Mr Macleod that Texas Instruments would be interested in acquiring National and that such a transaction would be beneficial to both Texas Instruments and National. Mr Macleod informed Mr Templeton that, although National was not for sale, he would advise our Board of Directors of any offer made by Texas Instruments and that our Board of Directors was aware of its responsibility to consider any offer that might be in the best interest of our stockholders. Mr Templeton and Mr Macleod also discussed the risks associated with exploring a potential transaction between Texas Instruments and National, including the impact on National's business and employees and the potential difficulties associated with maintaining National's business during an integration of National into Texas Instruments. Mr Templeton and Mr Macleod did not discuss price or any other material potential terms at this meeting.[. . .]

On January 26, 2011, Mr Templeton and Mr Macleod met together at the San Jose Airport. At the meeting, Mr Templeton conveyed his opinion that a sale of National to Texas Instruments was in the best interests of both companies and discussed the potential strategic advantages of combining the companies, including the potential increase in the scale and breadth of the combined company's product lines, the pooled engineering talent for the combined company, additional manufacturing capacity and an expanded sales force. Mr Templeton and Mr Macleod discussed next steps with respect to exploring a possible transaction. Mr Macleod indicated that the next step would be a formal proposal from Texas Instruments regarding the purchase of National, including a proposed per share price that could be shared with our Board of Directors. On February 7, 2011, Mr Templeton called Mr Macleod and told him that Texas Instruments was sending a written proposal to National. Mr Templeton initially declined to discuss the contents of the proposal, including the offer price; however, when pressed by Mr Macleod, Mr Templeton indicated the offer price would be in the range of $22.00 to $23.00 per share of National common stock. Mr Templeton reiterated his rationale for a transaction between National and Texas Instruments. [. . .]

On February 23, 2011, Mr Templeton called Mr Macleod and informed him that Texas Instruments was prepared to potentially increase its offer price. Mr Macleod responded that the value of National was significantly in excess of Texas Instruments' offer and that National would be unwilling to provide Texas Instruments confidential information without an assurance that Texas Instruments was prepared to increase its offer price. Mr Templeton stated that Texas Instruments believed that its offer price was fair and provided a significant premium to our stock price, but that Mr Templeton was prepared to recommend an increased offer price of $24.00 to $25.00 per share, if the information provided by National, including information about additional cost synergies, supported such an increase. Mr Macleod indicated that while he was not authorized by our Board of Directors to pursue a transaction in the range of valuation suggested by Mr Templeton, Mr Macleod would be willing to have a meeting between representatives of Texas Instruments and Mr Todd DuChene, our Senior Vice President, General Counsel and Secretary, Mr Chew and himself to discuss our business operations subject to the execution of an acceptable confidentiality agreement and so long as Texas Instruments understood National's position on the importance of speed, certainty of closing, and the process being conducted in a manner to maintain confidentiality and minimize disruption to National's business operations. Mr Macleod also emphasized that price remained an open issue and that Texas Instruments would have to increase its offer price for National to continue discussions regarding a potential transaction with Texas Instruments. Mr Templeton and Mr Macleod agreed to have the requested diligence meeting on February 25, 2011. [. . .]

On February 28, 2011, Mr Templeton called Mr Macleod to discuss the February 25, 2011 meeting and indicated that Texas Instruments would be prepared to increase its offer for National to $25.00 per share for National.

7.4.2 Break-up-fee clause

Break-up fees enable a buyer to be indemnified if the transaction is not concluded if, for example, the target company recommends a higher offer, the shareholders of the target company vote against the deal at the shareholders' meeting, or it is not possible to obtain a necessary administrative authorization. The sum (generally around 2–3% of the value of the transaction) compensates the buyer for the time and resources spent on carrying out the transaction.

The break-up fee is sometimes paid by the buyer if it is unable to obtain the authorization needed to conclude the transaction, as in the AT&T/Sprint deal (worth $39 billion), under which AT&T had to pay $3 billion to the seller (T-Mobile) in the event of a refusal from competition authorities.

Academic studies tend to show that break-up fees benefit the shareholders of the target company. A study by Micah Officer ('Termination fees in mergers and acquisitions', published in the *Journal of Financial Economics* in 2003) of 2,511 transactions that took place between 1988 and 2000 shows that the premium offered is 7% higher if the deal contains a break-up-fee provision. A buyer is more inclined to enter into a competitive process knowing that its costs will be covered in the event that the transaction does not go ahead. Of course, after the announcement of the transaction, the presence of a break-up-fee provision may discourage competitors from making a counteroffer, since it makes counteroffers more expensive.

Example: Break-up-fee clause in the Apax/Kinetic merger agreement:

(iii) this Agreement is terminated by the Company pursuant to Section 8.3(a); then the Company shall (A) in the case of clause (i) above, concurrently with the occurrence of the applicable event,

(B) in the case of clause (ii) above, no later than three (3) Business Days after the date of such termination and (C) in the case of clause (iii) above, immediately prior to or concurrently with such termination, pay Parent or its designee the Termination Fee (as defined below) by wire transfer of immediately available funds (it being understood that in no event shall the Company be required to pay the Termination Fee on more than one occasion). "Termination Fee" shall mean (1) an amount equal to $51,800,000 if the Termination Fee becomes payable in connection with the Company entering into an Alternative Acquisition Agreement with an Excluded Party and (2) an amount equal to $155,400,000 in all other circumstances.

7.4.3 Matching-rights clause

Matching-rights clauses, which are sometimes negotiated at the time of signing a merger agreement, give the buyer a significant advantage. The clause essentially amounts to a "preferential right," since it enables the buyer to outbid a superior offer made by a competitor. In the event of a bidding war following the announcement of an offer, the initial buyer therefore has the opportunity to counter the offers made by the other bidders. The formulation of this clause is very important, since it sets out the procedure to be followed for the target company in negotiating with a new buyer, the information rights granted to the initial buyer and the time frame for deciding on a rival offer. One of the most significant recent examples of such a clause was that involved in the battle between Dell and Hewlett-Packard to take control of 3PAR. The clause in the agreement was formulated as follows:

Notwithstanding the foregoing or anything to the contrary set forth in this Agreement, if, at any time prior to the Appointment Time, the Company Board receives a Superior Proposal or there occurs an Intervening Event, the Company Board may effect a Company Board Recommendation Change provided that (i) the Company Board determines in good faith (after consultation with outside legal counsel) that the failure to effect a Company Board Recommendation Change would reasonably be expected to be a breach of its fiduciary duties to the Company Stockholders under applicable Delaware Law, and in the case of a Superior Proposal, the Company Board approves or recommends such Superior Proposal; (ii) the Company has notified Parent in writing that it intends to effect a Company Board Recommendation Change, describing in reasonable detail the reasons, including the material terms and conditions of any such Superior Proposal and a copy of the final form of any related agreements or a description in reasonable detail of such Intervening Event, as the case may be, for such Company Board Recommendation Change (a "Recommendation Change Notice") (it being understood that the Recommendation Change Notice shall not constitute a Company Board Recommendation Change for purposes of this Agreement); (iii) if requested by Parent, the Company shall have made its Representatives available to discuss and negotiate in good faith with Parent's Representatives any proposed modifications to the terms and conditions of this Agreement during the three (3) Business Day period following delivery by the Company to Parent of such Recommendation Change Notice; and (iv) if Parent shall have delivered to the Company a written proposal capable of being accepted by the Company to alter the terms or conditions of this Agreement during such three (3) Business Day period, the Company Board shall have determined in good faith (after consultation with outside legal counsel), after considering the terms of such proposal by Parent, that a Company Board Recommendation Change is still necessary in light of such Superior Proposal or Intervening Event in order to comply with its fiduciary duties to the Company Stockholders under applicable Delaware Law. Any material amendment or modification to any Superior Proposal will be deemed to be a new Superior Proposal for purposes of this Section 6.3. The Company shall keep confidential any proposals made by Parent to revise the terms of this Agreement, other than in the event of any amendment to this Agreement and to the extent required to be disclosed in any Company SEC Reports.

In the event that the board of directors of 3PAR received a rival offer, it would have to follow a procedure that is set out clearly in this clause. Firstly, the board would have to issue an opinion on the quality of the offer and class it as either superior to the last offer received or not. If it were deemed superior, the board, in accordance with its duty to maximize the purchase price, would have to accept the new proposal. It would be then that the clause would play its part.

In the 24 hours following the receipt of any new proposal considered superior by the board of directors, the board would be obliged to provide Dell, the beneficiary of the clause, with details of the identity of the bidder and the terms of its offer. Any information or documentation submitted to the new bidder would also have to be supplied to Dell.

From that moment, Dell would have a maximum of three business days in which to formulate a new offer. In certain situations, these clauses can also be favorable to the target company, because a competitor may choose to raise its offer considerably in order to block a buyer with matching rights, thereby putting the initial buyer out of the race. In these transactions, the parties' reactions can be analyzed in the context of game theory, with each party attempting to anticipate its competitor's or competitors' next move.

7.4.4   Specific-performance clause

Specific-performance clauses enable the target company – once all the conditions precedent have been lifted – to use judicial means to force the buyer to complete the transaction. The formulation of this clause is very important. In LBOs, the co-contracting party of the target company is generally an ad hoc shell company created by the private-equity firm. The specific-performance clause is usually limited to the commitment to provide the equity part of the transaction, whereas it is actually often a lack of financing that is the problem.

> **Example: Specific-performance clause in the Apax/Kinetic merger agreement:**
>
> Section 9.10 Specific Performance. The parties agree that irreparable damage for which monetary damages, even if available, would not be an adequate remedy, would occur in the event that the parties hereto do not perform the provisions of this Agreement (including failing to take such actions as are required of it hereunder in order to consummate the Merger) in accordance with its specified terms or otherwise breach such provisions. The parties acknowledge and agree that the parties shall be entitled to an injunction, specific performance and other equitable relief to prevent breaches of this Agreement and to enforce specifically the terms and provisions hereof, this being in addition to any other remedy to which they are entitled at law or in equity; provided that the Company shall be entitled to seek specific performance as a third party beneficiary of Parent's rights against the Investors under the Equity Financing Commitments that relate to the equity commitment relating to a portion of the Merger Consideration, subject to the terms thereof, and to cause Parent and/or Merger Sub to draw down the full

proceeds of the Equity Financing and to cause Parent or Merger Sub to consummate the transactions contemplated hereby, including to effect the Closing in accordance with Section 1.2, on the terms and subject to the conditions in this Agreement, if, but only if: (A) all conditions in Sections 7.1 and 7.2 (other than those conditions that by their nature are to be satisfied at the Closing) have been satisfied, (B) Parent and Merger Sub fail to complete the Closing by the date the Closing is required to have occurred pursuant to Section 1.2, (C) the Debt Financing (or, if alternative financing is being used in accordance with Section 6.15, pursuant to the commitments with respect thereto) has been funded or will be funded at the Closing if the Equity Financing is funded at the Closing and (D) the Company has irrevocably confirmed that if specific performance is granted and the Equity Financing and Debt Financing are funded, then the Closing will occur. Notwithstanding anything herein to the contrary, it is hereby acknowledged and agreed that the Company shall be entitled to seek specific performance to cause Parent and Merger Sub to enforce, including against anticipatory breach, the obligations of the lenders to fund the Debt Financing under the Debt Financing Commitment, but only in the event that each of the following conditions has been satisfied: (i) all of the conditions set forth in Sections 7.1 and 7.2 have been satisfied (other than those conditions that by their nature are to be satisfied at the Closing), and Parent and Merger Sub fail to complete the Closing by the date the Closing is required to have occurred pursuant to Section 1.2 and (ii) all of the conditions to the consummation of the financing provided by the Debt Financing Commitment (or, if alternative financing is being used in accordance with Section 6.15, pursuant to the commitments with respect thereto) have been satisfied (other than those conditions that by their nature are to be satisfied at the Closing). Each of the parties agrees that it will not oppose the granting of an injunction, specific performance and other equitable relief as provided herein on the basis that (x) either party has an adequate remedy at law or (y) an award of specific performance is not an appropriate remedy for any reason at law or equity. For the avoidance of doubt, under no circumstances will the Company be entitled to monetary damages in excess of the aggregate amount of the Parent Fee.

7.4.5   Dissenters'-rights clause

Dissenters'-rights clauses enable a minority shareholder to oppose the transaction (even if the deal has been approved by a majority of shareholders) and to ask that its shares be valued and sold at a fair value decided by a court. In practice, obtaining a court decision is a very long and expensive process (due to the lawyer's and valuer's fees) and this option is rarely used.

Example: Dissenters'-rights clause in the Apax/Kinetic merger agreement:

(d) Notwithstanding any other provision contained in this Agreement, Shares that are issued and outstanding as of the Effective Time and that are held by a shareholder who has not voted such Shares in favor of the Merger and who is entitled to demand and properly demands the fair value of such Shares pursuant to, and who complies in all respects with (and has otherwise taken all of the steps required by) Subchapter H of Chapter 10 of the TBOC to properly exercise and perfect such shareholder's rights of dissent and appraisal ("Dissenting Shares") shall be deemed to have ceased to represent any interest in the Surviving Corporation as of the Effective Time and shall be entitled to those rights and remedies set forth in Subchapter H of Chapter 10 of the TBOC; provided, however, that in the event that a shareholder of the Company fails to perfect, withdraws or otherwise loses any such right or remedy granted by the TBOC, the Shares held by such shareholder shall be converted into and represent only the right to receive the Merger Consideration specified in Section 2.1(a) of this Agreement. The Company shall give Parent (i) prompt notice of any written notices to exercise dissenters' rights in respect of any Shares, attempted withdrawals of such notices, and any other instruments served pursuant to applicable law that are received by the Company with respect to shareholders' rights of dissent and appraisal and (ii) the opportunity to participate in and direct all negotiations and proceedings with respect to any such demands for payment of fair value under the TBOC. The Company shall not, without the prior written consent of Parent, voluntarily make any payment with respect to, or settle or offer to settle any such demands for payment of fair value under the TBOC.

As we have seen in this second part, the analysis of the risk that an M&A transaction will fail involves analyzing different elements: the financing, the regulatory risks (antitrust or other risks), and the legal clauses. These aspects are invariably found in all transactions. However, there are two types of transaction that both present distinctive features in each of the aforementioned elements: hostile takeover bids and LBOs. These two types of transaction will be the focus of the third and final part of the book.

8
Other Risks

There are many additional risks that threaten the completion of an M&A transaction, but they cannot be grouped together under one heading. In this chapter, we will look at four very specific types of risk. First, numerous M&A transactions require approval from administrative authorities other than the merger control bodies. There are lots of these administrative authorizations, and their number depends on the countries involved. Second, there is political risk, which applies most often to transactions in emerging nations. Third is the risk of a natural disaster, which cannot be foreseen but may cause the transaction to be completely abandoned. Finally, we will also discuss the risk of fraud or false accounting. Arbitrageurs must always consider two key elements: (i) the likelihood that the transaction will not be completed (this does not happen often, but we will look at some examples); (ii) the timetable that may arise from any problems, which is the main factor in evaluating the spread.

8.1 ADMINISTRATIVE AUTHORIZATIONS

8.1.1 United States

In the US, there are two areas of administrative formalities relating to M&A: the first is concerned with any investment by a foreign entity and is dealt with by the Committee on Foreign Investment in the United States (CFIUS); the second relates to sector-specific authorities.

8.1.1.1 The role of the CFIUS

The CFIUS investigates all M&A transactions instigated by foreign firms which target US companies, regardless of whether the buyer declares the bid voluntarily. The committee was established in 1975, during the presidency of Gerald Ford, with a view to monitoring and channeling foreign investment in the US, and protecting the country where necessary. We will examine the role of the CFIUS by studying the example of L-1 Identity Solutions, a US security company that was the subject of a takeover bid from French industrial group Safran.

In September 2010, Safran announced its intention to buy L-1, which specializes in biometric analysis and identity data services, for $1.2 billion. The parties expected the deal to be completed during the first quarter of 2011. In 2008, Safran had lost out to L-1 in a bidding war for Secure ID, a company specializing in identification products. The strategic aim of Safran was therefore pretty clear: penetrate the US security market and get its hands on L-1 technologies so it could merge them with its own Morpho business. Synergies from the transaction were estimated at $30 million per year. The deal was subject to the $303-million sale of L-1's intelligence services unit to UK defense and aerospace group BAE Systems.

As with any foreign investment, the transaction was also subject to CFIUS approval. On March 15, 2011, the committee wrapped up its initial investigation and requested additional information, thereby triggering a 45-day second investigation period. On May 2, in order to give the CFIUS more time to rule on the case, the parties withdrew their request and immediately filed a new one, with the committee's approval. This is a common strategy when more time is required as it resets the initial timeframe and opens a new 30-day window. However, a wave of panic gripped investors in the days that followed. With several requests made to the CFIUS, various demands for additional information refused and a 30% control premium, arbitrageurs feared big losses. The change in the spread during this period could not have been more chaotic, as Figure 8.1 shows.

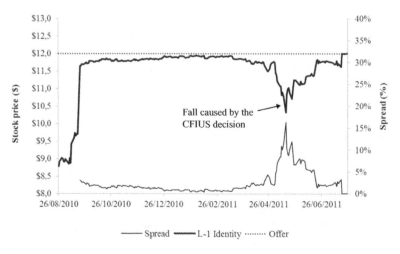

Figure 8.1   L-1 Identity Solutions: changes in share price and spread
Source: Bloomberg

The two parties filed their new request on June 20. The length of the process and the initial reluctance of the US authorities to wave through a transaction giving a foreign group (moreover, one that was 30% owned by the French government) access to sensitive assets can be explained by the specific nature of these assets and their connection to the US security system.

The new request put an end to speculation that Safran planned to pull the plug on the deal in light of the problems experienced at the beginning of June. Some observers had thought that the various obstacles would see the French group either pay the $75-million break-up fee and kill the deal or attempt to negotiate a price cut. This speculation did not allow for Safran's determination to see the deal through, not only to get its hands on L-1's assets but also to establish a presence in the US in the wake of its failed attempt to buy Secure ID. In the eyes of investors, Safran was debating whether such a purchase – taking into account (i) the remedies demanded by the CFIUS and (ii) the uninspiring results published by L-1 since the deal was announced – was still so attractive or whether it might be better to abandon the transaction and grow organically in its target businesses in the US, such as driving-license renewals and government contracts. In addition, any withdrawal by Safran would be made more difficult by the agreed sale of L-1 assets to BAE, which was already under way. Lastly, a price cut was simply not an option given that L-1 shareholders had already voted in favor of the deal and would be unlikely to accept a lower offer.

The CFIUS eventually gave its approval, subject to Safran accepting certain conditions. These conditions involved the French group spinning off some of the assets it acquired into a separate entity governed by an independent committee known as a proxy board. Safran accepted the remedies and completed the acquisition on 25 July 2011 – 10 months after it was first announced.

The CFIUS has flexed its muscles in recent times on the subject of foreign investment. In 2008 and 2010, the committee blocked several transactions instigated by Huawei in the US on the grounds of the Chinese firm's links to its national government.

8.1.1.2   Sector authorities

In the US, certain sectors have their own regulatory bodies that are required to rule on pertinent M&A transactions. Historically, these bodies were created in sectors that were once monopolies. In the examples to come, we will see some of these authorities at work:

the FCC in telecoms; the FERC in energy; and the PSC in public services.

In November 2008, AT&T announced its intention to buy fellow US telecoms group Centennial Communications for more than $900 million. Centennial operated in the US and, to a lesser extent, in the US Virgin Islands and Puerto Rico. It was Puerto Rico that was the cause of conflict with the FCC. Although Centennial was only the ninth-largest operator in the US, the combination of the two companies would have given the new entity a 40% share of the market in Puerto Rico. However, the real problem from a competition perspective was the relationship between AT&T and América Móvil SAB, the telecoms firm owned by Mexican businessman Carlos Slim. AT&T controlled 23% of América Móvil, and the proposed merger would have created a block controlling 70% of the telecoms market in Puerto Rico.

The FCC eventually approved the takeover of Centennial by AT&T in November 2009 after the buyer agreed to sell off some of its assets in order to avoid anti-competitive scenarios. AT&T got the green light from the FCC only after agreeing to offload its operations in Louisiana and Mississippi to its main rival Verizon Wireless. The FCC also ensured that ties between AT&T and América Móvil would be totally severed and that AT&T was fully committed to maintaining competition in Puerto Rico. The FCC paid a great deal of attention to this deal to ensure that the telecoms sector retained a high level of competition throughout the US.

The biggest concern for the FCC at the time of writing is AT&T's proposed $39-billion takeover of T-Mobile USA, which was announced in March 2011. The deal would create the largest telecoms operator in the US, with nearly 130 million subscribers. In anticipation of the likely obstacles the transaction would face, the parties announced on the day their merger agreement was published that the deal would take at least a year to clear all the administrative hurdles. The FCC approval process will surely be one of the biggest hurdles.

The Federal Energy Regulatory Commission (FERC) plays a similar role to the FCC in the energy sector. However, unlike its telecoms counterpart, the FERC is independent from the US government. We will examine the work of the FERC by looking at the example of Duke Energy's acquisition of Progress Energy.

On January 10, 2011, electricity producers Duke Energy and Progress Energy publicly announced their merger project, which was estimated at $26 billion and would create the largest electricity generation company in the US. The two parties filed their approval request with the FERC in April, and the regulator was charged with ruling on the proposed deal's compliance with the principles of free competition. If the filing is considered to be complete, the Commission generally announces its decision within six months. At the end of August, however, the FERC announced that it was still waiting for the parties to submit certain information and could not begin its investigation, thereby pushing back the decision date. We can see that the FCC and the FERC work similarly in their respective sectors. They are not, however, the only authorities that rule on M&A transactions in the US.

8.1.1.3   PSCs

One of the peculiarities of the US system is the partial decentralization of the M&A control authorities, particularly in the public-services sector. We have seen how the CFIUS, the FCC and FERC operate at federal level, but they are not the only authorities whose approval is needed.

Referring back to the Duke Energy/Progress Energy deal, the two parties required approval from the authorities in the two states where they both had operations: North and South Carolina (Figure 8.2). These authorities are usually known as Public Service Commissions (PSCs) or Utilities Commissions (UCs).

The concerns of some consumer groups and municipalities that are existing clients of one of the parties have a bearing on the consequences of the merger and on the market power of the resulting entity.

There were even more obstacles to the merger between Iberdrola and Energy East. The target company, Energy East, had most of its operations across the north-east of the US, meaning the project required approval from the PSCs in New York, Maine, Connecticut, and Massachusetts. The longest and most difficult process came in New York. The New York PSC eventually authorized the deal, albeit subject to certain conditions, after more than a year of legal and diplomatic struggles. The final decision went as high as the then Senator of New York, Hillary Clinton, following a personal intervention by Spain's ambassador to the US. As we can see, these state commissions also play a key role in the outcome of M&A.

8.1.2   Canada

Prior to the much-publicized attempted C\$39-billion takeover of Canadian firm PotashCorp by Anglo-Australian mining behemoth BHP

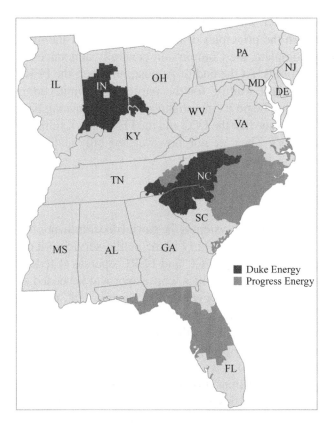

Figure 8.2   Duke Energy and Progress Energy service territories
Source: Company presentation

Billiton, few investors saw Canada as a protectionist country or had heard of the Investment Canada Act. This all changed in November 2010, when BHP withdrew its offer for the potash producer. The Investment Canada Act regulates foreign investment in Canada. Such investment is outlawed unless it brings a "net benefit" to the country.

The particular way in which the deal panned out was very much to the detriment of BHP. First, the Potash board rejected BHP's initial offer of $130 per share, claiming it was too low, and adopted a poison pill while leaving the door open to a higher bid. Many observers at the time thought BHP would have to offer $150 or even $160 per share to make the transaction a success.

At the same time, the provincial government of Saskatchewan (the home of Potash) and the national government of Canada declared that, in accordance with the Investment Canada Act, the transaction would need to result in a net benefit for the country in order to be approved. On September 20, in accordance with the provisions of said act, the Canadian Competition Bureau issued BHP with a request for additional information to help it make its decision. The regulator said it would announce its decision by November 18.

One of the reasons behind the reluctance of the Saskatchewan authorities to authorize the deal was the fear of a direct economic loss for the province. With the Potash headquarters located there, Saskatchewan receives significant amounts in royalties and taxes. On October 13, BHP issued a "Pledge to Saskatchewan," in which it committed to a certain number of practices that would be beneficial to the province. Among other things, BHP promised to keep the headquarters in Saskatchewan, participate in local programs, and buy from local suppliers. The case certainly stirred nationalist and provincial feelings.

On November 3, the Canadian government decided to block the transaction, deeming it to be not in the interests of Canada. Prime Minister Stephen Harper said: "The desire to have a Saskatchewan champion, the largest fertilizer company in the world, became paramount in our thinking." BHP took just 10 of the 30 days afforded it to abandon its takeover bid altogether. The mining group said that, in spite of its huge efforts to comply with the wishes of the Canadian regulators, their conditions had become too expensive and the group would not be submitting an improved offer.

BHP's fate was decided by the political climate in Canada at the time. The provincial government of Saskatchewan had to deal not only with opposition from its own people to the takeover but also with its own disputes with the national government. It was therefore the perfect opportunity to find political motives for opposing the BHP deal.

The example of BHP in Canada provides a nice conclusion to this section on the administrative authorizations needed for the completion of M&A transactions. While some cases appear straightforward, certain situations are particularly tricky and often far removed from mere financial or strategic considerations. As we have seen, the political climate is often a key factor. In 2010, US firm Danaher made a bid for French secure-payment specialist Ingenico. The then French industry minister, Eric Besson, thought it wise to issue a strong statement on Ingenico's strategic interest to France, even going as far as to talk about the government blocking the deal through its stake in Safran, which controlled 22% of Ingenico. As we can see, M&A can really stir patriotic (or maybe protectionist) feelings in national governments. This can present arbitrageurs with some very tricky problems.

8.1.3 Europe

In Europe, on top of supranational laws, each country has its own process for approving M&A transactions. Most countries have a list of "strategic" sectors, in which competent authorities need to give special approval to business combinations.

Traditionally, these strategic sectors include defense, energy, chemicals, infrastructure, and telecoms. Owing to the various authorizations required, the timetable for some deals can be significantly affected. Deals in the banking sector, for example, are among the longest because they tend to require many authorizations from banking regulators in the different countries involved.

In France, a list of strategic sectors was drawn up following PepsiCo's mooted approach for Danone, the biggest French food group. In July 2005, market rumors suggested the US giant wanted to take control of Danone. This prompted French politicians to raise their shields in an attempt to protect one of the crown jewels of French industry. PepsiCo soon announced that it had no intention of buying Danone, but the episode still led to the creation of a list of strategic sectors that would need certain special authorizations. The takeover of chemical company Rhodia by Belgium's Solvay in 2011 had to conform with the new rules given the highly sensitive nature of the target company's activities.

8.2 POLITICAL RISK

The BHP/Potash episode was just one example of the many ways in which political risk can manifest itself. It is one of the hardest risks for arbitrageurs to anticipate and evaluate. We will examine political risk by looking at two examples that had a major impact on the investors involved in the respective transactions.

In December 2009, Tongling Nonferrous Metals and China Railway Construction – both state-owned Chinese companies – announced a joint bid for Canadian firm Corriente Resources, a specialist in extracting copper in Ecuador.

The cash offer of C$8.60 per share valued Corriente at nearly C$650 million, which was a premium of 27% over the target company's average share price during the previous month. In order to be completed, the transaction required some fairly standard criteria to be met: a "yes" vote from 66.7% of target company shareholders; no MACs; and the approval of several government agencies, including the Chinese regulators. Corriente bosses, who controlled around 12% of their company, had already given their backing to the takeover. Deals involving Canadian natural-resource companies and firms from emerging nations are fairly common given the large weighting of the former among listed companies in Canada (despite many of them, including Corriente, not actually having any operations there) and also the desire of developing economies to get a secure supply of strategic natural resources. Buyers often come from China and India, for example.

On March 22, Corriente's shares slumped by more than 12% on the Toronto Stock Exchange, causing the spread to suddenly and considerably widen, as shown in Figure 8.3.

The reason for this was nothing to do with Corriente or even its Chinese suitors. On that day, the Ecuadorian government announced an end to negotiations with the Export-Import Bank of China concerning the financing of a $2-billion hydroelectric power station construction project. The Ecuadorian government cited "mistreatment" and the demand of certain financial guarantees. Investors' unease was heightened when

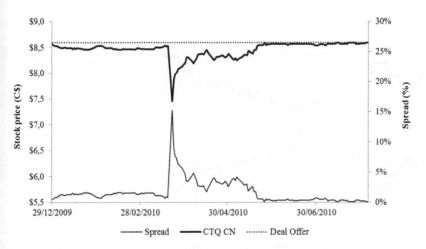

Figure 8.3   Corriente: change in share price and spread
Source: Bloomberg

several Ecuadorian ministers were fired by President Rafael Correa in the days that followed.

Observers felt that the decision by the Ecuadorian government called into question all previous agreements with Chinese companies and could therefore also put a stop to the takeover of Corriente Resources.

The transaction was completed in the end, and the share price once again converged towards the offer price, enabling the most perceptive arbitrageurs to generate healthy returns. As is often the case in these situations, the move by the Ecuadorian government gave it some leverage in the negotiations surrounding the hydroelectric project. It did not, however, have any impact on the Corriente deal.

Our second example took place in the Democratic Republic of Congo. Like the first, it also involved a Canadian-listed target company – mineral-extraction specialist Anvil Mining – and a Chinese buyer, Minmetals. The C$8-per-share offer valued the Canadian firm at close to C$1.5 billion and required approval from the shareholders of the two companies as well as from the competent regulators.

On October 31, 2011, the spread, which had previously been volatile but fairly narrow, suddenly widened and reached 11% (non-annualized). Figure 8.4 shows the share price of Anvil and the spread throughout the transaction:

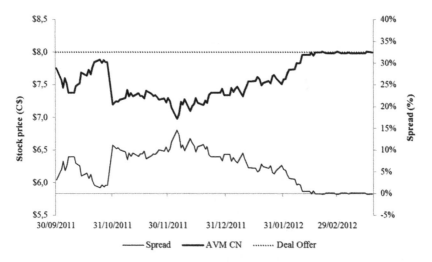

Figure 8.4 Anvil: change in share price and spread
Source: Bloomberg

On October 31, the parties involved received notification from Gécamines, the Congolese owner of a concession operated by an Anvil subsidiary, explaining that it was required to approve the Anvil/ Minmetals deal, and that without said approval, the concession agreements would be violated. Owing to the structure of Gécamines, the final decision rested with the Congolese government. In the eyes of the arbitrageurs, this announcement was a clear indication that the Congolese government wanted to have its say on the transaction rather than simply be affected by it – after all, neither party involved was Congolese. This introduced an additional risk to the transaction.

The spread was very volatile on the back of the announcement, and just to complicate matters further, the Congolese presidential elections were scheduled for the end of November. This meant that, as well as being uncertain, the decision of Gécamines would be significantly delayed. Minmetals was forced to put back the closure of the transaction on several occasions in order to accommodate the various parties involved and ensure that the deal received the multiple authorizations it needed.

The election results were announced on December 16 and an agreement was finally reached a month later. The deal provided for Anvil paying $55 million to Gécamines for concession rights. Now that all authorizations had been received, the transaction could be completed.

These two examples show clearly how political risk can manifest itself and how it can affect M&A and the resulting arbitrages. Several indicators, such as forthcoming elections or an unstable climate, mean that political risk can be anticipated to some degree, but it is hard to evaluate. It also varies according to the country in question and is yet another factor for arbitrageurs to take into account when making their investment decisions.

8.3 NATURAL-DISASTER RISK

By definition, natural-disaster risk is impossible to predict. Having said that, and despite it being statistically unlikely, every arbitrageur must be aware of its existence and potential occurrence. The takeover of Mariner Energy by Apache in spring 2010 is a perfect example.

On April 15, two days after announcing its intention to buy Devon Energy's assets in the Gulf of Mexico, Apache Corporation announced that it had agreed to acquire Mariner Energy for $2.7 billion. The payment for the transaction was structured as 30% cash and 70% Apache shares. The two takeovers would have given Apache a stronger position

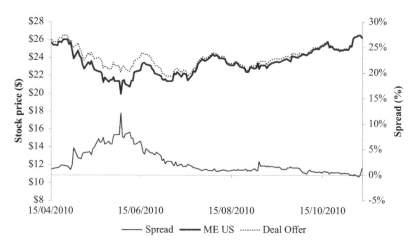

Figure 8.5 Mariner Energy: change in share price, offer value, and spread
Source: Bloomberg

in the deep-water natural gas and oil drilling business in the Gulf of Mexico.

At first, the Apache/Mariner Energy deal looked straightforward, but it turned out to be anything but. The deal was announced just five days before the disaster on the BP oil platform in the Gulf of Mexico, causing the explosion of a well and one of the worst oil spills in US history. The various people involved took several days to estimate the potential impact of the disaster on the transaction, and this can be seen in the delayed reaction of the spread in Figure 8.5. We can also see that it was a very volatile investment for the arbitrageurs involved in the deal.

The non-annualized spread was around 1.2% on the day after the takeover was announced. On June 1 – i.e. six weeks later and after the events in the Gulf of Mexico – it was more than 12%.

Certain sectors are clearly more susceptible than others to accidents or natural disasters that may significantly affect a transaction. The natural-resources and chemicals industries, for example, can be very exposed to such events. Arbitrageurs are clearly unable to predict these events, but they must be aware of their existence and be able to make a quick judgment should they actually occur: (i) the event is serious enough to threaten the completion of the transaction, and I should sell out of my position; or (ii) the transaction is likely to go ahead in spite of the event, and it is therefore a chance to build up my position at a better spread. Figure 8.5 shows very clearly that those arbitrageurs who went with the second judgment for the Apache/Mariner deal were very likely to have made excellent returns out of the unfortunate situation.

8.4   THE RISK OF FRAUD OR FALSE ACCOUNTING

One final, and not insignificant, risk is fraud or false accounting. If fraud or false accounting (even if not intentional) is uncovered during a transaction, the buyer is likely to pull out or at least negotiate a lower price. In most merger agreements, fraud and false accounting constitute MACs and therefore enable the buyer to get out of its obligations.

One particularly noteworthy example from recent times is the aborted sale of Procter & Gamble's Pringles division to Diamond Foods. California-based Diamond Foods specializes in peanut- and other nut-based biscuits and snacks, which are distributed all over the world. In April 2011, the company announced its intention to buy the Pringles division of Procter & Gamble for $2.35 billion. The acquisition was a major part of the California-based firm's growth strategy. It would more than double its turnover and make it the world's largest snacks producer. When the deal was announced, the two companies said they expected it to complete in 2011.

However, in October doubts began to emerge as to the regularity of Diamond Foods' accounts and its ability to carry out the transaction. On November 1, the company announced that the deal, which had been scheduled for completion in December, would instead be finalized in the first half of 2012. The announcement prompted a sharp fall in Diamond Foods' share price, as shown in Figure 8.6.

Given that part of the proposed payment was in Diamond Foods' shares, this fall in the share price also significantly affected the offer price, and Procter & Gamble began to study alternatives, including pulling the plug on the deal.

Once the announcement was made that the closure of the deal had been pushed back, no-one knew what to make of the situation at Diamond Foods. There was strong speculation that the company was a target for short sellers who wanted to capitalize on the downward pressure on its share price.

On February 8, Diamond Foods announced that it would restate its accounts after irregularities were flagged up by an independent committee. It also announced the departure of its chief executive and finance director. The chairman issued the following statement: "After an extensive and thorough investigation, the Audit Committee concluded that the

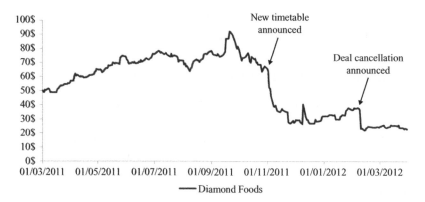

Figure 8.6 Diamond Foods: change in share price between March 2011 and April 2012
Source: Bloomberg

Company's internal controls were inadequate and that certain grower payments for the 2011 and 2010 crops were not accounted for in the correct periods."

The MAC clause in the merger agreement between Diamond Foods and P&G stated not only that any event with a significant impact over more than two financial years constituted an MAC, but also, and more unusually, that "any change in the employment status of Diamond's senior management that is likely to result in a material adverse change on Diamond's future prospects" would also be considered an MAC. Both these criteria were met: the accounting irregularities concerned 2010, 2011 and 2012, and the group's two most senior executives had been fired after the merger announcement.

Two days later, P&G announced its intention to abandon the transaction under the terms of the MAC clause in the merger agreement. The only issue to be resolved was potential penalties, but P&G chose to cancel the deal without seeking damages from Diamond Foods. Less than a week later, on February 15, the owner of the Pringles brand announced its sale to Kellogg's for $2.7 billion, enabling the cereal producer to become the world's second-largest snacks firm, behind PepsiCo.

The accounting irregularities at Diamond Foods not only cost it the Pringles deal with P&G, thereby losing ground in its competition with Kellogg's and others, but also saw more than half wiped off its market value, as shown in Figure 8.6.

Part III
Specific Transactions

The final part of the book focuses on two specific types of transaction: the hostile bid and the leveraged buyout. The various risks covered in Part II are applied to each of these transactions in order to find out more about their specific nature. Chapter 9 on hostile takeovers also covers the various defense mechanisms available to target companies in order to appreciate the tactical side of these transactions. Chapter 10 looks at the specific characteristics of leveraged buyouts and the private-equity industry, with a particular focus on investment situations for arbitrageurs.

9

Hostile Transactions

Although hostile transactions represent only a small proportion of takeover bids, they usually attract the most attention, as demonstrated by the vast amount of commentary recently on the Roche/Illumina, BHP/Potash, and Sanofi/Genzyme deals.

The uncertainties associated with the fate of these transactions (the success or failure of the planned takeover, the final price, the timetable, etc.) make them particularly complex and interesting deals, but also potential sources of huge profits, for arbitrageurs, which is why this chapter is so important.

In order to truly understand how these particular operations work and how they can influence the execution of hostile transactions, we will begin by presenting a general overview of hostile transactions, including the different parties involved and the numerous possible offer strategies. We will then look at the regulatory framework that governs them, which is strict and clearly sets out how the various parties involved should conduct themselves. After that, we will examine the various defense mechanisms available to target companies to counter hostile bids. There are a number of these mechanisms, which may be put in place either before or during the offer. Finally, we will look at how regulation on hostile transactions differs in different countries. These differences have a considerable influence on the execution of hostile transactions.

9.1   A GENERAL OVERVIEW OF HOSTILE TRANSACTIONS

Financial theory (see, e.g. Jensen and Ruback, 1983) teaches us that the financial market acts as a tool to sanction bad company managers. As a company grows in size, there is a risk that the objectives pursued by the shareholders (to maximize the creation of value) and the managers (to keep their jobs) may diverge. Consequently, the possibility of a takeover bid (in which a predator may offer a premium over the company's share price because it believes it can improve the target company's management) disciplines managers by encouraging them to run the company in such a way as to create value for the shareholders, i.e. by taking decisions that are likely to maximize its share price.

Hostile offers should be treated as "role plays" between the different parties concerned. They all begin with the announcement of an unsolicited buyout offer, followed by a dance between the two parties and any other potential buyers. In order to properly understand these situations, an arbitrageur must be able to clearly comprehend the parties' motivations, the "rules of the game" set out by the regulations, and the conduct that the players may adopt.

9.1.1 Profile of the target company

There are two opposing theories on the identification of companies that may be the target of a takeover bid.

The first is the inefficiency theory. This corresponds to the traditional view according to which the companies most likely to be the subject of a takeover bid are those companies whose performance is considerably weaker than that of their main competitors or of the markets. It may be tempting for the board of directors of a company to take an interest in the situation of a rival company whose results are less strong and think that, if it were at the helm, the management team of its company would operate the rival much more efficiently. This approach has much in common with the view of so-called turnaround funds (also sometimes referred to as distress funds), which acquire companies in a delicate operational and/or financial situation and help them to recover before selling them (via a flotation or via a sale to a competitor in the same sector, for example). Such operations have the potential to generate substantial profits.

This first view of the perfect target is also supported by a number of academic articles. Ambrose and Megginson (1992) show that institutional investors are generally present to a lesser extent in the shareholder structure of targets of hostile takeover bids, even well before the bid is announced. This shows that a deterioration in their performance leads institutional investors to abandon such companies. Similarly, certain articles (Hasbourck, 1985; Palepu, 1986) show that strong revenue growth, a high market-to-book ratio, a high level of debt, and a large company size are factors that make it less likely that a company will be the target of a hostile takeover bid. Finally, a comparison (Dahya and Powell, 1998) between friendly and hostile transactions shows that the targets of hostile bids present a higher level of management turnover and a lower level of profitability.

The rival theory, known as the investment opportunities hypothesis, claims that potential targets of hostile bids are simply companies that present interesting possibilities for development for a buyer at a given time, such as synergies or prospects for growth.

Certain academic studies also bear out this theory. Such studies invalidate the first theory by showing that hostile-takeover targets are not significantly different from other companies, and are certainly no less efficient (Schwert, 2000).

It would appear, therefore, that the profile of the targets of hostile takeover bids is not fixed, which is not surprising. Both theories are supported by numerous examples. While it is true that these companies are not the best-performing companies in their respective groups, they are also generally not in distress and at the mercy of an opportunistic buyer. Finally, as most articles mention, it seems that the quality of the company's governance is at least as important as the target company's recent performance.

9.1.2   The different parties involved in hostile offers

One way to approach the world of the "game" of hostile takeover bids is to list the players and their motivations. These transactions cannot simply be summarized as a battle between the buyer and the target company. They can be affected by the interactions between several different types of parties, which are described below.

9.1.2.1   The buyer

The buyer is the starting point for the events thanks to its decision to launch a hostile takeover bid for a given target company. Hostile buyers are often described as opportunists who are hungry for control. The role of the initial buyer is, of course, decisive, since its first offer may serve as a benchmark for other companies that may be interested in the target. We will see later on that there is a wide range of possibilities for the initial buyer with regard to the offer strategy and determining the amount of the consideration.

9.1.2.2   The target company and its constituent parts

This is the other major element of a hostile takeover bid. As we have seen, the target company may or may not be in distress. On the other hand, it will almost always be characterized by attractive assets for one or more potential buyers. These may be physical assets or patents and other intellectual property, for example. In any case, the buyer must be able to find synergies in the target company, as well as under-exploited or poorly exploited assets that could be sold, restructured, or used more efficiently.

A fundamental point for any observer is that the target company may not represent a homogeneous block and can sometimes be subdivided into several groups. There are usually numerous conflicts of interests between the stakeholders of a company. One of these is between the managers and the members of the board of directors. As a general rule, the management team of a company does not remain in place following a buyout, and if it does end up becoming part of the new group, its powers are often very much diminished. Consequently, the managers of a company are naturally often opposed to the buyout of their company. On the other hand, as we will see in more detail later on, the members of a company's board of directors are legally obliged to act in the interests of the company's shareholders and maximize their wealth. A buyout may make it possible to achieve these objectives. We can therefore already see a potential conflict beginning to appear between certain parties within the target company.

Other conflicts of interests also exist, one of which pits the so-called independent members of the board of directors against those affiliated with the management team. This second set of directors must therefore face two opposing forces, in light of the first conflict of interests we mentioned. Another type of conflict can arise between shareholders, depending on the size of their shareholding in the target company. The interests of the majority shareholders may be opposed to those of the minority shareholders, thereby fragmenting the shareholder structure. Some shareholders may also be able to influence the decisions made by the board of directors as a result of share ownership blocks and voting rights.

We can see, therefore, that the target company is not a homogeneous group and that the interests of the different parties that make up the company and the balance of power between them must be taken into account in order to obtain a clear view of the transaction.

9.1.2.3 Other potential buyers

These are investors that are likely to make an offer for the target company but have not yet done so. They can also act as hostile bidders by outbidding the initial buyer's offer. However, they may also act in concert with the target company (i.e. its management team and/or board of directors) in order to enable it to escape the hostile offer. We will discuss the different defense techniques later on, but a friendly buyer that takes total control of the target company is a "white knight" and a friendly buyer that merely acquires a shareholding in the target company that is sufficient to defend it against a hostile offer is a "white squire".

9.1.2.4 Arbitrageurs

Arbitrageurs are the last group that can influence the execution of a hostile offer. In fact, they may even be the most influential group in determining whether such an offer succeeds or fails, as we have seen on several occasions in this book.

Guy Wyser-Pratte, one of the most well-known merger arbitrageurs, describes his colleagues as follows (1982):

> An arbitrageur is not an investor in the formal sense of the word: i.e., he is not normally buying or selling securities because of their investment value. He is, however, committing capital to the "deal" – the merger, tender offer, recapitalization, etc. – rather than to the particular security. He must thus take a position in the deal in such a way that he is at the risk of the deal, and not at the risk of the market.

All these potential parties to the deal may have a significant impact on how the hostile bid develops and whether it succeeds or fails. As an arbitrageur, it is therefore essential to have a good knowledge of the parties involved and to attempt to anticipate their respective conduct.

9.1.3 The offer strategies

For the initiator of a hostile offer, the problem is very simple: how to take control of the target company as quickly as possible in order to minimize both the likelihood of a rival bid and the implementation of defense mechanisms by the target company? The bidder can employ several means of action.

9.1.3.1 Direct purchase on the market

A bidder may simply attempt to buy all the listed shares of the target company directly on the market. In the absence of regulation (on threshold crossings) and defense mechanisms and if all the target company's shares are listed (the floating stock is equal to the number of shares issued), this maneuver would enable the buyer to effectively take control of the target company. This is called a "street sweep".

A buyer may also attempt to take advantage of the confusion and panic that ensue following the failure or withdrawal of a buyout offer in order to enact its own strategy to buy shares in the target company directly on the market. This is called a "drop and sweep".

Another means of attack is the formation of a block of shares (or "toehold"). As a result of the regulation on threshold crossings, this strategy has lost any power to surprise, but it does still indicate the buyer's interest in the company, thereby potentially discouraging other bidders. If a higher rival bid is made, this strategy also enables the unsuccessful bidder to make a profit on its position.

This strategy of buying directly on the market is very rarely used in transactions in which the buyer intends to take total control. It is heavily regulated and may take time, since it is dependent on volumes traded. It is more frequently used to assemble blocks of shares.

9.1.3.2   Tender offer

As we have already seen, this is the principal mechanism used in hostile offers, since it allows the bidder to address the target company's shareholders directly, stating the purchase price, the method of payment, and the duration of the offer.

9.1.3.3   Directly approaching the board of directors

One means of attack is for a buyer to contact the board of directors of the target company directly. If the target company has put anti-takeover defenses in place, it will sometimes be possible for a buyer to negotiate directly with the body responsible for these mechanisms. There are different ways of carrying out this approach, depending on how aggressively the buyer wishes to proceed:

- The "Saturday night special" is a surprise offer made directly to the board of directors that is generally open for a short period of time, and therefore requires a quick response from the target company.
- The "bear hug" is an offer made without a public announcement.
- The "strong bear hug" is an offer made with a public announcement and a call to negotiate.

- The "super-strong bear hug" is an offer that threatens the target company with a drop in price in the event of any opposition or delays.
- Lastly, the "godfather" is a cash offer that is deliberately so high that it is difficult for the target company's board of directors to refuse it.

9.1.3.4 Proxy contest

This approach is usually carried out prior to a shareholders' meeting in order to present a list of candidates for the board of directors who support the buyer and get them elected by assembling the necessary votes. The acquisition may then be carried out if the candidates who support the buyer are elected, since the board of directors will now be in favor of the transaction.

There are two ways of holding the vote: a "proxy contest," which is based on a percentage of the votes cast, and "consent solicitation," which is possible in certain jurisdictions and is based on a percentage of the shares issued. It is more complicated for the buyer to achieve the desired result in the second situation, since many shareholders never vote.

9.1.3.5 Legal battle

The last means of attack for a buyer is to attempt to have a court remove the various defense mechanisms that may be adopted by a target company. Courts are generally opposed to defense measures taken without the shareholders' agreement as expressed in a vote, but it is rare for a buyer to win such a case.

The buyer's choice of means of attack is determined principally by four fundamental factors:

- The attitude of the target company's management team and board of directors: the more they are opposed to the idea of a transaction, the more it will be in the buyer's interest to offer its proposal directly to the shareholders of the target company. That way, it will avoid what would probably be a losing battle against its counterparts within the target company, which would result in considerable delays.
- The distribution of power within the target company: if the shareholder structure of the target company is made up of a number of blocks of majority shareholders only, then the buyer may prefer direct dialogue with these parties. On the other hand, a fragmented shareholder structure made up of a large number of small shareholdings

will be more conducive to the launch of a tender offer addressed to all the shareholders in the same terms.

- The strength of the target company's defenses: the buyer's conduct will vary depending on the nature of the defense mechanisms in place. In the next section, we will look at the different defense mechanisms and the responses they can trigger from the buyer.
- The possible presence of rival buyers: if the target company's managers can call for the assistance of a rival buyer as a white knight, it follows that it is in the bidder's interests to put its offer directly to the target company's shareholders. Similarly, if it is likely that rival offers will be made, the buyer will favor strategies that enable it to take control of the target as quickly as possible, sometimes even if it means paying slightly more.

9.1.4   The matter of price

The framework of game theory enables us to analyze these situations in which several potential buyers compete to buy the target company via offers and counteroffers. Game theory is concerned with the interactions between the players involved in the same situation and their responses to the choices made by the other parties. Its application to hostile offers is direct and prompts such questions as: how much should a potential buyer offer for the target company in order to discourage any competition but without overpaying? And what is a potential buyer's best response to the announcement of a rival offer? The answers to such questions are influenced by the degree of competition and the estimated profits from the transaction.

For strategic buyers, the matter of what price to offer is linked to that of the potential synergies involved. A buyer expecting a high level of synergies with the target company will be tempted to make a substantial offer in an attempt to eliminate the competition. If the level of synergies anticipated is lower, the offer made by the bidder, even if towards the upper end of its range, will be lower, and a buyer expecting more synergies may outbid it. In the vocabulary of game theory, these situations are known as non-cooperative equilibria with deterrence. This concept (Selten, 1975) applies when one of the parties is deterred from acting when faced with a threat from its competitor, even if the threat cannot be realized (which the party does not know *a priori*).

Figures 9.1 and 9.2 show the impact of synergies on the valuation of the group resulting from the merger between the two parties and, therefore, on the price that the buyer will potentially offer for the target

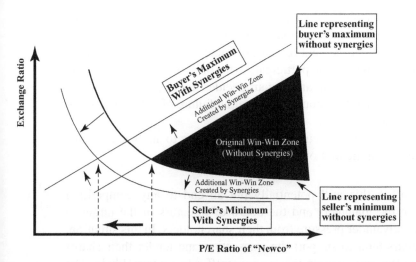

Figure 9.1 Impact of synergies on the maximum and minimum of the transaction
This material is reproduced with permission of John Wiley & Sons, Inc.

company. Figure 9.1 shows the impact that synergies have on the maximum and minimum of the transaction. The dark zone, known as the win–win zone, increases the greater the synergies are.

Figure 9.2 shows the same principle using the DCF approach. The greater the expected synergies, the greater the gap between the buyer's

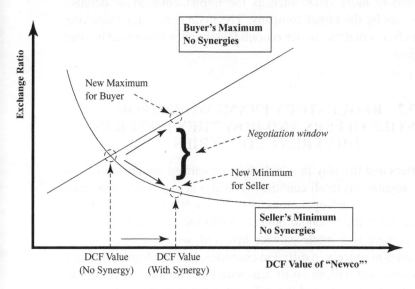

Figure 9.2 Impact of synergies using the DCF approach
This material is reproduced with permission of John Wiley & Sons, Inc.

maximum and the seller's minimum. This means that the greater the synergies, the higher the price the buyer will be prepared to pay.

From an arbitrageur's point of view, the matter of price is very different. The choice is whether to participate in the offer or not, in anticipation of higher rival offers. If an arbitrageur decides not to participate in the offer, he must take into account the potential failure of the offer and the losses that he would suffer.

Once again, the arbitrageur finds himself having to analyze two possible strategies on the part of the bidder:

- A high offer: this will potentially put an end to any competition and force the managers and the board of directors of the target to react quickly under pressure from their shareholders. In this situation, arbitrageurs tend to support the transaction and tender their shares into the offer, anticipating that a counteroffer is not very likely. The main disadvantage to this strategy for the buyer is that, at the end of the day, it does not know whether it could have achieved the same objective with a lower offer. Fear of counteroffers and impatience are the main reasons for launching an offer at a high price.
- A low offer: the bidder takes the risk of facing rival offers, but saves money compared with the high offer. This type of offer often leads to longer transactions than in the case of the above offer and the bidder is exposed to more risks, such as the implementation of defense mechanisms by the target company. The main reason for launching such an offer is that the bidder is confident that it will not face intense competition.

9.2   REGULATORY FRAMEWORKS FOR HOSTILE OFFERS AND HOW THEY DIFFER IN DIFFERENT COUNTRIES

Hostile offers and the way in which they are carried out are subject to very strict regulations in all countries. The aim is to protect companies that are the target of such operations, as well as to allow free competition to thrive between the potential buyers so that the best offer succeeds. This means there is a subtle balance involved, which, as we will see later on, varies massively in different countries. We will look at the case in the US first, and will go on to deal with the situations in European countries after having studied the different defense mechanisms.

We have already seen some of the fundamental rules of takeover bids, which obviously also apply to hostile offers, but there are also certain provisions that concern this type of transaction directly.

Mandatory disclosure of threshold crossings is a very widespread regulatory provision. In the US, the 13-D rule stipulates that all entities must notify the Securities and Exchange Commission of any acquisition of more than 5% of the share capital of the target company within 10 days. These mechanisms help to prevent creeping takeovers and alert the public about the acquisition of blocks of minority shares. They sometimes make it possible to reveal a buyer's intentions prior to an offer aimed at taking total control.

Other provisions concern how the offers are actually carried out. In accordance with the Williams Act, any tender offer, whether hostile or friendly, must be held open for at least 20 days. The act was introduced with a view to preventing quick and hostile takeovers by corporate raiders by giving the target company a certain amount of time to organize its defense. Moreover, a hostile tender offer is automatically extended by 10 days if a rival offer is made. In addition to this, during the first 10 days of a hostile tender offer, shareholders who have tendered their shares into the offer may overturn their decision and call back their shares for any reason whatsoever. This provision gives the target company's shareholders more flexibility with regard to their decision to participate in the offer or not. Lastly, the buyer must honor its obligations pro rata to the shares tendered into the offer, rather than according to the speed with which the shareholders tender their shares. This prevents shareholders from having to rush to tender their shares so as to be guaranteed the possibility to participate in the offer.

Regulations pay particular attention to the role of the members of the board of directors. Although these rules apply to them at all times, they are particularly important if the company is the subject of a hostile approach. In the event of a hostile offer, it is the members of the board of directors who put the company's defense in place, and their conduct often influences the shareholders' response. The two principles governing the conduct of the board of directors as a whole are equality and loyalty towards all the target company's shareholders. The first obligation concerns the disclosure of material information to the public. The assessment of whether or not a piece of information is material is often a source of confusion. However, the managers of a company are generally obliged to inform the board of directors of any hostile approach, and the board of directors must then decide whether or not to disclose it. In a number of cases, a company has failed to disclose such information only for it to be revealed to the public later on, often thanks to rumors. This then frequently gives rise to disputes, whether in court or not, between the different parties within the company (management and board of directors) and the shareholders, who may have wanted the company to be sold. The most recent example of this concerns biotechnology firm Amylin, which received an offer from major pharmaceutical group Bristol-Myers Squibb but did not disclose it. The approach was revealed thanks to rumors on the market, and Carl Icahn, one of the company's leading shareholders, subsequently initiated legal proceedings against it.

Another aspect of the obligations of the board of directors concerns its "Revlon duties." If the board decides that a sale of the company should be initiated in order to maximize the shareholders' wealth, then the sale must take place under the highest offer if several bids are received. This rule was born out of a ruling issued by the Delaware Supreme Court in the *Revlon vs MacAndrews & Forbes Holdings* case in 1986. Corporate raider Ronald Perelman, via his company, Pantry Pride, launched a hostile tender offer with a view to acquiring Revlon, a manufacturer and distributer of cosmetic and dermatological products. However, in order to thwart Perelman, Revlon's board of directors agreed to sell the company to Forstmann & Co. in a private-equity LBO, and put defenses in place against Pantry Pride. The court issued the following ruling:

> However, when Pantry Pride increased its offer to $50 per share, and then to $53, it became apparent to all that the break-up of the company was inevitable. The Revlon board's authorization permitting management to negotiate a merger or buyout with a third party was a recognition that the company was for sale. The duty of the board had thus changed from the preservation of Revlon as a corporate entity to the maximization of the company's value at a sale for the stockholders' benefit. This significantly altered the board's responsibilities under the Unocal standards. It no longer faced threats to corporate policy and effectiveness, or to the stockholders' interests, from a grossly inadequate bid. The whole question of defensive measures became moot. The directors' role changed from defenders of the corporate bastion to auctioneers charged with getting the best price for the stockholders at a sale of the company. [. . .]. The original threat posed by Pantry Pride – the break-up of the company – had become a reality which even the directors embraced. Selective dealing to fend off a hostile but determined bidder was no longer a proper objective. Instead, obtaining the highest price for the benefit of the stockholders should have been the central theme guiding director action.

The court ordered Revlon's board of directors to hold an auction sale of the company. The auction was won by Pantry Pride for a total of $2.3 billion.

As well as ensuring that the highest offer wins the bid, the directors must also ensure that the sale process itself is fair for all the participants.

Finally, in the event of legal proceedings brought against the members of a board of directors by a rejected potential buyer, for example, the onus is on the plaintiff to prove that the board of directors was at fault. In US case law, the doctrine known as the business judgment rule is proof of judges' reticence to interfere in the operational and other decisions of company managers or boards of directors. One of the only ways to win such a case is therefore for a plaintiff to prove that the alleged offenders have acted in breach of their various obligations, such as objectivity and equality of treatment.

All these rules strictly govern the decisions taken by the different parties involved in hostile transactions and, consequently, observers must be familiar with them in order to be able to correctly analyze such situations.

9.3 DEFENSE MECHANISMS

There are several different ways of categorizing the anti-takeover defense mechanisms that a target company can put in place. We are going to look at two different groups: defenses that can be put in place prior to a transaction and those that can be implemented while the offer is being carried out. We should note, however, that all these measures are not necessarily mutually exclusive and it is actually common to combine them. We will see an example of this in the case study at the end of this chapter on the Sanofi/Genzyme deal.

9.3.1 Preventive measures

The goal of preventive measures is to discourage potential buyers from launching an offer. They are therefore not customized to any one buyer in particular. They can have different objectives, such as raising the price to be paid or making the buyout longer and more complicated.

9.3.1.1 *Staggered vs unstaggered boards*

The difference between these two types of boards of directors concerns the frequency with which the members are up for reelection and how many of them are up for reelection at each election. In an unstaggered board, all the directors are elected each year. This means that the board of directors could be fully replaced each year. In a staggered board, only some of the members are up for reelection each year. Typically, the shareholders will vote each year on one-third of the members of the board of directors. Consequently, it will take at least three years to replace the entire board. This provision makes it possible to delay the process whereby a hostile buyer may take control of the board of directors following a proxy fight. It therefore enables the target company to gain some time and to keep its defenses in place for at least two years. The removal of the defense mechanisms can be decided only by a vote by the board of directors.

There is a current school of thought, led by the Harvard Law School Shareholder Rights Project, which seeks to encourage US companies to abandon staggered boards on the grounds that they constitute an obstacle to good corporate governance. The group's main argument is that a staggered board makes a company less attractive to a potential buyer and, consequently, without this possible sanction from the market for the company's managers, it will tend to be managed badly. Under the influence of this group, in the first quarter of 2012, one-third of S&P 500 companies with staggered boards decided to abandon the practice. In conclusion, it should be noted that there are no academic studies that are conclusively in favor of or opposed to staggered boards. Some studies have shown that companies with staggered boards tend to be less highly valued (Bebchuk and Cohen, 2005) and to erode value (Masulis, Wang, and Xie, 2006). Other articles (e.g. Becher, Bates, and Lemmon, 2007), on the contrary, have shown that these companies are no better protected against hostile offers than other companies.

9.3.1.2   Fair-price provision

Fair-price provisions ensure that, when a tender offer is made, all shareholders receive the same consideration in exchange for the shares that they tender into the offer. Such provisions prevent the launch of offers in which the shareholders who are the quickest to decide to tender their shares into the offer receive a predetermined consideration and the others, who are not as quick, receive a lower amount. This type of deal is called a two-tier or freeze-out offer. The buyer's goal is simple: to buy a majority block of shares as quickly as possible and then buy the minority shares at a lower price. However, most companies have now adopted fair-price provisions, rendering this type of offer obsolete.

9.3.1.3   Supermajority provision

Supermajority provisions stipulate that M&A transactions must be approved by a reinforced majority, such as 85% instead of the traditional 51% or 67%. The aim of these provisions is to allow a minority to cause a hostile transaction to fail, thereby giving the minority a decisive power. If the provisions are not sufficient to thwart a hostile offer, they can at least delay it, since a supermajority takes longer to assemble than a simple majority.

9.3.1.4   Dual-class recapitalization

The creation of different classes of shares makes it possible to allocate different voting rights depending on the class in question. For example, let's suppose that 10 voting rights are allocated to class A shares of company X, while class B shares entitle the holder to just one vote. Shares that carry a larger number of voting rights are typically distributed within the company's management team, or even to shareholders that support it. Blocks formed in this way can then counter potentially larger groups that hold fewer voting rights. The allocation of such share classes is often carried out to the detriment of the other shareholders, since they lose the equivalent of the value of the voting rights. They therefore generally receive an exceptional dividend, for example, to compensate for this.

9.3.1.5   Golden parachutes

A golden parachute is a promise to pay considerable sums to the managers of a company in the event that a change of control causes them to lose their jobs. This type of provision does not require a shareholder vote to be approved. On the upside, golden parachutes allow for better retention of a company's key employees and encourage managers to focus on the shareholders' interests. On the other hand, golden parachutes are often thought of as a reward for the mediocrity that led the company to be considered as a potential target. Academic research on the impact of adopting golden parachutes is divided, with regard both to whether or not they create wealth for the shareholders and to whether or not they make a company more attractive as a potential target. It therefore appears to be impossible to draw any conclusions, since the results depend on the research methods used and the periods examined.

9.3.1.6   Employee stock ownership plans

These plans can prove to be a very effective defense mechanism. One possible method is to incorporate the company's pension fund into its share capital in order to form a shareholder block made up of the company's own employees. The employees can therefore participate in the vote like any other shareholder and may be able to thwart a hostile offer.

9.3.1.7   Poison pill

The poison pill is one of the most commonly used and most effective defense mechanisms. Most current US companies have adopted a poison pill. Its basic principle is simple: in the event that a shareholder (the "interested person") takes control of a certain percentage of the company's share capital (the "triggering event"), the other shareholders reserve the right to issue shares at a below-market-value price and subscribe them in order to dilute the position of the aforementioned shareholder. The structure of the offer is such that the latter cannot participate in it.

This defense mechanism can be adopted at any time, whether in anticipation of or during a buyout offer. The poison pill is almost systematically the subject of legal proceedings in the event of a hostile offer. It therefore allows the target company to gain some time. It is not a means of completely thwarting a hostile offer, since it is not effective in the event of a particularly attractive offer. Moreover, since the board of directors has the power to put an end to the mechanism, it gives the bidder all the more incentive to negotiate with the board. In general, a poison pill enables the board of directors to negotiate more advantageous offer terms with the bidder or a rival buyer.

The following example will help us to better understand how the poison pill works. Clorox, the subject of an unsolicited approach by Carl Icahn, used the poison pill in July 2011.

According to the plan, if a shareholder or a group takes control of more than 10% of the share capital, the other Clorox shareholders will be entitled to subscribe preference shares pro rata to the number of shares they hold. The plan states that the other shareholders:

> will be entitled to purchase, at the then-current exercise price, additional shares of common stock having a value of twice the exercise price of the right. In addition, if Clorox is acquired in a merger or other business combination after an unapproved party acquires more than 10 percent of Clorox's common stock, each holder of the right would then be entitled to purchase at the then-current exercise price, shares of the acquiring company's stock, having a value of twice the exercise price of the right.

Consequently, Icahn was unable to acquire more than his existing 9.4% of Clorox's share capital without triggering the implementation of this plan, which would automatically reduce his shareholding.

A variation on the traditional poison pill is the "chewable" poison pill. This consists of a more or less similar mechanism, but also provides for the poison pill to be dissolved when faced with an offer considered to be high enough.

As with golden parachutes, the conclusions of academic research on poison pills are contrasting. While certain articles show that their adoption corresponds to an increase in shareholder wealth, others highlight a lack of impact on the company's share price. Similarly, no link can be established with the company's operational performance. Be that as it may, it appears that such provisions are universally adopted when a company's prospects improve.

9.3.2 Mechanisms adopted during an offer

These mechanisms are generally aimed at an identified buyer and are therefore specific responses. They aim either to thwart the transaction or to delay it for as long as possible.

9.3.2.1 The crown jewel defense

The principle of this defense technique is to sell some of the most attractive assets (the "crown jewels") of a company that is the target of a hostile offer to a friendly third party. Such clauses consequently call the economy of the transaction for the hostile buyer into doubt, therefore leaving said buyer with no option but to retract its offer. However, these provisions are so restrictive for buyers and constitute such a curb on free competition between potential buyers that they are very strictly regulated.

In 1989, Macmillan Publishing Company attempted to prevent its rival, Robert Maxwell, from executing a hostile takeover of it by concluding a friendly deal with Kohlberg Kravis Roberts, with a view to selling four of its divisions to the private-equity firm if the target were acquired by another party. However, Maxwell initiated legal proceedings in an attempt to have the provision repealed and take full control of Macmillan. The Delaware Supreme Court ruled in his favor, stating that the adoption of such a clause by the target company did not constitute an equivalent response to the threat posed by Maxwell, that the price indicated was not fair, and that its implementation would not maximize the shareholders' wealth.

Ever since this episode, the use of crown jewel defenses has practically disappeared as a mechanism commonly used by target companies to defend themselves.

9.3.2.2 Litigation

There are usually a great many reasons why a target company may initiate legal proceedings against a hostile buyer. The two main reasons behind legal action are that it is a way of slowing down the offer process and a way of increasing its cost to the buyer. These effects are even more exaggerated if legal proceedings are brought in multiple jurisdictions. As a general rule, bringing legal action can also force the buyer to reveal more material information than it otherwise would have done and can give the transaction more publicity, which does not work in a hostile buyer's favor. The different reasons for filing a suit can be:

- failure to comply with offer procedures;
- failure to disclose having crossed a threshold exceeding the regulatory level;
- the use of privileged information and/or failure to comply with confidentiality clauses;
- breach of competition regulations.

A traditional response from a buyer is to file its own suit in order to counter the target company's legal action.

The decision by the target company or the buyer to begin legal proceedings is often part of a strategy of negotiation between the parties with a view to arriving at a friendly transaction. Legal proceedings therefore make it possible to push the negotiations, often concerning the price, in one direction or the other.

9.3.2.3   Just say no

The "just say no" defense is an exclusively US mechanism that allows a company to simply refuse a buyout offer. Consequently, it gives boards of directors immense power. We will look at how it works using the example of the deal between Airgas and Air Products.

In February 2010, Air Products launched a hostile takeover bid for Airgas with a control premium of 38%, having already made two unsuccessful confidential approaches in the four previous months. The price of this new cash offer was $60 per share, compared with $60 and then $62 per share for the first two attempts. The company's board of directors rejected all three proposals, claiming that they undervalued Airgas based on its forecast long-term objectives.

The defense mechanisms in place prior to the offer seemed to be robust. Airgas had adopted a poison pill with a threshold of 15% and the company was registered in Delaware (a tiny state with 1 million inhabitants where most listed companies are registered due to its lenient tax rules), which means that the buyer would have to obtain the board's agreement to finalize the transaction. Consequently, if Air Products sought to replace the members of Airgas's board of directors, it could do so only by means of a proxy fight. In May 2010, Air Products proposed that three members of its choice be appointed to the board of directors at the vote held at the annual shareholders' meeting scheduled for August. In July, Air Products raised its offer to $63.50 per share with a view to encouraging as many arbitrageurs as possible to buy shares in Airgas, since they would be inclined to vote in favor of the directors proposed by Air Products in order to ensure the takeover bid would go ahead.

In September, the results of the shareholders' meeting vote were published and the three candidates proposed by Air Products were elected to Airgas's board. The buyer once again increased its offer, to $65.50 per share, a premium of more than 50% over the target company's preannouncement share price. Just like the previous proposals, this new offer was rejected by Airgas's board.

Air Products then wanted to bring forward the 2011 shareholders' meeting, which was initially scheduled for August 2011, to January 2011. There is only one shareholders' meeting per year, but there are no rules on when it must be held. Air Products' objective was to propose new candidates for the board of directors, who, if elected, would enable it to obtain a majority of votes on the board of directors, which could then recommend the offer. The Delaware Court of Chancery ruled in its favor and the date of the forthcoming shareholders' meeting was set for January. However, Airgas appealed against this decision. To everybody's surprise, Airgas won its appeal and the date of the 2011 shareholders' meeting was put back until September.

In December, Air Products made its "best and final" offer, at $70 per share, and requested that the Court of Chancery order Airgas to remove the poison pill and let its shareholders decide on the offer's fate. For Airgas's board of directors, there was no doubt that the offer still underestimated the company's true value, which it put at $78 per share. For Judge Chandler, the question was whether the members of Airgas's board had acted with the interests of the company's shareholders in mind, in an informed manner and in accordance with the various statutory and regulatory provisions.

On February 15, he issued a decision, without further right of appeal:

> as Delaware law currently stands, the answer must be that the power to defeat an inadequate hostile tender offer ultimately lies with the board of directors.

He concluded that the members of the board had reasonably valued Airgas's growth prospects and that the proposal made by Air Products therefore could undervalue the target company. He also concluded that, although most of the target company's shareholders were in favor of the transaction, the vast majority of these shareholders were arbitrageurs who were motivated by short-term gains. Ultimately, he ruled in favor of Airgas and its board of directors, reinforcing the provisions of the just say no defense.

This case demonstrates, on the one hand, the predominant role of the target company's board of directors in M&A transactions in the US, which explains why very few offers remain hostile until their completion. On the other hand, it illustrates the importance of the target company's domicile in such transactions in the US.

9.3.2.4   Countertender offer: Pac-Man

The Pac-Man defense mechanism involves a company that is the target of a hostile offer in turn launching a hostile takeover bid for the initial buyer. This defense technique, which shows the target company's resistance, was used frequently in the 1980s, but has been used very rarely, if at all, since. The disadvantages of this technique are that the target company can come up against all the defense mechanisms that we are currently analyzing and that such transactions can sometimes result in situations that are not very clear.

The best example of this is the attempted hostile takeover of Martin-Marietta by Bendix in 1982, which ultimately resulted in the takeover of the latter by the initial target. When it made its counteroffer, Martin-Marietta appealed to an ally, Allied Corporation, to finance the deal. At the close of the two hostile offers, Martin-Marietta and Bendix both held a controlling majority in their adversary, resulting in a particularly confusing situation when it came to the shareholders' vote. Allied Corporation came to Martin-Marietta's rescue and, via a share swap, took control of Bendix and returned to Martin-Marietta its own shares held by Bendix.

9.3.2.5   Asset restructuring

The target company may dispose of some of its assets in several ways: the flotation of a subsidiary, a sale or a total liquidation. Like the crown jewel defense, these potential changes to the nature of the company can call into doubt the economy of the transaction for the buyer. For example, such transactions can alter the synergies anticipated by the buyer or even destroy certain resources that it had hoped to exploit.

Asset restructurings can also have another consequence: generating cash for the target company, which can then be used to finance other defense mechanisms, such as greenmailing, which we will discuss later on, the distribution of an exceptional dividend, or the purchase of shares.

Buying assets is another way for a company to defend itself, since the purchased assets may make the target company less attractive to the buyer. These strategies may also result in competition issues when used in horizontal hostile takeover bids.

9.3.2.6   White knight and white squire

A "white knight" is a friendly buyer that agrees to purchase the target company in order to thwart the hostile bidder. Traditionally, a white knight agrees not to alter the structure of the target company. The white knight is usually one of the target company's rivals that is attracted by the potential for considerable synergies or by the chance to preserve strategic relations. In the above example of a Pac-Man defense, Allied Corporation coming to the rescue of Martin-Marietta is an example of a white knight.

A "white squire" is very similar to a white knight. The only difference is that the former acquires only a minority stake in the target company to protect it against the unwanted predator, whereas the latter takes a majority interest.

9.3.2.7   *Going-private transaction/LBO*

Another defense method consists of the purchase of the target company by its own management team, which subsequently continues to run it outside of the financial markets. This type of transaction requires the participation of a financial partner, such as a private-equity firm, and the use of large amounts of debt to finance the buyout.

We will examine this type of transaction in more detail in the next chapter, which is entirely dedicated to LBOs. While this strategy was used particularly frequently in the 1980s, its use has since diminished, as strategic buyers are able to justify higher control premiums than private-equity firms thanks to the synergies involved.

9.3.2.8   *Greenmailing*

In greenmailing, a target company facing a hostile offer can buy back blocks of shares purchased by the buyer at a premium over the current share price. It therefore essentially involves the target company paying the buyer in order to put an end to the hostile offer.

This mechanism has frequently led to legal proceedings being brought against target companies that use it, and it is now forbidden in some states in the US. Similarly, certain US companies have included a ban on adopting greenmailing practices in their internal regulations.

9.4   REGULATORY DIFFERENCES IN DIFFERENT COUNTRIES

We have seen how regulation plays an important role in the execution of hostile offers and in how target companies can respond. Consequently, it is only natural that different legislative systems lead to different mechanisms. Having widely explored the situation in the US throughout this chapter, we will now look at the situation in Europe, drawing a distinction between the case in the UK and that of the countries of continental Europe.

9.4.1   The UK

In the UK, the regulations on defense mechanisms are set out in the City Code on Takeovers and Mergers issued by the Takeover Panel. However, the implementation of these measures and the other provisions relating to anti-takeover defenses is also governed by the rules on the conduct of members of company boards of directors.

Pursuant to General Principle 3 of the City Code, the board of directors of a company that is the target of a takeover bid must act in the interests of the company as a whole and must not deny the shareholders the right to judge whether or not a buyout offer is a good one. Consequently, whether the offer is already under way or is expected, the board of directors is not authorized to adopt measures that aim to thwart the offer unless such measures receive the support of the company's shareholders. This is often referred to as the passivity rule.

Article 21.1 of the City Code lists a number of such actions that could hinder the offer process, including the issuance of shares, options or any other security that has a component that can be converted into shares. The text also prohibits the sale of assets of significant value, as well as making contact with strategic partners outside of the company's ordinary activities.

The result of these actions is to dilute a potential buyer's position, like a poison pill, or to make the target company less attractive (by selling strategic assets, for example). Although the article lists a certain number of these actions, it states that members of the board of directors should refrain from taking any action that could impede the proper execution of the offer.

In addition to their duty to remain neutral, the members of the board of directors are subject to a certain number of duties towards the company and its shareholders. They must also facilitate access to and publish all important information relating to the transaction.

The members of the board do have some measures available to them, however. They can attempt to persuade the shareholders that the offer is inadequate and urge them to reject it if they believe that the offer is not appropriate. The directors can also seek strategic partners to buy the company, or white knights. This conduct is not considered unlawful if the members of the board act in the target company's best interests. An alternative technique is to seek white squires, which, unlike white knights, do not take control of the target company, but acquire a stake in its share capital by buying shares on the market or subscribing specially issued shares.

Aware of the massive imbalance between targets and buyers in the latter's favor, in July 2011 the Takeover Panel announced a shake-up of certain mechanisms relating to the execution of takeover bids. This battle to defend UK companies facing hostile takeover bids was launched by Roger Carr, the former chairman of Cadbury, the UK confectionery company acquired by US group Kraft in February 2010. In this case, Cadbury's board of directors had twice rejected a cash-and-share offer made by Kraft, believing both offers to be unacceptable and opportunistic. Five months later, after having lowered the minimum acceptance threshold from 90% of the votes to 50% plus one vote, in accordance with the provisions of UK legislation, more than 70% of Cadbury's shareholders voted in favor of the buyout by Kraft, which was finalized on February 5. During the course of the offer, hedge funds acquired around 31% of Cadbury's share capital (compared with 5% previously), thereby supporting the buyout and prompting Roger Carr's speech in February 2010, after the closing of the offer.

For Mr Carr, changes needed to be made to the takeover bid procedure in the UK so as to better protect the interests of companies facing hostile offers. In his famous speech at Oxford University, he proposed three measures which, in his opinion, would effectively protect the targets of takeover bids and would enable them to resist such bids. Firstly, he proposed lowering the regulatory threshold for disclosing share transactions from 1% to 0.5%. This would enable the parties involved in the offer to be identified directly and publicly. Mr Carr's second proposal was to raise the minimum acceptance threshold for an offer, then fixed at 50% plus one vote. In his speech, he proposed a threshold of 60% of the votes. His final proposition was more specifically aimed at hedge funds, which, in his opinion, had made the buyout of Cadbury possible. He mentioned the possibility of withdrawing the voting rights associated with shares in the target company purchased during the offer period. According to Mr Carr, this proposal would enable only the base of historic shareholders to decide on the transaction's fate. Although it was based largely on his own experience during the buyout of Cadbury by Kraft, Roger Carr's speech did spark a debate on the defense mechanisms available to companies targeted by takeover bids in the UK, a debate that was unquestionably necessary given the massive imbalance between the parties.

The amendments made to the City Code did not incorporate Mr Carr's proposals, but did have the objective of slightly redressing the balance of power between target and buyer. They came into force on September 19,

2011. These provisions stipulate, inter alia, that, during negotiations between potential buyers and the target company, the name of the interested buyer must be revealed, except in certain specific circumstances. Consequently, this mechanism formalizes the buyer's interest very early on and is therefore a much more restrictive measure than the previous provision. On the one hand, the potential buyer must face the market's reaction to the transaction, which can be seen through the performance of its share price. The measure also accelerates the timetable of the deal. Under the previous regulations, the interested entity could contact the potential target confidentially and ask that this contact remain private, thereby gaining access to the company's documents. This stage did not involve any notion of time, and target companies were therefore at the mercy of the potential buyers' will. The principle of revealing the buyer's identity therefore makes it possible to correct part of the imbalance of power between the parties.

The second provision of this principle stipulates that, by the 28th day after its identification at the latest, the buyer must choose either to announce its firm intention to make an offer or to withdraw ("put up or shut up"). However, the buyer is exempted from this obligation if the Panel grants it an extension for whatever reason. This acceleration of the offer timetable also makes it possible to put an end to the vast freedom previously granted to the buyer. Lastly, the text reaffirms the prohibition on any type of break-up fee or reverse break-up fee arrangement, which constitutes the third amendment.

To finish off this section, we shall have a look at Table 9.1 on the next page, which gives an overview of the various regulatory thresholds.

9.4.2 Continental Europe

While the balance leans towards target companies in the US and towards buyers in the UK, the balance of power is more or less even in the countries of continental Europe, balancing shareholder defense mechanisms with movements to take control of a company.

There is a wide range of defense mechanisms that a target company can put in place, either before or during a hostile offer. One of the fundamental principles is that of giving the shareholders' meeting responsibility for adopting defense measures during the course of an offer. There is, however, an exception to this principle of neutrality on the part of the management and directorial bodies of the target company during an offer: the reciprocity clause. This may be invoked if the buyer fails

Table 9.1 Overview of the various regulatory thresholds

Regulator	Threshold for launching a mandatory takeover bid	Minimum scope of the takeover bid	Option to impose conditions on the takeover bid	Squeeze-out possible	Defense measures must be authorized by the shareholders' meeting during the takeover bid...	... even if the buyer is not subject to the same restriction
Takeover Panel	30% of the voting rights. Increase of stake between 30% and 50%	100% of the share capital and all securities convertible into or exchangeable for shares	Approval of the regulatory body mandatory for all conditions	Yes, if the offer secures more than 90% of the shares	Yes	Yes

to comply with the principle of neutrality or implements "equivalent measures" to those adopted by the target company. The problem with applying this principle lies in assessing the equivalence of the measures. The fact remains that, in the event that the reciprocity clause is applied, the managers and directorial bodies of the target company regain their prerogatives with regard to the adoption of anti-takeover measures.

Table 9.2 provides a summary of the measures that we have just looked at, as well as some of the advantages and disadvantages of each measure.

Finally, Table 9.3 summarizes the details of the procedure, for different countries, in the event that a buyer is obliged to launch a takeover

Table 9.2 Overview of defense mechanisms

Measure	Advantages	Disadvantages
Measures involving the search for alternative solutions to the offer		
Search for a counteroffer	Probable failure if the initial buyer does not outbid Positive impact of the communication on the target company's share price More room for maneuver for the managers Immediate maximization of value	Limitation on information that can be transmitted to potential partners Partial or total loss of autonomy for the group
Counteroffer for the buyer (Pac-Man)	The offer will be thwarted if the timetables coincide Development of an alternative business plan to that of the buyer	Requires shareholders' meeting vote Gives credibility to the buyer's strategic position Focuses the debate on management issues
Measures likely to increase the cost of the offer		
Issuance of share subscription warrants by way of defense	No shareholders' meeting vote necessary if an issue has been authorized within the 18 months prior to the offer Dilution of the buyer's position to the benefit of the current shareholders Increase in the board's negotiating power	Can be used without authorization from the shareholders' meeting during an offer only if the reciprocity clause is applied

(continued)

Table 9.2   (*Continued*)

Measure	Advantages	Disadvantages
Measures likely to change the essence of the target company		
Spin-off/disposal of significant assets	Substantial change that could result in the withdrawal of the offer Possibility to transfer the proceeds of the disposal in the form of an exceptional dividend	Extra time needed for the transaction to be executed Requires a shareholders' meeting vote
Acquisition of significant assets/exit of minority shareholders from certain subsidiaries	Substantial change that could result in the withdrawal of the offer Possibility of anti-trust problems for the buyer Increase in the cost of the offer at the least	Extra time needed for the transaction to be executed Requires a shareholders' meeting vote
Measures aimed at securing the loyalty of the target company's shareholders		
Payment of an exceptional dividend during the offer	Allows for debate on the future expansion of the distribution policy Attracts attention to the quality of the buyer Creates confusion over the cash component offered	Automatic adjustment of the offer price generally planned by the buyer Lack of impact unless the amount is high and substantially changes the target company Requires a shareholders' meeting vote
Payment of an exceptional dividend in the event that the offer fails	Loyalty dividend, encourages shareholders not to accept the offer	Does not directly thwart the offer Requires a shareholders' meeting vote
Statutory amendments (increase in dividend, etc.)	Secures the loyalty of the target company's shareholders	Requires a shareholders' meeting vote More of a preventive measure than a defense during an offer
Buyback of shares with a view to cancellation	Increase in earnings per share Attracts attention to the quality of the buyer's shares Creates confusion over the cash component offered	Reduction in the cost of the offer to the buyer Requires a shareholders' meeting vote
Capital increase	Increase in the cost to the buyer	Requires a shareholders' meeting vote

Table 9.3 Summary of hostile takeover procedure

Country	Regulator	Threshold for launching a mandatory takeover bid	Minimum scope of the takeover bid	Option to impose conditions on the takeover bid	Squeeze-out possible	Defense measures must be authorized by the shareholders' meeting during the takeover bid . . .	. . . even if the buyer is not subject to the same restriction
Germany	BAFin	30% of the voting rights	100% of the shares	Success threshold, shareholders' meeting, antitrust, none if the offer is mandatory	Yes, if more than 95% of the voting shares	No	No
Belgium	CBFA	30% of the voting rights	100% of the shares	Success threshold, shareholders' meeting, antitrust	Yes, if more than 95% of the voting shares	Yes	Yes
Spain	CNMV	30% and 50% of the voting rights, or less if right to appoint more than 50% of the directors in the following 24 months. 5% between 30% and 50%	100% of the shares	Success threshold, antitrust	Yes, if more than 90% of the voting rights	Yes	No

(continued)

Table 9.3 (*Continued*)

Country	Regulator	Threshold for launching a mandatory takeover bid	Minimum scope of the takeover bid	Option to impose conditions on the takeover bid	Squeeze-out possible	Defense measures must be authorized by the shareholders' meeting during the takeover bid . . .	. . . even if the buyer is not subject to the same restriction
France	AMF	30% of the share capital or voting rights, 2%/year between 30% and 50% of the share capital or voting rights	100% of the share capital or of securities giving access to the share capital	Success thresholds, antitrust, shareholders' meeting (if share issue), none if offer mandatory	Yes, if more than 95% of the share capital and voting rights	Yes	No
Italy	CONSOB	30% of the share capital, 3% per year between 30% and 50%	100% of the voting shares	Antitrust, thresholds	Yes, if more than 95% of the share capital and voting rights	Yes	No
Netherlands	AFM	30% of the voting rights	100%	Thresholds	Yes, if more than 95%	Yes	Yes
Switzerland	COPA	33.3% of the voting rights	100% of the share capital	Threshold, antitrust, MAC clause	Yes, if more than 98% of the voting rights	Yes	Yes

bid after having crossed a certain threshold. We are presenting these details at the same time, since they are very similar in all the countries of continental Europe.

CASE STUDY: The Sanofi/Genzyme Deal

Background

In May 2010, the chairman of Genzyme, Henri Termeer (aged 64), found himself in a delicate situation: his company was bogged down in a viral-contamination problem at its Allston plant and was unable to restart production, its share price (which had reached $83 in August 2008) had fallen to $47, Carl Icahn[1] was carrying out a proxy fight and demanding a seat on the board of directors, and on May 23 he received a phone call from Chris Viehbacher, chairman of Sanofi, asking him to think about a possible transaction.

Henri Termeer founded Genzyme in 1983 with a simple idea: to develop medicines to treat orphan diseases, extremely rare diseases that were of no interest to any of the major pharmaceutical companies. From this crazy gamble, selling extremely expensive (but reimbursable) treatments to several thousand patients, Mr Termeer created a group with more than 12,000 employees and turnover of $4.5 billion.

At the same time, the strategic position of Sanofi-Aventis could be described as worrying. Like all major global pharmaceutical groups, the French firm was facing a threat from the expiration of patents for its bestselling drugs (Plavix, Taxotere, Stilnox), since the arrival of generic versions of these products would cost it 20% of its turnover by 2013. Filling this "gap" would not be easy, since the group had not yet recovered from the failure of its latest two blockbusters: anti-obesity pill Acomplia, which was withdrawn from the market in 2008 after one year because it was leading to suicides; and Multaq (a heart medication), which had its authorization reevaluated after some cases of liver damage came to light. However, behind this economic phenomenon was a much deeper movement, characterized by two major trends: the end of large mass medications and the explosion of demand in emerging countries. As a result, like all its competitors, Sanofi turned its back on its strategy of specialization and vertical integration via research in order to diversify its activities.

It was against this background that the new CEO arrived. Chris Viehbacher, a German-Canadian, came from UK pharmaceutical group GSK with a two-pronged plan of attack: to cut costs and to make acquisitions (which became possible thanks to the group's access to cheap, abundant finance). The business model of the major pharmaceutical companies was evolving: from now on, the model would not be to find new products (a risky, expensive gamble), but to develop and distribute products produced by independent research firms, which soon run into problems due to the growing costs involved in testing thousands of patients. A form of implicit agreement came into being between these firms and the major pharmaceutical groups: the former would do the research, while the latter would take care of the marketing. Essentially, faced with the forthcoming expiration of their patents, the giants of the pharmaceutical sector looked instead to buy ready-made research.

How the Transaction Unfolded

On June 9, 2010, Genzyme announced that it had reached an agreement with Carl Icahn and granted him two seats on the board of directors. During the week of June 28, Chris Viehbacher called Henri Termeer again to reiterate Sanofi's interest in Genzyme and suggest that they meet at an industry conference in mid-July that both chairmen were scheduled to attend. On July 2, market rumors circulated that Sanofi was preparing a deal worth "around $20 billion" in the US. At that point, Henri Termeer asked his advisory banks (Goldman Sachs and Credit Suisse) to study the different options available to Genzyme in the event of an attempted buyout by Sanofi. The banks presented their conclusions at a strategic committee meeting on July 9: bearing in mind the difficulties facing Genzyme and its depressed share price, it was not the right time to sell. On July 10, Henri Termeer called Chris Viehbacher to explain the company's position and decline the invitation. On July 23, news agency Bloomberg and the *Wall Street Journal* both revealed that Sanofi had approached Genzyme informally about a takeover bid. On July 29, Chris Viehbacher called Henri Termeer to inform him that a bear hug letter was being sent containing a buyout proposal. Below are several extracts from the letter:

> [. . .] Genzyme has historically been a true success story in biotech, and the company has become the world leader in providing novel treatments for genetic diseases. In addition, the company built a positive reputation within the scientific community and developed strong relationships with patient advocacy groups, physicians, patients and the broader healthcare community. However, the company now faces a number of significant and well-documented challenges that were discussed thoroughly during this year's proxy campaign. An acquisition by Sanofi-Aventis would not only position the company to overcome these challenges quickly and successfully by applying Sanofi-Aventis' global resources and expertise to help realize and accelerate Genzyme's business strategy, but also deliver near-term compelling value to your shareholders that takes into account the company's future upside potential. [. . .]
>
> Substantial premium: We are prepared to pay $69 for each of the issued and out-standing common shares of Genzyme. This is a premium of 38.4% over the share price as of July 1, 2010, the day prior to press speculation regarding Sanofi-Aventis' potential acquisition plans for a large US biotech company. It also represents a premium of 30.9% over the one month historical average share price through

July 22, 2010, the day prior to press speculation that Sanofi-Aventis had made an approach to acquire Genzyme. [. . .]

In addition to these compelling reasons, we believe there are many others that demonstrate why Sanofi-Aventis is the right partner for Genzyme. Sanofi-Aventis has significant expertise executing and integrating transactions, and a strong track record creating value through those transactions by enhancing their performance through leveraging Sanofi-Aventis' capabilities. Sanofi-Aventis has demonstrated that it is a good corporate partner by enabling its affiliates to maintain their distinctive culture and focus on their core strengths. Sanofi-Aventis is strong financially with a market capitalization of approximately $77 billion, revenue of approximately $38 billion and EBITDA of approximately $16 billion. From Sanofi-Aventis' perspective, the proposed transaction would provide a new sustainable growth platform. [. . .]

On August 11, Genzyme sent a reply to Sanofi:

Dear Chris,

As I promised in my August 2 letter, the Genzyme Board of Directors reviewed your unsolicited, non-binding $69.00 per share proposal to acquire Genzyme. With the assistance of our financial and legal advisors, the Board unanimously rejected your offer. Without exception, each member of the Genzyme Board believes that this is not the right time to sell the Company because your opportunistic takeover proposal does not begin to recognize the significant process underway to rectify our manufacturing challenges or the potential for our new product pipeline.

We recognize that Genzyme's share price has been depressed as a result of manufacturing setbacks the Company experienced last year. In reaching a decision to reject your offer, the Board not only reviewed the timeline and remaining steps necessary to address the manufacturing challenges, but also the potential of our new product pipeline, in particular the outlook for our MS treatment Alemtuzumab. We are confident that these factors coupled with our newly announced discipline for deploying capital and significant opportunity to reduce costs will soon be recognized by investors.

The Board is resolute about maximizing Genzyme's future value for our share-holders.

Sincerely,
Henri Termeer

On August 29, Sanofi sent a second letter to Genzyme, reiterating its $69-per-share offer and this time making it public:

We are disappointed that you rejected our proposal on August 11 without dis-cussing its substance with us. [. . .] As I have mentioned to you, we are committed to a transaction with Genzyme, and, therefore, we feel we are left with no choice but to take our compelling proposal directly to your shareholders by making its terms public. [. . .]

It is our preference to work together with you and the Genzyme Board to reach a mutually agreeable transaction. As we have consistently stated, we place value on the ability to engage in a constructive dialogue and to conclude a successful outcome that would ensure a timely and smooth integration.

The same day, in a press release, Genzyme announced that it had received this offer letter and reiterated its board's opposition to the offer.

On September 16, Chris Viehbacher called Henri Termeer and suggested that they meet. His invitation was accepted.

The meeting took place on September 20. Below is a summary of the meeting, as written up by Genzyme's lawyers:

The meeting between Mr Termeer and Mr Viehbacher took place on September 20, 2010, and included Mr Wirth and Sanofi's Chief Financial Officer, Jérôme Contamine. During the meeting, Mr Viehbacher focused his remarks on elaborating on his previously expressed position that the unaffected Share price of the Company prior to rumors of Sanofi's interest in acquiring the Company fairly reflected the Company's prospects and the risks inherent in its recovery from the manufacturing interruption at its Allston Landing biologics manufacturing facility, requested that Mr Termeer provide a price range at which a deal could be consummated, and proposed that the parties agree to a price range of from $69.00 per Share to $80.00 per Share. Mr Termeer, consistent with the Strategic Planning Committee's instructions and the Company Board's position with respect to Sanofi's proposal, declined to agree to Mr Viehbacher's proposed price range of $69.00 per Share to $80.00 per Share or to suggest any other price range, but he discussed at length the intrinsic value of the Company, reiterated the Company Board's unanimous view that $69.00 per Share was an inappropriate price at which to commence negotiations or diligence and encouraged Mr Viehbacher to demonstrate his commitment to acquiring the Company by raising his offer to a price that would more fairly reflect the Company's intrinsic value and persuade the Company Board to enter into discussions with Sanofi. In the course of the discussion, Mr Viehbacher also noted that as a result of his discussions with shareholders of the Company, he believed a transaction between Sanofi and the Company was of interest to the Company's shareholders but avoided any statement that the Company's shareholders had any interest in such a transaction at a price of $69.00 per Share. Mr Viehbacher further indicated that Sanofi was potentially willing to raise its proposed per Share consideration from $69.00 per Share, but not until he was provided by the Company with a range at which the Company believed a deal could be consummated. Mr Termeer, consistent with the Company Board's direction, again declined to discuss any particular price range, and instead focused his remarks on the intrinsic value of the Company, the progress the Company was making in recovering from its manufacturing interruption and resupplying the market for Cerezyme and Fabrazyme, the potential recovery in the Company's financial results expected during 2011 that was not yet fully reflected in market expectations and the substantial commercial potential of alemtuzumab in MS. Throughout the meeting, Mr Viehbacher stated that his proposed price range of $69.00 per Share to $80.00 per Share was manageable, but that, based on his current understanding, he could not get to $80.00 per Share. At the end of the meeting, Mr Viehbacher noted that he believed Sanofi had three options: (1) to walk away from a possible deal with the Company, which

Mr Viehbacher indicated was an unacceptable option in light of the value of the transaction to Sanofi and the substantial time he had put into the proposed deal; (2) to try to engage further with the Company and the Company Board, which seemed difficult in light of the Company's position; or (3) to launch a public tender offer. Mr Viehbacher indicated at that time that he was of the view that Sanofi had no choice but to commence a tender offer.

On October 4, Sanofi launched a takeover bid for Genzyme at a price of $69 per share, which was once again rejected by Genzyme's board as inadequate.

On November 8, the tension was mounting and Sanofi sent another letter asking Genzyme not to put any poison pill measures in place and to let the shareholders decide whether or not the takeover bid was suitable.

On December 14, Sanofi extended its takeover bid until January 21, 2011.

In mid-December, rumors began to surface that an offer containing a CVR was being considered.

On January 12, 2011, certain articles in the press claimed that progress had been made in the negotiations. The following day, the transaction was approved by the European competition authorities.

On February 16, an agreement was signed between the parties: Sanofi increased its offer to $74 per share, plus a CVR entitling shareholders to payments of up to $14 per share depending on the achievement of certain objectives (detailed in Figure CS9.1), particularly with regard to the level of sales of Lemtrada.

Genzyme's Defense

Genzyme considered several anti-takeover defense mechanisms:

Legal defense: adoption of a poison pill

Genzyme is registered in Massachusetts, and is therefore subject to the regulations of that state. The state's regulations are more favorable than those of Delaware towards target companies and have, since 1990, obliged companies to have a staggered board (a board of directors in which one or more members, usually one-third, are up for reelection each year, on a rotating basis). This

	Production Milestone	Approval Milestone	Sales Milestone #1	Sales Milestone #2	Sales Milestone #3	Sales Milestone #4
Cash Payments	$1.00 per CVR	$1.00 per CVR	$2.00 per CVR	$3.00 per CVR	$4.00 per CVR	$3.00 per CVR
Triggers	Paid if specified Cerezyme®/ Fabrazyme® Production levels are met in 2011	Paid upon final FDA approval of Lemtrada™ for multiple sclerosis (MS) indication	Paid if Lemtrada™ net sales post launch exceed an aggregate of $400m within four specified quarters per territory	Paid if and when Lemtrada™ global net sales exceed $1,800m	Paid if and when Lemtrada™ global net sales exceed $2,300m	Paid if and when Lemtrada™ global net sales exceed $2,800m
Estimated Timing of Potential Payments	Jan 2012	~H2 2012	~2014	2014-2020	2015-2020	2016-2020

Figure CS9.1 CVR objectives and consideration description
Source: Company presentation

mechanism forces a buyer to wait for two years and two board elections to be able to take control of a company's board of directors. However, in 2006, Genzyme – under pressure from its shareholders – destaggered its board, switching to a system under which all the directors were up for reelection each year. Moreover, Genzyme let a poison pill expire in 2009 and did not opt for the Massachusetts control share acquisition statute.

Of course, all its defense mechanisms could be reactivated, and Sanofi warned Genzyme to think carefully about this via a letter dated November 8, 2010:

> You have expressed publicly (and, we understand, directly during your conversations with Genzyme shareholders) that you are committed to maximizing shareholder returns and that you value shareholders' voices. However, we note certain comments in your Schedule 14D-9 that appear to be inconsistent with that objective.
>
> First, you indicated that you believe that the Genzyme Board can, at any time, opt to immediately stagger the terms of its members, extending the terms of two-thirds of Genzyme's current directors for an additional one to three years. This action would deprive shareholders of the opportunity to elect the full Genzyme Board at the 2011 annual meeting of shareholders, a right they expressly demanded. As you know, in 2006, holders of more than 85% of the outstanding shares of Genzyme common stock voted to approve an amendment to Genzyme's Articles of Organization to provide that all directors would be elected annually. Given this, we do not believe that it would be appropriate for the Genzyme Board to disenfranchise shareholders by unilaterally staggering the terms of directors.
>
> Second, you stated that the Genzyme Board retains the ability to adopt a "poison pill". As you are well aware, if adopted, the poison pill would prevent Sanofi-Aventis from acquiring Genzyme, regardless of your shareholders' support for a transaction.
>
> Third, you indicated that the Genzyme Board may wield the Massachusetts anti-takeover statutes in a manner that would, as a practical matter, prevent Sanofi-Aventis from acquiring Genzyme without the cooperation of Genzyme's Board, notwithstanding your shareholders' support of a transaction.
>
> We believe it would be inappropriate for the Board to take these defensive actions. If we are unable to have a direct dialog with you, in all fairness you should allow your shareholders the opportunity to decide for themselves whether or not to accept our proposal.
>
> Your shareholders should know with certainty that you will not interfere with their right to benefit from our offer by taking any of the actions described above. Therefore, we ask that you take action to make the Massachusetts anti-takeover statute inapplicable to our offer and confirm that Genzyme's 2011 annual meeting of shareholders, including the election of all directors, will be held on schedule on the fourth Thursday of May (May 26, 2011), as provided in your Bylaws.
>
> It remains our preference to work together with you to reach a mutually agreeable transaction. We continue to believe that a transaction is in the best interests of the shareholders of both Genzyme and Sanofi-Aventis, and we look forward to hearing from you.

White knight

One possible defense mechanism for Genzyme was, naturally, to find another buyer prepared to launch a takeover bid at a higher price. Letting Sanofi think that other buyers could enter the race would also be a good way for Genzyme to put pressure on Sanofi to improve its offer, since Sanofi did not want to "outbid itself", as Chris Viehbacher put it.

Throughout the course of the process, several names were mentioned, including Johnson & Johnson, Glaxo and, more specifically, in November, Japanese firm Takeda (which allegedly offered $82 per share), but the value of the transaction ($20 billion), Genzyme's situation (the company was operating under a consent decree from the FDA), and the timetables of the various potential buyers (Pfizer was in the process of acquiring Wyeth, Roche was already present in the sector via Genentech, Novartis was busy with Alcon, etc.) limited the intensity of the competition over the deal, and in the end no white knight appeared.

Stand-alone or just say no strategy

The main defense strategy for Genzyme was probably to convince its shareholders that it was not the right time to sell the company, that Sanofi's offer underestimated the intrinsic value of the company's assets, that the manufacturing problem would soon improve, and that, in the medium term, its shares could trade at higher than the proposed price of $69. After all, Genzyme's shares had been trading at around $83 in August 2008. The stand-alone strategy was also put in place via legal defense mechanisms (see above) in agreement with the shareholders.

Remember that, under US law, the board of directors has a sovereign power to assess the offer price and may therefore consider the offer to be inadequate, even if a majority of shareholders tender their shares into an unsolicited takeover bid (see the Agrium/CF Industries and Air Products/Airgas precedents).

The implementation of this strategy was to come up against several obstacles:

- The presence of activists within the shareholder structure and on the board of directors. Carl Icahn and Relational Investors bought their shares at around $55 per share and around $60 per share respectively. They would obviously be receptive to a cash offer involving a significant premium over their share purchase price, rather than waiting several years for a complicated and unpredictable recovery.
- The portion of the share capital held by arbitrage funds would continue to increase, particularly once the offer was formally submitted by Sanofi (some funds still doubted Sanofi's determination prior to the launch of the offer). These funds were naturally looking for a short-term return and were not long-term shareholders. Their investment theory was that Sanofi and Genzyme (for different reasons) both needed the deal and that the parties would ultimately

reach an agreement on a higher price. The stand-alone strategy – which assumes a withdrawal by Sanofi – would obviously involve a sharp fall in Genzyme's share price, which would be catastrophic for the arbitrage funds.
- Genzyme's historic shareholders (mutual funds such as Fidelity and Invesco), which could on the face of it have supported the management in its desire to remain independent, were obviously put off by two factors: (1) the management's errors in handling the Allston plant contamination crisis (the managers failed to realize the seriousness of the events and did not take corrective decisions quickly enough) and the subsequent FDA investigation and steep fines accepted in November 2010; and (2) the publication of the company's quarterly results, in which it lowered its forecasts. It was probably at that moment that the historic shareholders "broke away from" Henri Termeer and sent him the message that the stand-alone strategy no longer had their support.

Price improvement strategy

Since no defense mechanism really enabled Genzyme to retain its independence and no white knight had appeared on the horizon, it was up to the board of directors to negotiate the best possible deal with Sanofi. Trying to find a transaction price was not easy due to the different viewpoints of a major pharmaceutical group and a biotech firm in 2010. To give an exaggerated description of the situation, we could say that the shareholders of a major pharmaceutical group had a rather "prudent" or even pessimistic view of the future (expiration of patents, increased competition from generics, not many pipeline projects, an end to reimbursement of the cost of some medications, etc.), which explains the fairly modest P/E ratios and generous dividends of such companies. The shareholders of biotech firms, on the other hand, generally had a fairly optimistic view of their company's prospects, since these companies tended to have a vast potential for growth and a large number of pipeline projects, and "saw a rosy future," which explains their very high P/E ratios and lack of dividends. Reaching an agreement on price between a buyer that was pessimistic (but rich and with access to almost unlimited and very cheap finance) and a target company that was optimistic (but operating under a consent decree and with a founder on the brink of retirement!) would not be easy. The solution came through the use of a CVR, enabling the parties to share the risk regarding the prospects of Lemtrada (a medication for multiple sclerosis): Genzyme saw potential for peak sales of $3.5 billion, while Sanofi (and most analysts) put the figure closer to $700 million.

Epilogue

As a matter of interest, the code names used in the deal (known as "Grand Cru") were "Petrus" for Sanofi and "Margaux" for Genzyme.

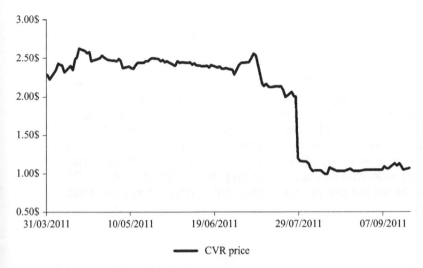

Figure CS9.2   Change in the CVR price and impact of the first default
Source: Bloomberg

Figure CS9.3   Genzyme: change in share price and spread
Source: Bloomberg

When the transaction was announced, Chris Viehbacher promised that, if Sanofi had to make all the CVR payments, he would personally deliver the last cheque to Henri Termeer along with a bottle of his favorite wine.

However, on July 28, 2011, Sanofi announced that the first CVR payment, of $1 per share, would probably not take place due to Genzyme's production delay. This failure to make the first payment, considered to be the most secure, resulted in a fall of more than 40% in the CVR price. Figure CS9.2 shows the change in the CVR price and the impact of the first default. It looks like the objectives set were rather aggressive, and the chances of Henri Termeer enjoying a bottle of his favorite wine were very slim. Figure CS9.3 presents the evolution of the spread. It significantly widened in the wake of Genzyme putting in place its defenses. The spread was turned negative after Sanofi increased its offer and then converged towards zero.

Note

1   Carl Icahn is a US investor who repeatedly features in the Forbes list of the world's wealthiest individuals and specializes in shareholder activism, i.e. acquiring significant shareholdings with a view to influencing a company's strategy. He is known for his decisive role in a number of M&A transactions, such as those involving RJR Nabisco, TWA, Texaco, and, more recently, Motorola Mobility and Yahoo! (without success).

10

Leveraged Buyouts

The number of leveraged buyouts (LBOs) has grown sharply over several years, earning them a key role in the M&A market. They are therefore now a common investment scenario in M&A arbitrage strategies. Just like M&A, LBOs are cyclical by nature, with their reliance on debt making them even more sensitive to market conditions. Figures 10.1 and 10.2 show the change in LBO volumes and the amount of funds raised in recent years.

In the first part of this chapter, we will look at the main characteristics of LBOs, and then we will shift our focus to how these operations affect the arbitrage process.

10.1   MAIN CHARACTERISTICS OF LBOs

10.1.1   Principles

An LBO can be defined as the purchase of a company, financed partly by debt, within a tax-efficient and specific legal framework where the managers of the company form a partnership with specialist professional investors.

Several investors buy a company using an ad hoc holding vehicle, which borrows as much as the target company's self-financing capability will allow and is capitalized by the buyers in the amount of the balance of the acquisition price (financial leverage).

In France, the new group – comprising the parent company and the target firm – can benefit from fiscal consolidation, enabling it to reduce its tax base by the amount of interest on the acquisition debt (fiscal leverage).

The implementation of a specific governance structure separates power and equity in the LBO holding company and provides a hierarchy for the financial interests and respective powers of the different investors: management, sponsors, and creditors (legal leverage). Figure 10.3 shows the different relationships between the parties involved in an LBO transaction.

Figure 10.1   LBO volumes (billions of dollars)
Source: Thomson Financial

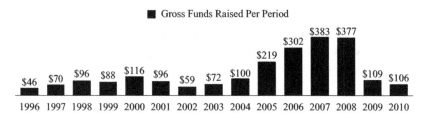

Figure 10.2   Funds raised (billions of dollars)
Source: Thomson Financial

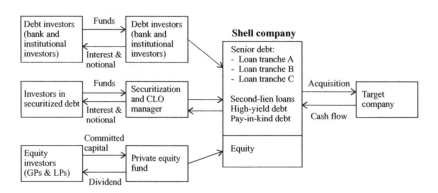

Figure 10.3   Typical structure of an LBO operation

The final stage of the operation involves merging the shell company with the target firm.

Management teams are often investors in LBOs. They run operations at the target company and usually play a part by contributing capital. Implementing a management package dependent on the capital gain made by the private-equity firm aligns the interests of the parties and gives the managers an incentive to carry out their business plan (managerial leverage).

There are several types of LBO, which vary according to the level of involvement of the target company's management. If the operation is carried out with the support of the management, it is known as a management buyout (MBO). Where the investment fund brings managers from outside the target company, it is a management buy-in (MBI). Finally, the operation is known as an owner buyout (OBO) where the target company's majority shareholder squeezes out the minority interests.

Private-equity firms historically generate healthy returns, and several reasons have been suggested as to why these firms are able to run certain companies better than their management teams or other corporate-finance organizations:

- The benefits of debt: the amount of money borrowed makes the management teams more disciplined. They know that, in order to perform and achieve the goals set by their sponsors, particularly in relation to paying off the debt, they must keep a tight rein on costs and spending. Debt is also beneficial from a fiscal perspective because the interest can be deducted from taxable income, enabling firms to improve their cash flow.
- Managerial leverage, which we will come back to later in the chapter.
- The perfect alignment between the control of companies and their shareholder structure. The funds do not only take ownership of the companies; they control them, take part in decision making and closely monitor performance. For example, KKR partners have historically sat on the boards of directors of the companies in which they have invested, representing a huge shift from the passive approach of many board members.
- Less regulation and the long-term outlook: delisting companies enables private-equity firms to avoid many obligations in relation to shareholder disclosure. There are drawbacks, however, in that access to the debt markets is no longer possible and there is no analyst coverage. It should be stressed, though, that these are secondary

considerations for the funds. Operating away from the stock market also removes some of the pressure of meeting stated financial objectives and allows companies to have a long-term operational outlook.

10.1.2   The different parties

10.1.2.1   The target company

As the guiding principle of an LBO is to finance a large part of the acquisition price through debt, it is essential that the target company has a healthy and constant cash flow. The other investment criteria that buyers generally look for are:

- A growing or mature sector that can guarantee healthy demand throughout the operation and therefore consistent financial results with a view to paying off the debt.
- A strong market position, meaning that the company has a well-established brand, strong commercial ties with its partners, and high-quality goods or services.
- Significant entry barriers, which result not only from the profile of the sector but also the strength of the company's brand, etc. Such entry barriers also guarantee a certain stability and predictability with regard to future cash flow and revenues.
- Little or no risk of disruptive innovation.
- A high-quality management team that is committed to such a transaction.
- The scope for improving profits.
- Transformation of EBITDA into free cash flow (i.e. low capital expenditure and working capital; ideally, the latter will be negative like it is in the retail sector).

10.1.2.2   The investment funds

The shareholders of the holding company that contribute capital to the operation tend to be specialist private-equity investors. They can also take on other guises, such as divisions of investment banks (although this trend is changing rapidly at the moment) or hedge funds. These funds raise money (commitment) from investors (mainly pension funds, insurance firms, funds of funds and family offices) by promising them attractive returns in exchange for their money being tied up for a certain period, generally 10–12 years.

The funds buy (during the investment period, usually lasting four or five years) and then sell (during the divestment period, lasting a similar amount of time) companies with the aim of generating a capital gain. This gain comes from:

- The recourse to leverage (let us say that a company generating $100 million of free cash flow each year is bought for $1 billion in year n, using $500 million of debt and $500 million of equity. If the company is able to pay off $100 million of the debt each year, and if the fund sells the company in $n + 5$ at the purchase price, the return on equity is 15% per year).
- Improved market conditions, which may lead to a higher valuation multiple.
- Increased profits at the target company and more organic growth.
- More external growth (build-up).

The investment teams in the private-equity firms make their money from management fees (2% per year) and carried interest, i.e. part of the capital gain realized by the investors if a minimum return is achieved (hurdle rate, generally around 8% per year). The investment team usually buys access to parts of the carried interest for around 1% of the fund's value.

Private-equity firms are all different. It is possible, however, to categorize them based on several distinctive criteria:

- The size of the operation: there are small-cap funds (operations below €100 million), mid-cap funds (operations between €100 million and €1 billion), and large-cap funds (operations above €1 billion). The size of the operation is directly linked to the size of the fund: a fund with €500 million of assets under management generally invests equity of €50 million (10% of the fund), making the operation worth between €100 million and €200 million.
- The geographical area of investment, which is outlined in the fund prospectus. Many funds are pan-European or global.
- Sector specialization: some firms specialize in certain sectors where they have built up expertise, e.g. technology/telecoms (Apax), property (Colony), retail (Lion Capital), and infrastructure (Macquarie).

Some firms agree to invest in turnarounds or restructuring scenarios, or perhaps in operations requiring new management (management buy-ins). Other firms stick to less risky operations. The November 2005 buy-out of Converteam (formerly Alstom Power Conversion, an engineering firm specializing in the design and installation of systems for converting electrical energy into mechanical energy) from Alstom by Barclays Private Equity may have appeared risky because the target firm was making operating losses. In 2007, Converteam bought Minneapolis-based Electric Machinery. This acquisition enabled the firm to consolidate its presence in North America. In September 2008, Converteam opened its capital to new investors, prompting Barclays' stake to be diluted at the expense of LBO France. In 2010, Converteam turned over $1.5 billion and generated EBITDA of $239 million. The investors sold their controlling interest to General Electric in March 2011 for $3.2 billion, generating one of the biggest capital gains in the history of French LBOs.

10.1.2.3   The banks

The banks play a crucial role in LBOs because they put up most of the investment. On a secondary level, they also advise during M&A transactions. Most banks have therefore developed specialist LBO financing services. In major LBOs, the banks syndicate financing, meaning that they sell or transfer part of the loan that they have underwritten to a group of lenders (generally other banks). This enables banks to reduce their exposure and, therefore, risk.

The loan is usually split between:

- Senior debt, which is paid back first and benefits from sureties (pledging of securities, certain assets, etc.). It represents around 40% of the purchase price and is divided into two tranches: tranche A, which amortizes over six or seven years; and tranche B, which is paid off over up to seven years. This senior debt is underwritten by the arranging banks on the basis of a loan agreement that contains the principal covenants (clauses limiting investments or dividend payments, minimum credit ratios: debt/EBITDA, EBITDA/interest expense, etc.).
- Subordinated debt, which is paid back after the senior debt. This can be either mezzanine debt or high-yield debt placed on the bond markets. Companies such as Europcar, Rexel, Pages Jaunes, and Picard Surgelés have had recourse to this type of high-yield debt.

10.1.2.4   The management

The managers of the target company play a key role in the operation because they are responsible for the day-to-day running of the company throughout the LBO (the private-equity firms can play their part as shareholders by deciding on the overall strategic direction, but they are not entitled to manage the company; if they did, they would be liable as de facto managers should the company fold). An LBO is often a chance for the management team to be true entrepreneurs and make money out of the management package.

LBOs resolve agency conflicts between shareholders and managers (i.e. potential differences in opinion) by aligning their interests:

- The stick is the significant amount of debt that needs to be paid off in regular installments.
- The carrot is the management package, which enables managers to take part of the capital gain realized by the private-equity firm.

The details of how a management package is implemented go beyond the remit of this book. Essentially, managers are offered stock purchase warrants as a way of gradually owning more of the company depending on the private-equity firm's total return on investment. The private-equity firm agrees to award part of its capital gain to the managers if the operation goes better than expected.

10.1.3   Exit opportunities

Opportunities to get out of the investment can also impact the buyout. The main focus of the private-equity firm, i.e. the return on investment, may depend on the investment exit conditions (generally after two to five years). The exit may be carried out by an IPO or the sale of the company to an industrial player or another private-equity firm. Sometimes, sponsors make a loss-making exit through the bankruptcy of the company. If the target company is no longer generating sufficient cash flows for the parent company to service its debt, and the shareholders cannot agree on a rescue plan, bankruptcy is the only option.

The different exit options depend not only on the actions of the LBO fund, which may or may not have improved the performance of the target company, but also on market conditions at the time of the exit.

10.2   A BRIEF HISTORY OF PRIVATE EQUITY

The history of M&A in the US is generally divided into six waves, running from the end of the nineteenth century to the present day, with each one founded on the new regulations that arose from the previous wave. We discussed these waves in Chapter 1. The explosion of private-equity transactions corresponds with the sixth and final wave, which began in 2004 and ended with the financial crisis in 2008. Before we look at the details, let us first examine why private equity emerged and how it changed in the run-up to this sixth wave.

10.2.1   Emergence and growth of private equity

The origins of private equity date back to a practice implemented by Jerome Kohlberg and his cousins Henry Kravis and Georges Roberts at their then employer, the investment bank Bear Stearns. Over several years, the three bankers developed what at the time was a highly prized method of transferring the ownership of companies. The targets were companies that were too small to be listed on the stock exchange and whose founders were looking for a way out but did not want to sell up to rivals. Federal tax laws rendered it particularly unappealing to transfer ownership of a company from one generation to the next.

In 1965, Kohlberg organized the buyout of dental-equipment supplier Stern Metals for $9.5 million. A group of investors paid $500,000 to enter the share capital, and the remaining money came from bank loans. The founding Stern family held on to a majority stake and retained operational control of the company. Four years later, the family sold its stake during a capital increase, making a profit of $4 million. In Kohlberg's eyes, these operations allowed the founders to get some money back on their initial investment while introducing new investors to help the company grow under the existing management. The practice proved so profitable that the three cousins set about developing it rapidly within Bear Sterns.

At the start of the 1970s, they added another type of transaction to their repertoire. Many conglomerates were formed during previous M&A waves, but their results were much worse than their rivals. The new trend for these groups involved splitting them into several independent, better-performing divisions. Kohlberg and his cousins used exactly the same approach for these groups as they had for small companies, putting together ad hoc groups of investors in order to buy parts of the group and financing most of the operation with debt.

In 1976, the three cousins attempted to develop their methods within Bear Sterns in order to operate on a larger scale. The bank refused, prompting the trio to set up KKR. Two years later, KKR finished raising $38 million for its first ever fund. The first large-scale LBO was carried out in 1982. Legend has it that the group of investors involved put up only $1 million of the $80 million needed to buy greetings-card manufacturer Gibson Greetings. Just 16 months later, the company completed a $330-million IPO.

The first private-equity boom took place in the 1980s, with more than 2,000 LBOs taking place over the course of the decade. As they relied extensively on debt for their transactions, private-equity firms quickly developed a need for major financing to support their growth. Michael Milken and his bank Drexel Burnham Lambert attempted to fill the void. For around a decade, as there was no other source of financing, attempts had been made – in vain – to develop the junk bond market, which at the time was restricted to small issuers or unrated companies. From 1980 onwards, LBOs grew in size, thanks partly to the financing offered by Mr Milken and his bank, and private equity took off concurrently with the junk bond market.

The 1980s was also the period in which the biggest private-equity names that we know today were founded: Bain Capital (founded by, among others, Mitt Romney) in 1984; Hellman & Friedman also in 1984; Blackstone in 1985; and Carlyle in 1987.

The standout deal of the era came just before the credit markets imploded and the savings and loans crisis of 1989. Valued at more than $31 billion (including debt), the takeover of RJR Nabisco by KKR remained the largest ever LBO for several years. The deal made an even bigger impact on market operators because KKR's offer came out of a battle of bids (and egos) between the private-equity firm and a group of investors led by Ross Johnson, the chief executive of the target company. The crisis took hold soon after, putting a temporary stop to LBOs. However, the RJR Nabisco/KKR episode was not finished. With the company taking on massive debts during its buyout, it ran into trouble and KKR, having already registered big losses, was forced to invest another $1 billion.

10.2.2 The explosion of private equity

The private-equity explosion took place during the sixth M&A wave, starting in 2003. Between 2004 and 2007, private equity represented around 20% of all M&A in the US, conducting deals worth more than $1,000 billion. The industry was able to dominate because of the extremely favorable lending conditions at the time in the wake of the Federal Reserve's decision to lower interest rates after 9/11.

Nine of the 10 biggest ever LBOs were announced and finalized in 2006 and 2007. The three largest were: TXU by KKR, TPG, and Goldman Sachs for $44 billion; Equity Office by Blackstone for $38 billion; and hospital operator HCA by KKR, Bain Capital, and Merrill Lynch for $33 billion.

As these examples show, this new era was marked by greater collaboration between private-equity firms for the major deals – a direct consequence of the fallout of KKR's purchase of RJR. Another notable transaction in this period was the buyout of SunGard, a company specializing in software and IT services. It was a game-changing deal for private equity for two reasons. First, it was one of the first ever LBOs of a technology company. The $11.5-billion deal for SunGard saw seven private-equity firms form a consortium: Silver Lake Partners, Bain Capital, Blackstone Group, Goldman Sachs Capital Partners, Kohlberg Kravis Roberts & Co., Providence Equity Partners, and Texas Pacific Group (TPG). As it was a first for the industry, SunGard's legal advisers, Sherman & Sterling, expressed doubts as to the buyers' ability to finance the transaction. Consequently, the financing condition was withdrawn from the agreement, to the significant benefit of the target company. In order to re-establish some balance, the buyers inserted a $300-million reverse termination fee clause into the buyout agreement, enabling them to pull out of the deal for whatever reason. This was an historic first for private equity and for LBOs. As we have seen earlier in the book, reverse termination fees were subsequently used widely and are still a key part of merger agreements today.

However, the reliance on debt that brought about the heyday of private equity with the accommodating interest rate policy of the Fed came back to bite the industry when lending conditions deteriorated in the summer of 2007. This marked the end not only of the sixth wave of M&A but also of private equity's dominance of these transactions.

10.3   HOW LBOs AFFECT ARBITRAGE

LBOs raise specific issues for arbitrageurs:

10.3.1   The reasons for the transaction

Unlike a merger between two companies, LBOs are motivated by the search not for synergies but for a financial return, albeit by way of an intelligent structure. In other words, LBOs are on much less solid grounds than strategic operations. If, for example, economic and market conditions worsen significantly, most strategic operators adopt a long-term outlook and reiterate their desire to press ahead with the acquisition. The synergies will still be there and the good strategic reasons for the deal (economies of scale, more market power, etc.) have essentially not changed. Faced with the same situation, however, a private-equity firm will almost certainly pull out of a deal. It will do so either reluctantly, because it cannot secure financing from the banks, or deliberately, because the transaction will no longer deliver the hoped-for returns and thus no longer adheres to the firm's criteria. This is why LBOs are far more dangerous for arbitrageurs than strategic deals and require very close attention. As LBOs are, by nature, more risky, the spreads involved are generally wider.

10.3.2   Financing

Without going over our analysis of financing risk from Chapter 5, the main criteria for analyzing the financing of an LBO are:

- How aggressive the financial package is: the higher the debt (and therefore the lower the equity), the more the risks are borne by the banks and therefore the more likely the lenders are to pull out if there is a problem. The structure of the financing (debt tranches, rates, covenants, etc.) and the presence of a bridge loan are key factors to take into consideration.
- How committed the lending banks and sponsor are: is there a lending condition (yes, generally), and at what stage is the process: comfort letter, underwriting, pricing, marketing, syndication, etc.
- The solidity of the banking pool and the reputation of the private-equity firm.

10.3.3   Competition risk

This is generally minimal unless the private-equity firm already has a stake in the same sector and plans to group together its operations. Private-equity firms sometimes look to consolidate or add to the activities of companies in their portfolio, with new acquisitions often their preferred method. Competition risk manifests itself, therefore, only when the fund already has a company operating in the same sector in its portfolio.

10.3.4   Agreement terminology and the use of reverse termination fees

We have already examined legal risks in Chapter 8. With regard to LBOs, special attention should be paid to the drafting of MAC clauses (often used to renegotiate a deal), reverse termination fee clauses (the amount and the language used), which render many LBOs in the US purely optional for buyers, and "go-shop" clauses (which raise hopes of a counter-bid, perhaps from an industry operator looking for synergies and able to offer more money).

Some operations introduce unprecedented terms. In 2005, private-equity firms TPG Capital and Warbug Pincus agreed a modified reverse termination fee with their target company, Neiman Marcus. There was a low amount, in the event that the transaction was cancelled because of a lack of financing, and a higher amount if the buyers pulled out for whatever reason.

This reverse termination fee structure brought a huge element of choice to LBOs for private-equity firms. When we looked at MAC clauses, we saw how some funds tried to use these clauses to cancel deals.

10.3.5   Management and a potential conflict of interests

Let us consider a public-to-private transaction involving a listed company. A private-equity firm partnered with the management of the target company offers cash to this company's shareholders to buy them out. In this type of transaction, there is a potential conflict of interests for the management of the target company because it is involved in the LBO, so it must choose whether to defend the interests of its current shareholders or its new partners. This raises questions about the offer price (is it as high as it could be, and has the sale process been competitive enough), the legal conditions of the agreement (scope of MAC clauses, language used for the matching rights, etc.), and the possibility of a counterbid (a rival getting access to information).

This situation is dealt with very differently in the US and France:

- In the US, these "take private" transactions take on a very particular structure that attempts to limit conflicts of interest. This happens through: (i) the creation of an independent committee of directors that is separate from the management and charged with conducting the sale process and ensuring it is fair. The committee can appoint its own legal and financial advisers; and (ii) the shareholder approval thresholds at the target company being based on "the majority of the minority," i.e. completing a transaction requires a majority of votes from minority shareholders.

- In France, on the other hand, regulation issued by the AMF is a lot more flexible, and some deals have hit the headlines:
  - Apax's investment in GFI was based on a fairly "curious" package that was not beneficial to minority shareholders;
  - Cinven's attempt to buy Sperian Protection involved a cash offer of €70 per share, which represented extremely low valuation multiples and yet received the backing of major shareholders and the management. Honeywell then came in with a bid of €117 per share, demonstrating clearly that the sale process had been biased towards the LBO funds and to the detriment of shareholders.

CASE STUDY: LBO as an Arbitrage Opportunity: Del Monte Foods

Background

The takeover of Del Monte Foods by a private-equity consortium comprising KKR, Centerview, and Vestar Capital, which was announced at the end of November 2010, remains to this day one of the biggest post-crisis LBOs.

Del Monte Foods is a US food production and distribution group based in San Francisco. The group has two major product lines: canned fruit and vegetables (its tinned tomatoes and pineapple rings are particularly well known) and pet food. After selling its RJR Nabisco division to private investors in 1989, the group underwent several changes to arrive at its structure before the transaction in November 2010. In 1997, Del Monte appointed Richard Wolford as CEO – a man who had worked in the food industry and then in venture capital at TPG Capital, the firm with which he took control of the San Francisco-based group. He successfully managed Del Monte's IPO and then oversaw the acquisition of several brands from Heinz in 2002. This all-share deal, with an estimated value of almost $2 billion, enabled Del Monte to treble its size and gave Heinz shareholders a stake of around 75% in Del Monte. In 2006, Del Monte became the second-largest pet food firm in the US on the back of several acquisitions. The last of these deals saw the group buy Pets at Home from Bridgepoint Capital in 2010. Richard Wolford had therefore transformed Del Monte into a major player in the US food market, with a portfolio of well-known brands and a distribution network comprising the largest chains in the country.

The buyout by the private-equity consortium was announced on November 25, 2010, with the offer of $19 per share amounting to a total of more than $3.7 billion. Taking into account the 45-day go-shop period, during which Del Monte could solicit rival bids, and the time needed for the vote of the target

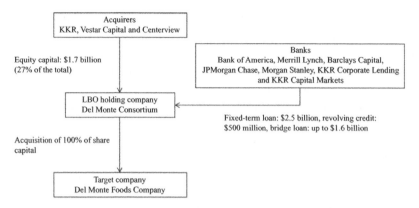

Figure CS10.1   Structure of the operation

company's shareholders and getting competition approval in the US (under the HSR Act) and China (from MOFCOM), the parties expected the deal to be completed in the first quarter of 2011.

Del Monte was the ideal target for an LBO. With its recognizable brands, the company generated significant annual cash flows and operated in the fast-growing pet food market (63 million US households have a pet; there are an estimated 90 million cats and 73 million dogs). The ability of the target company to provide large dividends to the holding company is crucial to the structure of an LBO. This is because it is the holding company that takes on the debt, and the dividends it receives must enable it to pay this debt off. Figure CS10.1 shows how the operation was structured as well as the different players involved. Figure CS10.2 shows the evolution of the spread. We can see that buyout rumors two days before the official announcement sent the stock price higher, materializing over half of the bid premium.

Bid Timetable

Del Monte received an initial approach from one private-equity firm in January 2010. In response, the target company contacted five potential private-equity buyers to ascertain whether they would be interested in making a move. During preliminary discussions, KKR declared its interest and that it may submit a joint bid with Centerview. At the same time, Vestar and a strategic buyer also informed Del Monte that they were potential buyers.

In March, the five private-equity firms submitted preliminary offers to Del Monte, but the US group said it was not interested in a sale. KKR and Centerview kick-started the process in October by making another offer. Del Monte rejected the bid but this time announced that it would continue negotiations. The two firms then had yet another offer rejected in the following month, but Del Monte authorized them to conduct due diligence and add Vestar to the consortium.

On November 24, the three private-equity firms announced their final bid of $19 per share, which was accepted by the Del Monte board and recommended to shareholders.

Financing

The financing of the transaction was split into two parts. Each of the sponsors undertook to put up shares in an equity commitment letter. This combined contribution came to nearly $1.7 billion.

The second part of the financing came from bank debt. The sponsors secured a $3-billion loan, comprising $2.5 billion of senior debt and $500 million of revolving credit. There was also an unsecured bridge loan of up to $1.6 billion. The lending banks were: JPMorgan, Barclays Capital, Morgan Stanley, Bank of America, Merrill Lynch, KKR Corporate Lending, and KKR Capital Markets.

Their obligations were subject to a clause, which read as follows:

The obligations of the lenders to provide debt financing under the debt commitment letter are subject to a number of conditions, including, without limitation: (i) a condition that, since May 2, 2010, there shall not have been any change, event, occurrence or effect which has had or would reasonably be expected to have a material adverse effect (defined in the debt commitment letter in a manner substantially the same as the definition of "material adverse effect" in the merger agreement, which is described under "The Merger Agreement – Representations and Warranties" beginning on page 68); (ii) negotiation, execution and delivery of definitive documentation with respect to the appropriate loan documents consistent with the debt commitment letter and specified documentation standards; (iii) the accuracy of certain specified representations and warranties; (iv) receipt of equity financing consistent with the equity commitment letters (which to the extent constituting other than common equity interests shall be on terms and conditions and pursuant to documentation reasonably satisfactory to the lead arrangers of the debt financing to the extent material to the interests of the lenders thereunder); (v) consummation of the merger in accordance with the merger agreement (without giving effect to any modifications, amendments or express waivers to the merger agreement that are materially adverse to the lenders under the debt financing without the reasonable consent of the lead arrangers of the financing) substantially concurrently with the initial funding of the debt facilities; (vi) delivery of certain customary closing documents (including, among others, a customary solvency certificate), specified items of collateral and certain Company financial statements; (vii) payment of applicable costs, fees and expenses; and (viii) with respect to the bridge facility, (x) receipt of a customary offering memorandum with respect to the senior unsecured notes offering, and (y) expiration of a 20 calendar day marketing period following the delivery of such offering memorandum. The final termination date for the debt commitment letter is the same as the termination date under the merger agreement.

Merger Agreement Clauses

Under the terms of the merger agreement between the two parties, Del Monte would have to pay a break-up fee of $60 million if it found another buyer during the go-shop period. In all other situations (e.g. if the shareholders voted against the operation), the target company would have to compensate the buyers to the tune of $120 million. KKR would have to pay Del Monte a reverse termination fee of $249 million if it backed out of the deal.

The go-shop period ended on January 8, 2011, with Del Monte not receiving an alternative offer. The consortium of KKR, Centerview and Vestar was therefore the only option, and the closure of the deal was confirmed for the first quarter of 2011.

Shareholder Vote

There were no barriers to this transaction in the form of competition authorizations. Getting such approval was a formality given the extremely competitive nature of the food industry and the fact that the buyers' portfolios had little in the way of food sector assets. The deal did not require approval from the European Commission because it was not a concentration under EU law. As the parties had expected, the Chinese competition authorities approved the transaction at the end of January. The only real problem was the vote by Del Monte shareholders.

The deal needed approval from the majority of these shareholders in order to be completed. The vote was initially scheduled for February 15, but a judge at the Chancery Court in Delaware – the state with jurisdiction over the merger agreement and where Del Monte is based – postponed it by 20 days until March 7.

As we have seen throughout this book, a delay in the vote or in any other event required for the completion of an M&A transaction is a massive risk for arbitrageurs. It tends to be a negative sign for the parties involved and always has a major impact on the returns that can be generated.

In order to understand why the Delaware judge intervened, we need to look at the role of Barclays.

The Controversial Role of Barclays Capital

Barclays Capital had its fingers in more than one pie in this transaction. Not only was the bank advising Del Monte on the sale, it was also one of the lenders. The Delaware judge made his decision based on the inappropriate conduct of Barclays (and KKR, as we will see) in performing these two roles.

The ruling raised the specter of the 1989 buyout of publisher Macmillan by its management and KKR, which was blocked by the Delaware Supreme

Court. At the time, judges ruled that the private-equity firm and the management of the target company had manipulated the bidding process behind the board's back with a view to strengthening their position and delisting the company.

The facts raised by the judge in the Del Monte case were eerily similar. He ruled that KKR and Barclays had manipulated the sale process in order to secure nearly $24 million in additional fees.

The judge found that Barclays initially suggested a sale of Del Monte in January 2010 and put forward a certain number of private-equity firms as potential buyers. As a long-standing client of the bank, KKR was naturally on this list. Barclays therefore used its ties with the parties to advise the target company and one of the buyers, while also participating in the financing of the deal without these parties being informed. Such behavior brings to mind the controversial practice of staple financing, whereby the bank advising the seller offers financing for the deal to the various buyers. In such a way, the financing agreement is directly "stapled" to the merger agreement. Banks clearly have a conflict of interests in these situations. It was also Barclays that added Vestar to the consortium, despite Vestar and KKR having signed confidentiality agreements with the bank preventing them from teaming up without Del Monte's approval. We can safely assume that the collusion between the potential buyers (a nightmare for any investment banker trying to increase the offer price in a bidding process) reduced the competitive intensity of the process and therefore the final offer price put to shareholders.

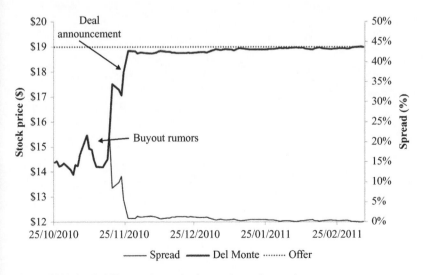

Figure CS10.2   Del Monte: change in share price and spread

The judge said:

Although Barclays' activities and nondisclosures in early 2010 are troubling, what indisputably crossed the line was the surreptitious and unauthorized pairing of Vestar with K.K.R. In doing so, Barclays materially reduced the prospect of price competition for Del Monte.

The judge postponed the shareholder vote and nullified the $120-million reverse termination fee. He refused to block the deal because he felt it was not right to leave the Del Monte shareholders without an offer. On March 7, 2011, the shareholders voted almost unanimously (99%) in favor of the transaction, meaning the deal could be completed.

On October 7, 2011, more than six months after the transaction was completed, Del Monte and Barclays announced their intention to pay nearly $90 million to investors that had shares in Del Monte when the deal closed. This payment of around $0.30 per share enabled the two groups to settle lawsuits connected to the role Barclays had played in the transaction and to allegations that Del Monte shareholders had not been paid enough in the buyout. In their press releases that followed the announcement, Del Monte and Barclays denied any wrongdoing.

Conclusion

As we have seen throughout the book, arbitrageurs must be multi-skilled individuals. When evaluating an M&A transaction, there are so many things to take into consideration: the financial scale of the deal, of course, but also legal, fiscal, accounting, industrial, and strategic aspects.

Arbitrageurs must always be up to speed with the latest changes in M&A practice, regulatory developments, and the strategies used by the various new entrants to the market such as buyers from emerging nations, sovereign wealth funds, or private-equity firms.

There is no substitute for the practice and experience that an arbitrageur accumulates over time. There are, however, indicators that show up transactions with risks that we have not studied in great detail.

As the market is generally fairly efficient, the safest deals from an objective viewpoint are also those with the narrowest spreads. Conversely, deals entailing certain risks have wider spreads. Arbitrageurs aim to identify spreads that have been mispriced by the market and therefore by their competitors. These are either deals that they consider to be safe but the market considers to have a certain degree of risk, or deals that they consider to be dangerous but about which the market has no concerns (if this is the case, an arbitrageur can bet against the deal).

As the ultimate judge of transactions, especially hostile ones, arbitrageurs are often courted (or manipulated) by the M&A parties to come down on a particular side of the fence: a potential buyer threatening to pull out of the deal in order to reduce the share price (and dissuade arbitrageurs from buying too high); and a target company attempting to create a bidding war (to attract arbitrageurs and encourage them to buy as high as possible). This triangle can be analyzed in terms of game theory, with each party subject to its own constraints and incentives and plunged into an uncertain situation with contradictory information.

The financial crisis that took hold in the summer of 2007 has changed the job of the arbitrageur in several ways. First, the increased transaction failure rate (or the "claims" rate, if we compare arbitrage with the insurance trade) has had a negative impact on some market operators, and several investors have discovered to their own cost that there is no such thing as a free lunch. Second, there are fewer operators in this particular market. The proprietary trading desks of the major investment banks have abandoned the market, and some funds (especially those using a lot of leverage) have shut down. This has, in some way, purified the market. In the words of Warren Buffett, "it's only when the tide goes out that you learn who's been swimming naked".

Lastly, the deals that are announced are generally better quality than they were before the crisis. As they are harder to finance, structure, and sell to the market, they are generally more solid.

In the current acute financial crisis, with the cards being re-dealt globally (emerging nations are more powerful, and private-equity firms and sovereign wealth funds are playing a greater role), this investment strategy, which is one of the oldest in the hedge fund universe, allows us to get back to basics: For what reasons (good or bad) have two listed companies decided to wed? What are the risks of the marriage failing to go ahead?

Merger arbitrage is a tried and tested investment strategy that has proven over several decades that it can consistently deliver alpha and returns that are not tied to the performance of the financial markets. It is a classic, timeless strategy, and one that all investors should consider to be indispensable, whatever the future holds.

Glossary

Alpha   the abnormal return of a stock or a fund in excess of what would be expected by an equilibrium model. It is measured as the intercept between the security characteristic line (i.e. the excess return of a stock or fund) and the security market line (i.e. the excess return of a benchmark index).

Arbitrage   simultaneously buying and selling the same stock on two different markets at a different price, and generating a risk-free profit at zero cost. M&A arbitrage involves gambling on the success of a transaction and taking advantage of the gap between the offer price and the target company's share price.

Beta (β)   a volatility coefficient or measure of a stock's sensitivity to systematic risk, i.e. the relationship between the fluctuations in the value of said stock and market fluctuations. Beta is an indicator of financial risk.

Bidder   the company that initiates an M&A transaction. In a takeover, the entity that submits the takeover bid.

Bidding war   a situation in which several buyers fight for the control of a target company by way of bids and counterbids.

Board of directors   the body responsible for overseeing the functioning of a company. It comprises several members, including a chairman. The board operates in accordance with the bylaws of a company.

Break-up fee   the amount the seller must pay if it decides to pull out of the transaction, to cover the costs incurred by the jilted buyer during due diligence.

Bridge loan   a loan taken out pending the arrangement of a longer-term financing that will also pay off the bridge loan.

Call option   an option giving its holder the right, but not the obligation, to buy an asset at a pre-arranged price on a pre-arranged date or during a pre-arranged window.

Carried interest   the part of the capital gain realized by an investment fund which goes to its managers.

Cash merger   a merger between two companies which is financed by cash.

Cash offer   a stock-market operation where cash is offered in exchange for all the shares in a target company.

Certain funds   the potential quality of a buyer's financing for an M&A transaction. The funds are said to be "certain" if they are confirmed by a bank.

CFIUS   Committee on Foreign Investment in the United States, a government body regulating investment by foreign companies in US companies or assets, where such investment affects areas of national security.

Chinese deal   a strategy whereby an arbitrageur bets on the failure of an M&A transaction.

Closing   the final phase of an M&A transaction which involves transfer of ownership.

Collar   a type of share offer involving a degree of fluctuation in the conversion ratio. A fixed-exchange-rate offer (FX) is where the target company's shareholders receive a fixed number of the buyer's shares as long as the buyer's share price remains within specified boundaries. The ratio can also be calculated over a specified period. A fixed-value offer (FV) is where the target company's shareholders receive a fixed amount (expressed as cash) for each share held.

Competition, or antitrust, regulation   laws that aim to ensure compliance with the principle of free trade and industry. It bans concentrations and anti-competitive practice. In terms of M&A, it is applied if the new entity will acquire too much market power in the wake of a transaction.

Conditions precedent   conditions which, if they are not satisfied, enable the bidder to withdraw its offer (where this offer is voluntary).

Conversion ratio   in a share offer, the conversion ratio is the share-swap ratio deriving from the value of these shares, used to pay the target company's shareholders. This ratio is established when the deal is announced and is the direct result of the relative size of the two companies, which is established during negotiations.

Covenant   clause in a loan agreement which, if conditions are not met, could trigger early repayment of the loan.

Dissenting rights   the right of shareholders to oppose a bid for the company in which they hold shares and to seek valuation from a judge.

Dual track   a process in which a company simultaneously prepares its IPO and invites a bidding war among industrial and financial investors. This technique is used mainly by private-equity firms.

Efficiency defense   a principle stating that the negative impact of an M&A transaction on competition can be offset by economic benefits for consumers, such as lower prices.

Efficiency offense   a principle stating that an M&A transaction increases the market power of the newly formed entity and therefore reduces competition within a sector.

Euribor   Euro interbank offered rate, the benchmark money market rate in the eurozone.

Event-driven strategy   a hedge fund strategy that aims to profit from particular events taking place during the life of a company, e.g. takeovers, mergers, restructuring.

FCC   Federal Communications Commission, the independent agency responsible for regulating the telecoms industry in the US.

FERC   Federal Energy Regulatory Commission, the federal agency responsible for regulating the energy sector in the US.

Financial leverage   the use of credit to increase the value of investments, and therefore of profits or losses.

Flowback   the sale of a bidder's shares, with payment also in shares, after the closure of an M&A transaction. The reduction, or flowback, in the share price is the result of the sale of shares by long-only funds that are shareholders of the target company and are not permitted to hold shares in companies listed on foreign stock exchanges.

Friendly bid   an offer that has received prior approval from the management bodies of the target company.

FTC   Federal Trade Commission, an independent US agency responsible for enforcing competition law and controlling anti-competitive commercial practice.

Go-shop period   the period following the announcement of a takeover during which the target company may, if permitted by the merger agreement, solicit rival bids.

Hart–Scott–Rodino antitrust clearance   approval required for the completion of M&A in the US. This approval, which comes from either the Department of Justice or the Federal Trade Commission, confirms that the transaction complies with US antitrust law.

Hedge fund an investment fund that implements "alternative" strategies in its quest to deliver absolute returns that are not tied to the performance of the financial markets.

Herfindahl–Hirschman Index (HHI) an index that measures the level of concentration of a particular market. It is the sum of the squares of the market share of each participant in a sector. The higher the HHI, the more concentrated the sector.

Hostile (unsolicited) bid an offer that has not received prior approval from the management bodies of the target company.

"Just say no" a defense mechanism available to boards of directors in the US, enabling them to foil a hostile bid. It involves never entering into negotiations with a bidder.

Leveraged buyout (LBO) the takeover of a target company by a holding vehicle that has taken on a lot of debt to finance the transaction. The holding company pays the interest on the debt and pays off the capital using dividends from the company it has acquired. A primary LBO is the first LBO of a given company.

Libor London interbank offered rate, the benchmark money market rates of different currencies.

Liquidity the ability to trade a large volume of shares on the market in a short space of time, without affecting price.

Long position buying shares.

MAC clause a clause in a merger agreement which enables the parties to cancel a deal in the event of a material adverse change.

Matching rights these give their holder a pre-arranged timeframe to match any rival bid for the target company.

Merger the combination of the goods or assets of two or more companies in order to create a single company.

Merger agreement a contract signed by the bidder and the target company, formally announcing their agreement.

Pac-Man an anti-takeover defense mechanism whereby the target company turns the tables and offers to buy the bidder.

Passivity rule an obligation imposed on the members of the target company's board of directors to abstain from any action that may harm the successful conclusion of a takeover bid.

Poison pill a mechanism implemented by a company in order to ward off and eliminate hostile bids. In general, a poison pill gives shareholders the chance to buy additional shares for less than the market price or gives managers the option to sell core assets.

Private equity   the sector of finance focusing on investments in unlisted assets. Private equity comprises: venture capital, capital investment, leveraged buyouts and turnaround financing.

Put option   an option giving its holder the right, but not the obligation, to sell an asset at a pre-arranged price on a pre-arranged date or during a pre-arranged window.

"Put up or shut up"   UK stock-market regulation forcing a bidder to reveal its intentions and announce a firm offer before a certain date. If it fails to do so, it is deemed to be no longer interested and is not permitted to make an offer for the target company for a given period.

Reverse break-up fee   the amount of compensation to be paid by the bidder if it pulls out of the transaction.

Reverse takeover   the acquisition of a public company by a private company, where the controlling shareholder of the private company becomes the major shareholder of the new entity. This shareholder may be exempted by the stock-market regulator from launching a compulsory takeover bid for the remaining shares.

Reverse termination fee   see Reverse break-up fee.

SEC   Securities and Exchange Commission, the federal body responsible for controlling and regulating the financial markets in the US.

Second lien   a type of loan used in leveraged buyouts. It is a long-term loan that is ranked between traditional senior debt and mezzanine debt. It is guaranteed by the same assets as the senior debt, but is paid back later.

Share offer   stock-market operation where shares in the bidder are offered in exchange for all the shares in a target company. No cash is involved, but a share offer does entail a restructuring of the bidder's shareholder structure by way of a reserved capital increase.

Short-form merger   a merger process available in some US states, enabling the transaction to be completed without a vote by the target company shareholders.

Short position   selling shares.

Short selling   the sale of financial securities that have been borrowed. The position is unwound by buying back the securities on the market and returning them to the lender.

Specific performance   a clause that may feature in a merger agreement. It obliges the buyer to complete the transaction under certain conditions.

Spread   the gap between the target company's share price and the offer price.

Squeeze-out   the compulsory purchase of remaining shares by the majority shareholder of a public company, where said shareholder controls (in France) more than 95% of the company's share capital and voting rights.

Stand-alone   the valuation of a company without taking into account possible synergies resulting from a merger. It can also mean a defense mechanism against a takeover bid, whereby the target company's board of directors attempts to convince its shareholders that the current management team can deliver more value by staying independent.

Substantial lessening of competition (SLC)   a test of how compliant an M&A transaction is with the competition rules of a country. There is every chance the deal will be blocked if it threatens to significantly reduce competition in a sector.

Takeover Panel   UK regulatory body responsible for enforcing the City Code on Takeovers and Mergers. The Takeover Panel also ensures that all shareholders are treated equally during M&A transactions.

Tender offer   see Cash offer.

Termination fee   see Break-up fee.

Top-up   an option enabling a target company to issue shares to the bidder in order to push it over the 90% share capital threshold that allows it to conduct a short-form merger.

Underwriting   a service whereby investment banks raise funds from investors on behalf of corporations and governments that are issuing securities (shares or bonds).

Volatility   the rate at which the price of a security varies, whether up or down. It is calculated using the annualized standard deviation of the price of an asset.

White knight   in a hostile takeover situation, a white knight rides to the aid of the target company by offering it a friendly solution.

References

Achleitner, A.K. (2009) *Value Creation in Private Equity*. Centre for Entrepreneurial and Financial Studies – Capital Dynamics.

Ambrose, B. and Megginson, W. (1992) The role of asset structure, ownership structure, and takeover defenses in determining acquisition likelihood. *Journal of Financial and Quantitative Analysis*, 27, 575–89.

Asquith, P., Bruner, R., and Mullins, D. (1983) The gains to bidding firms from merger. *Journal of Financial Economics*, 11.

Bagnoli, M., Gordon, R., and Lipman, B. (1989) Stock repurchase as a takeover defense. *Review of Financial Studies*, 2, 423–43.

Baker, M. and Savasoglu, S. (2002) Limited arbitrage in mergers and acquisitions. *Journal of Financial Economics*, 64.

Barrett, A. and Young, B. (2006) *M&A Special Committees: Structure and Compensation*. The Corporate Library.

Beaufort, V. de (2006) *Les OPA en Europe*. Economica.

Bebchuk, L. and Cohen, A. (2005) The costs of entrenched boards. *Journal of Financial Economics*, 78(2).

Bebchuk, L., Coates, J., and Subramanian, G. (2002) The powerful anti-takeover force of staggered boards: Theory, evidence, and policy. *Stanford Law Review*, 54, 857–951.

Becher, D., Bates, T., and Lemmon, M. (2007) Board classification and managerial entrenchment: Evidence from the market for corporate control. HKUST Business School Research Paper No. 07–05.

Berkovitch, E. and Khanna, N. (1990) How target shareholders benefit from value-reducing defensive strategies in takeover. *Journal of Finance*, 45.

Berkovitch, E. and Narayanan, M. (1993) Motives for takeover: An empirical investigation. *Journal of Financial and Quantitative Analysis*, 28.

Bessière, V. (2008) Création de valeur et motivation des acquisitions d'entreprises. *Banque & Marché*, 94.

Betton, S. and Eckbo, E. (2000) Toeholds, bid-jumps, and expected payoffs in takeovers. *Review of Financial Studies*, 13.

Bhagat, S. and Jefferis, R. (1991) Voting power in the proxy contest: The case of antitakeover charter amendments. *Journal of Financial Economics*, 30.

Bhagat, S., Brickley, J., and Loewenstein, U. (1987) The pricing effects of interfirm cash tender offers. *Journal of Finance*, 45.

Bielinski, D. (1992) Putting a realistic dollar value on acquisitions synergies. *Mergers & Acquisitions*, Nov/Dec.

Block, S. (2006) Merger arbitrage hedge funds. *Journal of Applied Finance*, 16.

Boesky, I.F. (1985) *Merger Mania*. New York: Holt Rinehart & Winston

Born, J., Trahan, E., and Faria, H. (1993) Golden parachutes: Incentives aligners, management entrenchers, or takeover bid signals? *Journal of Financial Research*, 16.

Boschin, N. (2009) *Le guide pratique du LBO*. Paris: Edition d'Organisation.

Bouayad, A. and Legris, P.Y. (2007) *Les alliances stratégiques: maîtriser les facteurs clés de succès*. Paris: Dunod.

Bozzo, M. (2007) Les strategies de blocage utilisées par les hedge funds lors des offres publiques. *HEC Club Finance, les études du club* 72.

Branch, B. and Yang, T. (2003) Predicting successful takeovers and risk arbitrage. *Quarterly Journal of Business and Economics*, 42.

Branch, B. and Yang, T. (2006) Merger deal structure and investment strategy: Collar merger. *Journal of Alternative Investments* 9(3).

Bruner, R. (2004) *Applied Mergers and Acquisitions*. Chichester: Wiley Finance.

Byrne, J. and Galuszka, P. (1999) Poison pills: Let shareholders decide. *BusinessWeek*, May.

Canivet, G., Martin, D., and Molfessis, N. (2009) Les offres publiques d'achat. *Droit 360*. London: LexisNexis Litec.

Capen, E., Clapp, R., and Campbell, W. (1971) Competitive bidding in high-risk situations. *Journal of Petroleum Technology*, June.

Capocci, D. (2004) Introduction aux hedge funds. Economica Gestion.

Carlton, D. and Perloff, J. (1998) *Economie Industrielle*. Brussels: De Boeck Université.

Caves, R. (1989) Mergers, takeovers, and economic efficiency. *International Journal of Industrial Organization*, 7(1), 151–174.

Ceddaha, F. (2010) *Fusions Acquisitions: Evaluation, Négociation, Ingéniérie*. Economica Finance.

Chadefaux, M. (2008) *Les fusions de sociétés: régime juridique et fiscal*. Groupe Revue Fiduciaire.

Chenain, L. and Pochon, J. (2009) Situation actuelle et prospective du financement des LBO. *Analyse financière*, 30.

Cherif, M. (2004) *Leveraged Buy Out: Aspects financiers*. Revue Banque Editions.

Chernow, R. (1998) *Titan: The Life of John D. Rockefeller, Sr*. New York: Random House.

Cornelli, F. and Li, D. (2002) Risk arbitrage in takeovers. *Review of Financial Studies*, 15.

Dahya, J. and Powell, R. (1998) Ownership structure, managerial turnover and takeovers: Further UK evidence on the market for corporate control. *Multinational Finance Journal*, 2, 63–5.

Davidoff, S. (2009) *Gods at War, Shotgun Takeovers, Government by Deal and the Private Equity Implosion.* Chichester: John Wiley & sons, Ltd.

De Luyck, P., Garnier, G., Giotakos, D., and Petit, L. (2001) General Electric/Honeywell – An insight into the commission's investigation and decision. Competition Policy Newsletter. Brussels: European Commission (No.3, October), p. 9.

Dresner, S. and Kim, K. (2006) *Reverse Mergers, and Other Alternatives to Traditional IPO.* New York: Bloomberg Press.

Dukes, W., Frohlich, C., and Ma, C. (1992) Risk arbitrage in tender offers: Handsome rewards – and not for insiders only. *Journal of Portfolio Management*, 18, 47–55.

Dussauge, P. and Garrette, B. (1995) *Stratégies d'alliance.* Paris: Editions d'Organisation.

Eckbo, E. (2006) Bidding strategies and takeover premiums: A review. *Journal of Corporate Finance*, 12.

Emery, G. and Switzer, J. (1999) Expected market reaction and the choice of method of payment for acquisitions. *Financial Management*, 28.

Ernst & Young (2008) How do private equity investors create value? A global study. Etude réalisée par Ernst & Young.

Federal Trade Commission. Early termination notices under the Hart–Scott–Rodino Act, www.ftc.gov/bc/earlyterm/index.shtml.

Fich, E. and Stefanescu, I. (2003) Expanding the limits of merger arbitrage. University of North Carolina Working Paper.

Gaughan, P. (1999) *Mergers, Acquisitions and Corporate Restructuring*, 2nd edn. New York: John Wiley & Sons, Inc.

Gomes, A. (2001) Takeovers, freezeouts, and risk arbitrage. University of Pennsylvania Research Papers, March.

Hasbourck, J. (1985) The characteristics of takeover targets. *Journal of Banking and Finance*, 9.

Hoffmeister, R. and Dyl, E. (1980) Predicting outcomes of cash tender offers. *Financial Management*, 9.

Hsieh, J.L. (2002) *Merger Arbitrage: Profits, Holdings and Impact on Takeovers.* Columbus, OH: Ohio State University.

Hsieh, J.L. and Wakling, R. (2005) Determinants and implications of arbitrage holdings in acquisitions. *Journal of Financial Economics*, 77.

In re IBP, Inc. Shareholders Litigation, 789 A.2d. 14, Del. Ch. 2001.

Jacquillat, B. and Levy-Garboua, V. (2009) *Les 100 mots de la crise financière.* PUF.

Jensen, M. (1989) Eclipse of the public corporation. *Harvard Business Review*, 67.

Jensen, M. and Ruback, R. (1983) The market for corporate control – The scientific evidence. *Journal of Financial Economics*, 11.

Jetley, G. and Ji, X. (2010) The shrinking merger arbitrage spread: Reasons and implications. *Financial Analyst Journal*, 66.

Jindra, J. and Walking, R. (2004) Speculation spreads and the market pricing of proposed acquisitions. *Journal of Corporate Finance*, 10.

Jorion, P. (2008) Risk management for event-driven funds. *Financial Analysts Journal* 6.

Karolyi, A. and Shannon, J. (1998) Where's the risk in risk arbitrage? Richard Ivey School of Business, University of West Ontario Working Paper.

Kaslow, A. (2000) The best defense for takeover pressure: Be prepared. *Community Banker*, 9.

Kirchner, T. (2009) *Merger Arbitrage, How to Profit from Event-Driven Arbitrage*. Chichester: Wiley Finance.

Kreps, D. (1996) *Leçons de théorie microéconomique*. PUF.

Kummer, D. and Hoffmeister, R. (1978) Valuation consequences of cash tender offers. *Journal of Finance*, 33.

Kyle, A.S. and Vila, J.-L. (1991) Noise trading and takeovers. *RAND Journal of Economics*, 22, 54–71.

Lamoreaux, N.R. (1985) *The Great Merger Movement in American Business, 1895–1904*. Cambridge: Cambridge University Press.

Larcker, D. and Lys, T. (1987) An empirical analysis of the incentives to engage in costly information acquisition: The case of risk arbitrage. *Journal of Financial Economics*, 18, 111–26.

Lhabitant, F.S. (2008) *Hedge funds: Origines, stratégies, performance*. Paris: Dunod.

Lipton, M. (2007) Shareholder Activism and the "Eclipse of the Public Corporation". 25th Annual Institute on Federal Securities, Miami, Florida.

Maheswaran, K. and Yeoh, S.C. (2005) The profitability of merger arbitrage: Some Australian evidence. *Australian Journal of Management*, 30.

Marshall, R. (2004) *Corporate Governance at Family Firms*. The Corporate Library.

Martin, K. (1996) The method of payment in corporate acquisitions, investment opportunities, and management ownership. *Journal of Finance*, 51.

Masulis, R.W., Wang, C., and Xie, F. (2006) Corporate governance and acquirer returns. ECGI-Finance Working Paper No. 116.

Mitchell, M. and Pulvino, T. (2001) Characteristics of risk and return in risk arbitrage. *Journal of Finance*, 56, 2135–75.

Moore, K. (1999) *Risk Arbitrage, an Investor's Guide*. Chichester: Wiley Finance.

Moulin, J.M. (2009) *Le droit de l'ingénierie financière*. Gualino éditeur.

Mueller, D. (1985) Mergers and market share. *Review of Economics and Statistics*, 67.

Nelson, R. (1959) *Merger Movements in American Industry 1895–1956*. Princeton: Princeton University Press.

Oesterle, D. (2006) *Mergers and Acquisitions in a Nutshell*. Thomson West.

Officer, M. (2003) Termination fees in mergers and acquisitions. *Journal of Economics*, 69.

Officer, M. (2007) Are performance based arbitrage effects detectable? Evidence from merger arbitrage. *Journal of Corporate Finance*, 13.

Palepu, K. (1986) Predicting takeover targets: A methodological and empirical analysis. *Journal of Accounting and Economics*, 8, 3–35.

Parrat, F. (2010) *Reprise et transmission de l'entreprise, aspects stratégiques, juridiques et fiscaux*. Economica.

Pearl, J. and Rosenbaum, J. (2009) *Investment Banking; Valuation, Leveraged Buyouts and Mergers and Acquisitions*. Chichester: Wiley Finance.

Poitrinal, F.D. (2010) *Le capital investissement: guide juridique et fiscal*. Revue Banque Edition.

Porter, M. (1992) The five competitive forces that shape strategy. *Harvard Business Review*, Janvier 2008.

Raimbourg, P. and Boizard, M. (2009) *Ingénierie financière, fiscal et juridique*. Dalloez.

Rankine, D. and Howson, P. (2006) *Réussir une acquisition*. Village Mondial.

Reed, S. and Reed Lajoux, A. (2007) *The Art of M&A: A Merger Acquisition Buyout Guide*. New York: McGraw-Hill.

Ricol, L. (2010) *Observatoire des offres publiques*. March.

Salans Corporate Group (2009) *Governmental Approvals and Third Party Consents in Corporate Transactions*. Salans Corporate Group Editions.

Schmidt, D. and Moulin, F. (2009) *Les fonds de capital investissement: principes juridiques et fiscaux*. Editions Gualino.

Schugart, W. (1998) The government's war on mergers. Policy analysis. Washington DC: Cato Institute (No. 323)

Schwert, W. (1996) Markup pricing in mergers and acquisitions. *Journal of Financial Economics*, 41.

Schwert, W. (2000) Hostility in takeovers: In the eyes of the beholder? *Journal of Finance*, 55.

Selten, R. (1975) A reexamination of the perfectness concept for equilibrium points in extensive games. *International Journal of Game Theory*, 4.

Sherman, A. and Hart, M. (2006) *Mergers & Acquisitions from A to Z*. Amacom.

Shleifer, A. and Vishny, R. (1997) The limits of arbitrage. *Journal of Finance*, 52.

Shleifer, A. and Vishny, R. (2003) Stock market driven acquisitions. *Journal of Financial Economics*, 70.

Sirower, M. and Rappaport, A. (1999) Stock or cash. *Harvard Business Review*, 77.

Topsacalian, P. and Gensse, P. (2006) *Ingénierie financière*. Economica.

Travlos, N. (1987) Corporate takeover bids, methods of payment, and bidding firm's stock returns. *Journal of Finance*, 42.

Tuan, J., Hsu, J., Zhang, J., and Qiusheng, Z. (1995) *Merger Arbitrage Profitability in China*. International Conference on Management Science and Engineering, Press of Harbin Institute of Technology.

Turk, T., Goh, J., and Ybarra, C. (2007) The effect of takeover defenses on long term and short term analysts' earnings forecasts: The case of poison pills. *Corporate Ownership & Control*, 4.

Vallée, B. (2007) *La contestation des offers publiques en France*. Club Finance HEC Février, 71.

Varaiya, N. and Ferris, K. (1985) Overpaying in corporate takeovers: The winner's curse. *Financial Analysts Journal*, 43.

Vernimmen, P. (2011) *Finance d'entreprise*. Dalloz.

Viandier, A. (2006) *OPA et OPE et autres offres publiques*. Editions Francis Lefebvre.

Walking, R. (1985) Predicting tender offer success: A logistic analysis. *Journal of Financial Quantitative Analysis*, 20.

Walking, R. and Edmister, R. (1985) Determinants of tender offer premiums. *Financial Analysts Journal*, 45.

Walsh, J. (1988) Top management turnover following mergers and acquisitions. *Strategic Management Journal*, 9.

Wang, K., Wang, S., and Tsai, C. (2008) Profitability and characteristics of risk arbitrage: Evidence from leveraged buyouts in the US National Chiao Tung University.

Watkins, M. (2003) *Negotiation*. Cambridge, MA: Harvard Business School Press.

Wei, D., Ferguson, M., and Chichernea, D. (2011) Deal risk, liquidity risk, and the profitability of risk arbitrage. Temple University Legal Studies Research Paper.

Weston, F., Mulherin, H., and Mitchell, M. (2010) *Takeovers, Restructuring and Corporate Governance*. Prentice Hall.

Wyser-Pratte, G. (1982) *Risk Arbitrage II*. Monograph. New York University, Salomon Brothers Center for the Study of Financial Institutions.

Index

Index compiled by Terry Halliday

Printed and bound by CPI Group (UK) Ltd, Croydon, CR0 4YY

23/04/2025

14660961-0001